Taken Hostage

Politics and Society in Twentieth-Century America

Series Editors

William Chafe, Gary Gerstle, Linda Gordon, and Julian Zelizer

A list of titles in this series appears at the back of the book

DAVID FARBER

THE IRAN HOSTAGE CRISIS AND AMERICA'S
FIRST ENCOUNTER WITH RADICAL ISLAM

Taken Hostage

PRINCETON UNIVERSITY PRESS
PRINCETON AND OXFORD

Library of Congress Cataloging-in-Publication Data

Farber, David R.
Taken hostage : the Iran hostage crisis and America's first encounter
with radical Islam / David Farber.
p.   cm.   —   (Politics and society in twentieth-century America)
Includes bibliographical references and index.
ISBN 0-691-11916-3 (alk. paper)
1. Iran Hostage Crisis, 1979–1981. 2. United States—Foreign relations—Iran.
3. Iran—Foreign relations—United States. 4. United States—Foreign
relations—1977–1981. 5. Islam and politics—Iran. I. Title. II. Series.
E183.8.I55F37 2004
955.05'42—dc22   2004046639

British Library Cataloging-in-Publication Data is available.

This book has been composed in Sabon and Helvetica Neue Family

Printed on acid-free paper. ∞

www.pupress.princeton.edu

Printed in the United States of America

1   3   5   7   9   10   8   6   4   2

Contents

Acknowledgments

THIS BOOK would not have been possible without the support and encouragement of many people. First, my thanks to the talented team of archivists at the Jimmy Carter Presidential Library. Without their helpful suggestions this book could not have been written. Thanks, too, to the library staff at Zimmerman Library, University of New Mexico, who kept finding the books and journals I needed.

Diplomatic historians Fred Logevall and Richard Immerman read the penultimate draft of this book and pushed me to think harder about the Carter administration foreign policy team and to understand the context of U.S.-Iranian relations. I am honored to have had these two superb scholars review this work. I am indebted to all the readers selected by Princeton University Press to review the manuscript and to the series editors, who supported this project throughout the publication process. The prose is stronger, the analysis keener, and the facts straighter because of their efforts. This project would never have flown without the commitment of Princeton University Press editor Brigitta van Rheinberg. Her careful read of the manuscript was immensely encouraging and helpful. I would also like to thank my international colleagues, especially Jun Furuya, Fumiaki Kubo, Melani Budianti, and Pia Alishibana, who have over the last few years invited me to give talks on recent American history and politics in France, Japan, and Indonesia. In particular, questions I received from Islamic students in Padang, West Sumatra, about American policy in the Middle East influenced my views on international perceptions of the United States and contributed to my desire to write this book. I also think the many students who asked such probing questions at Keio University in Tokyo and at the University of Indonesia in Jakarta. My thanks to the Centre National de la Recherche Scientifique, the Fulbright Commission, the Organization of American Historians, and the Japanese Association for American Studies.

My son, Max, read several sections of the manuscript and insisted that I keep the prose taut. Having someone read the manuscript who does not remember the 1980s (except Teenage Mutant Ninja Turtles), let alone Jimmy Carter's presidency, was quite useful in historicizing the story. Once again, Beth Bailey read every word of the many drafts of this book and thought through every aspect of the project with me. She urged me to spend as much time as I needed in Atlanta at the Carter Library and to take some time off to bicycle through Vietnam. Nineteen years, fourteen homes (a conservative estimate), thirteen jobs, thirteen books, and counting.

I decided to write this book after the September 11 attack. I was scheduled that day to give a lecture about race in early twentieth-century American history; instead, my students and I mainly talked about what drives people to commit such cruel and despicable acts and what, if anything, history could tell us about such horrors. The hostage-taking that took place on November 4, 1979, and the terror that was unleashed on September 11, 2001, are very different kinds of events. Nonetheless, this book does aim to explain how one kind of fierce anti-Americanism developed in one part of the Islamic world and, in turn, how Americans responded to it. Seeing the Iran hostage crisis as the first major act in an international struggle might, I hope, help us all gain perspective on the tortured relationship between the United States and the forces of political Islam.

Taken Hostage

Introduction

THE RUSTIC philosopher Calvin Coolidge observed that if you see ten troubles coming down the road, you can be sure that nine will turn off before they reach you. In the 1970s, though, the troubles all kept on coming. It was a game of chicken no one seemed to know how to escape and the head-on crash was not a pretty sight. The American people survived the wreckage (politically, the era's presidents were not so lucky) but not without scars and not without bitter memories.

The Iran hostage crisis, which lasted from November 4, 1979, until January 20, 1981, was but one of the many troubles Americans faced during a difficult time. The Iranian imbroglio, in fact, affected the American people less directly than any of the others. Unlike the energy crisis, inflation, economic stagnation, industrial dislocation, and presidential scandal and resignation, it happened faraway and caused little immediate pain to any but the hostages (sixty-six Americans were held in one form or another of captivity at the beginning of the ordeal; six other Americans escaped the immediate embassy takeover but were forced into hiding) and their families. Yet, as measured by public concern, emotional outpouring, and simple fascination, the Iran hostage crisis captivated the American people more than any other of the era's difficulties. By the millions Americans expressed their ongoing solidarity with the hostages. They wrote letters of sympathy to the hostages and their families. They wrapped yellow ribbons around trees in their front yards, pinned them on their clothes, tied them to their car radio antennas as symbols of concern for the hostages' plight.

Though television talk shows, the evening news, drive-time radio, and almost every other forum of public conversation, Americans followed the latest twists and turns of the Americans' captivity in Iran. The nation, itself, was held hostage by the crisis.

From the beginning, a great many Americans felt the hostage crisis was about more than the plight of a few dozen of their fellow countrymen. The event was an obvious symbol, an easily understood example of the nation's inability to control its own fate, maintain its dignity, and pursue its independent course in the world. The United States could not protect its own people; it could not get them out of harm's way; it could not bring them home safely. Had America really become just a "pitiful giant," first defeated by the ragtag armies of Vietnam and then stymied by a bunch of fanatical student hostage-takers who—with complete impunity—burned the American flag, screamed, "Death to America!" and scorned the American government's every attempt to negotiate a rational solution? Was the Ayatollah Khomeini, a figure who seemed to most Americans a crazy fanatic living in a time warp, really going to be able to outwit and make a mockery of the U.S. government? Did the Carter administration's aborted attempt to rescue the hostages—a fiasco that cost eight soldiers their lives—prove that the Carter administration was inept and that the U.S. military was a hollowed-out force incapable of looking after the nation's security? As Americans watched the hostage crisis unfold, most became increasingly certain of one thing: the United States had lost its way—economically, culturally, politically, and even militarily.

This account of the Iran hostage crisis offers an analysis of the specific unfolding of that event within a broader account of an era of failed expectations. Rather than cast blame on the key actors, I explain how the political context of the late 1970s reduced the Carter administration's options in managing and resolving the Iran hostage crisis and show how Americans made sense of the hostage crisis within their understandings of America's predicament at the end of the 1970s. My account is a grim reminder of a tough time, an explanation of why so many people in the United States, back then, felt that they, too, were being held hostage by Iranian fanatics—as well as by the OPEC cartel, stagflation, and all the other troubles that kept coming down the road.

This account also provides a framework for understanding why Ronald Reagan's optimistic rhetoric during the 1980 presidential election campaign made sense to many Americans who were living through the so-called Age of Limits. During the 1970s and for some time after, social critics castigated Americans for being selfish, self-absorbed narcissists. In popular magazines and best-selling books, the 1970s were excoriated as the era of the "Me" generation. In part, the critics were comparing the 1970s to the 1960s, when, they argued, Americans had selflessly worked together for the common good in social change movements. (Few of these critics recognized the vitality of the 1970s era's grassroots movements, which ranged across the political spectrum and included the New Right as well as the women's movement and the gay liberation movement.) Americans' outpouring of concern for the hostages, at least in part, belies the accusation of endemic selfishness among the American people.

The outpouring of empathy for the hostages and their families revealed that millions of Americans at the end of the 1970s had maintained a powerful desire for bonds of national community. The patriotic forms that bond took—while demonstrating at times an ugly chauvinism, xenophobia, and racism—also exposed how prevalent love of country remained in American society. While many Americans had, in the aftermath of the Vietnam debacle and the Watergate scandal, grown cynical about their political leaders, they had not necessarily grown similarly cynical about the United States itself. Overwhelmingly, politicians and social critics in the 1970s missed that difference.

One individual who did not was Ronald Reagan. Dismissed by most political pundits in the late 1970s as a has-been out of touch with the American political mainstream, Reagan campaigned brilliantly against the federal government but fervently for America as a shining ideal. Critics (and I include myself) argued that his vision of that ideal was often willfully blind to U.S. foreign policies that contradicted American principles. And while championing the ideals of the United States, Reagan seemed woefully unrealistic about—or dangerously ignorant of—the domestic inequities that plagued American society. But the rightness or wrongness of his policy predilections is not the point. Reagan preached a faith in the underlying idealism of the American way at a time when other leaders did not. His insight into the American people's continuing patriotism, even at a time when so much was going wrong, helped put Ronald Reagan in the White House.

In addition, what makes this history of the Iran hostage crisis different from the accounts written soon after the hostages' release is the critical importance I place on the rise of Islamic fundamentalism in Iran and on the Carter administration's troubled attempts to respond to its theocratic impulses within the prevailing cold war paradigm. At the time, most Americans had no way to know that the Iran hostage crisis was not a bizarre one-off encounter with an exotic form of Islam about which few had ever before thought. Now we know differently. Dozens of newly declassified documents show that Carter administration officials, especially National Security Council Advisor Zbigniew Brzezinski, had begun to think through the geopolitical importance of a politicized Islam in the region. But the indignities of the hostage-taking, followed by the Ayatollah Khomeini's embrace of the hostage-takers, made it hard to consider the long-term strategic challenges that a militant, politicized Islam posed for U.S. international interests.

The Soviet invasion of Afghanistan at the end of 1979 made a long-term policy response to Islam as a geopolitical reality in the region more difficult yet. American policymakers, still focused on the cold war threat of the Soviets, chose to arm the Islamic fundamentalists fighting Soviet troops in Afghanistan. Now we know that factions within these forces of Jihad would soon thereafter turn their fury on the United States. Still, even if U.S. policymakers had been all-knowing about the trajectory of militant Muslims in the region, they could not have easily defused the fierce anti-Americanism that motivated both the Islamic student militants who took over the U.S. embassy in Tehran and the older mullahs who con-

trolled the Iranian government that had emerged from the overthrow of Shah Pahlavi's regime. A quarter century of American
complicity and faith in the Shah's repressive—but also modernizing
and secular—regime could not have been easily overcome, even
supposing that President Carter had tried (and he did not). Nor, it
should be noted, would it have been effective for the Carter administration to condone—or demand—that the Shah slaughter rebel-
ling Iranians in sufficient numbers to halt the revolt. While the Shah
loyalists likely could have produced a mighty slaughter, it is unlikely that a bloodbath would have saved the Shah; it certainly
would not have contributed to the good name of the United States
in the region.

Most of all, in analyzing America's first major confrontation
with the forces of militant Islam, I have foregrounded the difficulty
American policymakers had recognizing how devoted Islamic militants in Iran were to creating an Islamic State. Over and over,
American policymakers kept expecting the Iranians to realize that
the real danger in the region was the Soviet Union. As I'll argue in
the chapters that follow, when Americans looked at Iran and the
region more generally, they saw Soviet Red and not Islamic Green.
Khomeini and his followers were, in fact, worried about communist and leftist factions within Iran. They were aware of the Soviet
threat to their rule. But they saw their real battle as against secular
modernism and they recognized, correctly, that the United States
was the major force spreading this cultural and political creed
throughout the world.

Carter and many of his key advisors seemed to really believe that
Khomeini was crazy and irrational. They kept hoping that wiser,
saner, and more rationally self-interested men would take over
Iran. Khomeini was not crazy. But what he wanted was so inimical
to American government officials' understanding of how the world
did and should work that he might as well have been, at least from
the stance of American negotiators.

Facing up to this cultural gap does not make the Islamic fundamentalists' beliefs, during the Iran hostage crisis and in the years
since, more palatable to most Americans. But it could allow for

more effective communication to take place. And although American policymakers should not be in the business of making generous deals with unpalatable ideologues or theocrats (and should never make deals with murdering terrorists), it is useful to see such people for what they are rather than simply see them, as some contemporary American pundits and policymakers do, as insane demons given over to evil. In Iran, the student hostage-takers, while no angels, killed no one, tortured no one, and generally (with some exceptions) treated their hostages reasonably well. Treating *hostages* "reasonably well," I want to underline, does not negate the despicable nature of the hostage-takers' acts. And the American government at that time could not be sure that the hostage-takers would continue to treat their captives decently. Still, American negotiators could have made the relative safety of the hostages clearer to the American people and they could have better explained that the American diplomats and soldiers being wrongly held in Iran had understood the risks involved in being in a country that was undergoing a furious political and cultural revolution. Part of my task in writing this book is to explain why the Carter administration did not try to calm the American people's response to the hostage-taking in 1979 and 1980.

In 1979 and 1980, pundits and policymakers played the game of "who lost Iran?" In retrospect, it is remarkable that the United States had been able to maintain a useful ally in the region for so long. But eventually—a quarter of a century after the U.S. backed the coup that put Reza Pahlavi on the Peacock Throne—the chickens had come home to roost. The only obvious lesson of the Iran hostage crisis is that when a failed policy blows up spectacularly the best solution is to determine why it happened and then act with extreme prudence so long as nothing catastrophic really occurs. And if you are the president, Jimmy Carter's miscalculations should be a grim reminder: in the event of troubles that cannot be easily resolved in faraway places involving Americans in harm's way, make sure somebody else in your administration is charged with handling the problem while you carefully explain to the voters why good results take time and that patience is always a virtue.

One other issue: much is made, in the more academic accounts of the hostage-taking, of media misrepresentations of the Iranian struggle and general mass media manipulation of Americans. I was surprised to see just how much appeared in the mass media about Iran—about the malevolence of the Shah's security forces, the misrule of the Shah, and the multiple motives of the anti-Shah forces. I was also surprised by the number of televised interviews with the Ayatollah Khomeini and his various followers. Newspapers even gave a decent amount of space to the hostage-takers' views and their various communiqués. Coverage of the story by the *New York Times*, admittedly the best source for daily news in that era, while not unflawed, stands up quite well as complex and nuanced reporting. ABC's nightly specials on the crisis, hosted by Ted Koppel (the show that would become *Nightline* in March 1980), also were full of incisive background on the revolution and the motives of the militant Islamic students and various officials running revolutionary Iran.

Not all coverage of the hostage-taking was stellar. A great deal of it traded in emotionalism. Many television and radio broadcasts featured anguished interviews with members of the hostages' families. In the final analysis it was not, I think, the quality of the coverage of the hostage crisis that needs critiquing but simply the excessive quantity of it. But the fact that the television networks, news weeklies, radio stations, and newspapers covered the hostage-taking so extravagantly cannot be blamed on some nefarious motive. Americans were fascinated by the story and emotionally pulled by it. By the late 1970s, the mass media had the capacity to feed that fascination—though its capacity was far less than it is today. For better and for worse, the mass media's capacity to trade on Americans' fascination with certain kinds of spectacle (and celebrity) is now a fact of American and, indeed, international cultural life. And in the late 1970s this new capacity made it possible for Americans to follow the Iranian hostage story, albeit sometimes obsessively.

Americans' inability to fully reckon with the Iran hostage crisis and to see it as a complex international relations fiasco does not, I think, rest with bad media coverage. Back then, despite Vietnam (or maybe in response to it?), Americans were not well equipped for or much interested in reckoning with the political complexity of their government's power. And the democracy's leaders, most particularly Jimmy Carter, did not have the tools, talents, or desire to explain effectively what can happen when powerful interjections and interventions into other peoples' lives are not appreciated. The Iranian hostage crisis could have been an interesting lesson in international affairs. Most Americans, however, including Jimmy Carter, treated it instead as (to paraphrase) the mad act of evildoers. As a partial result, American policymakers did not respond directly to the underlying problems that produced the Iran hostage crisis. That failure led, indirectly, some two decades later, to an evil act by vicious killers morally blinded by fanaticsm. Thinking past the act of terrorism to the strategy of prevention has not been an American strength. It is all the more important, therefore, to take another look at America's first major confrontation with Islamic fundamentalism.

Chapter One

CRISIS, CHAOS, AND JIMMY CARTER

*To burn or not to burn, that was the question. For several months,
the CIA station in the U.S. embassy in Iran had been under a strict
"read-and-burn" order. No cables or other materials were to be kept
in drawers, filed away, or even locked in secure vaults. But by the early
summer the high anxiety produced by the revolution and by the brief
February takeover of the embassy had cooled. A "three-month-retain"
status order had been instituted. There was a caveat. The total retained
material could not exceed that amount which could be burned in thirty
minutes.*

*The CIA station of the American embassy in Tehran was on the sec-
ond floor of the chancery, a nondescript, rectangular building just to
the right of the embassy's main entrance. Soon after the revolutionary
mobs had taken to the streets, the entire building had been "hardened"
by welding steel bars to the window frames and building sand-filled
bullet traps in front of the lower halves of each window. Trouble was
not unexpected.*

On Sunday morning, when the Iranians came over the walls and made their way through the front gates, the CIA personnel knew the drill. Four of them were on duty in the chancery. The CIA chief of station began to destroy the cryptography keys and other secret communication materials. At the other end of the floor, in a large walk-in vault, Bill Daugherty—with the station's operations support assistant—was trying to burn everything the Iranians should not see.

Daugherty had been in Tehran for fifty-three days; Iran was his first assignment. He was good but he was also very green. Documents were destroyed by hand-feeding them into a "barrel-shaped device about twice the size of a home furnace." Coolly, but not without a sense of urgency, Daugherty got to work. Iranians had breached the steel bars and were already in the building. He reports: "Ignoring the various sounds from the hallway as well as the mob's shouting outside the building, I began slowly dropping papers into the disintegrator. After digesting just a handful of documents, the temperamental device went ka-chonk and shut down."

Now what?[1]

IN THE 1970s, Americans too often felt that they faced nothing but bad choices. It was not one of those *Tale of Two Cities* eras, like the 1960s, with its "best of times," "worst of times." Especially in the last years of the decade, it was mainly just hard times. Events lent themselves to a litany of despair: inflation up, employment down; oil prices out of control, American-made automobiles breaking down; factories closed, marriages over, homicide rates soaring; President Gerald Ford. A band of snarling British musicians made a trans-Atlantic name for themselves singing in 1977, "No future for you, no future for me." By the late 1970s, industrial workers, home buyers, grocery shoppers, factory owners, storekeepers, and young people looking for their first real jobs were treading water, trying to find their way to a distant shoreline. While they struggled for direction, an unlikely leader named Jimmy Carter had an uneasy hold on the ship of state.

In 1976, after a parade of disasters—Watergate, the fall of Saigon, President Ford's pathetically ineffective Whip Inflation Now campaign—the former one-term Georgia governor, Jimmy Carter, had surprised everyone but himself by becoming president of the United States. In Democratic primaries and then in the general election he'd won voters to his side by telling them again and again: "I'll never lie to you." Just a couple of years after Richard Nixon ("I am not a crook") had been forced to resign from the presidency, personal honesty seemed the stuff of presidential heroism. Carter combined his campaign promises with an unbroken record of never having served the United States in any position of national leadership. In an era that had seen traditional leaders and established authorities lose much of their credibility, Carter's "outsider" candidacy won the day.

Though relatively untested, President Carter, not surprisingly, was a man of many gifts. He would never have risen so far and so fast without them. His modesty veiled a rapier sharp intelligence. His decency was as deep as his Baptist faith. Though fiercely ambitious, he was also incorruptible and incontestably dedicated to serving the people of the United States. If a measure of integrity, tenacity, discipline, and IQ points added up to presidential greatness, then Jimmy Carter would have been one of America's most extraordinary leaders.

Alas, in the game of presidential leadership, brainpower and character usually count for less than political skill. And in the latter category, Carter was no genius. More important, as the Bible-reading president knew well, "the race is not to the swift, nor the battle to the strong, neither yet bread to the wise, nor yet riches to men of understanding, nor yet favor to men of skill; but time and chance happeneth to them all." President Carter, during his one term in office, would face events through "time and chance" that allowed for no easy answer and, too often, for no solution at all.

The fall of the Shah of Iran and the subsequent taking of American hostages at the U.S. embassy in Tehran by followers of the Islamic fundamentalist Ayatollah Ruhollah Khomeini, on top of and in the midst of many other national difficulties, was President

Carter's most agonizing problem. In his memoirs, Carter blamed the 444-day-long hostage crisis for destroying his chances of winning a second term in office. For tens of millions of Americans, the 1979–1981 hostage crisis marked the spectacular failure of the Carter administration. Worse, it hammered home how far the American nation had fallen in the 1970s. Neither the president nor the American people knew that the fierce conflict between Iranian revolutionaries and the American government was just the first, relatively distant skirmish in America's ongoing struggle to resolve its differences with the Islamic world.

For Americans, the Iran hostage crisis came suddenly, claiming attention in the midst of all the other worries of a difficult decade. The first media reports were sketchy. On the morning of November 4, 1979, a mob rallied outside the American embassy in Tehran. There were thousands of people; they appeared to be students, mostly men but women, too. The women were in black, shrouded in chador. A small group cut the thick chain that secured the main gates and filed into the twenty-seven-acre embassy compound. Hundreds, then thousands, followed them, swarming over the eight-foot fence that guarded the embassy grounds. Iranian police, supposedly there to protect the American property, offered no resistance, called for no assistance, and received no support from other Iranian security forces. Compared to its heyday just a year earlier, the embassy was nearly deserted. And the few dozen U.S. embassy personnel who were still there were no match for the angry mob. They were grabbed and blindfolded. Their captors tied their hands behind their back. The 444 days of captivity had begun.

Americans watched the first news reports with indignation, as day after day the nightly news showed pictures of angry mobs at the U.S. embassy, waving crude anti-American placards and shouting anti-American slogans. The hostage-taking was an open wound on the American body politic and the press, politicians, and the American people could not leave it alone.

Walter Cronkite, anchor of the *CBS Evening News* and the most trusted man in American broadcasting, brought almost ritual quality to the passing days. In his marvelous stentorian voice, Cronkite ended each broadcast of the *CBS Evening News* with a solemn intonation: "And that's the way it is, [for example] Friday, January 4, 1980, the 61st day of captivity for the Americans hostage in Iran." Night after night, until the 444th night when the hostages were at last freed, Walter Cronkite counted the days of America's humiliation, feeding Americans' angry preoccupation with the Iranian hostage-takers and their captives.[2]

While November 4, 1979, marked the beginning of the crisis for America, Iranians (at least those who cheered on the takeover) saw it differently; they would choose other days to mark the beginning of all that followed. The student militants who took the embassy insisted that the crisis began on October 23, 1979. That was the day the American president allowed the deposed Shah of Iran, a man these militants saw as corrupt and evil, to seek sanctuary in the United States. "By allowing the shah to enter the U.S. the Americans have started a new conspiracy against the revolution," said one of these young militants in the days leading up to the embassy takeover. "If we don't act rapidly, if we show weakness, then a superpower like the U.S. will be able to meddle in the internal affairs of any nation."[3] The takeover, said the militants, was the second act of the drama, a defensive act to protect the Iranian revolution from American interference.

Following this model of causality, Iranians also pointed much further back. The crisis really began, the student militants explained to the world's media, on August 19, 1953. On that day the Iranian government of Muhammad Mossadegh, the Soviet-friendly, nationalist prime minister, was overthrown. Muhammad Reza Pahlavi, the Shah of Shahs, regained control of Iran. Operation Ajax, as it was known, had been approved by President Eisenhower and smartly directed by Kermit Roosevelt of the relatively new American Central Intelligence Agency (and grandson of President Theodore Roosevelt). Old hands at the British Secret Intelligence Service assisted where they could. According to the militants' logic, the U.S. embassy, from 1953 through November 1979, was not the home of American officials correctly pursuing proper missions of diplomacy. It was, as they said again and again, "a nest of spies" whose intelligence agents must be stopped before they plotted another coup against Iranian self-determination.

Henry Kissinger, national security advisor and then secretary of state under Richard Nixon—and no friend to Jimmy Carter—found such claims beneath contempt. He directed influential Americans' attention to a very different date. In a variety of remarks made after the fall of the Shah and during the hostage crisis that followed, he obliquely suggested that if one day were singled out as the beginning of the Iranian crisis, that day was almost exactly three years before the hostages were seized. It was November 2, 1976, the date the former governor of Georgia was elected to an office for which, Kissinger believed, he was ill prepared and poorly suited. Well before the Iranian militants took the embassy and made captives of Americans, Kissinger had been lambasting Carter's ambivalent support for the Shah and dismissing the president's call for greater international human rights. Carter, said Kissinger and other allied veterans of the foreign policy establishment, had reaped what he had sown in Iran.

Each of these beginnings—and others, as well—suggests a particular historical trajectory, a different set of "what-if" questions, a specific political or ideological focus. Each reveals its own truths or half-truths. Nonetheless, the meaning and impact of the hostage crisis in the United States cannot be reduced to the events of any one day, the deeds or misdeeds of one man, or even the bilateral history of Iran and America.

Americans perceived the outrageous treatment of their countrymen at the hands of Iranian Islamic fundamentalists as a national crisis because they believed that the United States, at the end of the 1970s, was already a nation in crisis. The American captives in Iran became a living symbol and a pointed daily reminder of what had gone wrong in the United States. So, before turning to the Iran hostage crisis, contested as its time line is, it is imperative to first recapture the national uncertainty and disappointment that preceded and accompanied the hostage-taking. Without a feel for the causes and character of what some then called America's national "malaise," Americans' angry preoccupation with the hostage crisis cannot be understood.

Given the bad name the 1970s have in most pop histories of the recent American past, it is worth at least noting that life in post-Watergate America was not all bad clothes, bad hair, and bad times. Compared to almost any other nation in the world, much was still very right about the United States in the fall of 1979. Plenty of people around the world looked with envy at Americans' standard of living, the nation's cultural vitality, and the recent progress American society had made in rectifying some of its more obvious flaws. It does no interpretative good to paint too overly bleak a picture of the 1970s in order to set off the angry hues of the hostage crisis. That said, Americans had plenty in the 1970s about which to complain.

In the 1970s, almost every certainty Americans brought to their everyday lives was up for grabs. Economic expectations were up-ended. America's global role was under fire. Culture wars were breaking out at school board meetings and around dining room tables. The president committed felonies, children smoked marijuana, men wore gaudy jewelry around their necks, and communist Chinese pandas were the star attraction at the National Zoo.

In the 1970s Americans began to work out the practical legacy of the radical mass movements and the liberal federal legislation of the 1960s. It was not easy. In most regards, the fireworks were over: nobody was going to sic German Shepherds on little black children seeking a modicum of social justice; white politicians were not going to stand in schoolhouse doors screaming racial epithets; and women had the legal right to equal treatment in the workplace. But no consensus had emerged in the United States about how to implement all the new laws or how far to carry the vaguely accepted new ideals of tolerance and inclusivity. What should equality before the law mean? Affirmative action? School busing? Was Black Power just a discredited slogan or a new political agenda? From whom and what should women be liberated? All women? Who else got a place at the table where decisions were made and resources allocated? Above all, these changes in the 1970s were personal; they affected people's families, their workplaces, their churches, their schools, and their intimate lives. Depending on your point of view, the cultural and political changes were exhilarating, unsettling, or frightening.[4]

In the 1970s, building on the grassroots activism, liberal federal legislation, and the countercultural movements of the prior twenty years, Americans had made stunning progress in bringing to life ideals of civic inclusivity, economic opportunity, and cultural diversity. It was good news for some; it was disquieting or even infuriating to others. At a minimum, in the 1970s no one could declare (as so many had done in the 1950s) that the nation enjoyed a calm, confident cultural consensus.

Similarly, the cold war ideological unity that had ruled American foreign policy from the Truman administration onward had broken apart. America's failed war in Vietnam had, obviously, done much to break the ideological spell of anti-communism. John Kennedy's thrilling certainties—"we shall bear any burden, pay any price" to defeat global communism—had died with America's failed commitment to Vietnam. In 1975, Americans watched in horror and embarrassment shocking images of Americans fleeing Saigon on overloaded helicopters, beating off terrified South Vietnamese allies, just moments before the city fell to communist forces. The "victory culture" that had emerged out of World War II and the first two decades of America's cold war battle against the Soviet Union and international communism was largely discredited. Pundits described a "Vietnam syndrome": defeat haunted America and made Americans across the political spectrum loathe to make strong international commitments to anyone.

In the early 1970s, President Richard Nixon and his key advisor, Henry Kissinger, had tried, with cunning and brilliance, to replace simple anti-communism with a more pragmatic realpolitik. Disregarding all pretenses of operating American foreign policy on the basis of morality, Nixon had embraced anyone in the world who gave the United States even short-term advantages. Thus, Nixon sidled up to racist regimes in Rhodesia and South Africa (though support was later tempered when events changed). Nixon further demonstrated his flexibility by seeking a measure of cooperation with the Soviet Union and opening up relations with the long despised and unrecognized communist government of mainland China. Nixon built American foreign policy on issues of expediency and narrowly cast national self-interest.

Nixon's Democratic opponent in the 1972 presidential election, South Dakota Senator George McGovern, had vigorously attacked Nixon's realpolitik approach. In a campaign speech McGovern called for a return to principle and morality in American foreign policy: "Our children look to us for moral guidance—for America's true ideals. But we protect the prestige of warmongers. And we pay with the soul of our nation."[5]

In 1974, at the tail end of the scandal-ridden Nixon presidency, investigative journalist Seymour Hersh revealed that the CIA, at Nixon's bidding, had helped overthrow the legally elected Chilean government and had, as well, engaged in numerous illegalities in the United States. Idaho Senator Frank Church followed up Hersh's reporting with a Senate investigation that revealed decades of CIA involvement in coups and covert operations against numerous foreign governments, including those of Guatemala, Ecuador, Cuba, Indonesia, and, of course, Iran. While radicals in the United States and around the world had long decried such CIA involvements, few Americans had ever heard their charges and most of those that had felt confident in dismissing them as communist propaganda. The charges were all true. Liberals, as well as many conservatives, were shocked. What was America's role in the world? Was it the defender of democracy and freedom, fighting against the tyranny of communism? Or was it just another underhanded nation that sought advantage wherever it could, however it might? The combined force of the "Vietnam syndrome," Nixon's nasty, if usually effective, *realpolitik*, and the revelations about CIA covert operations around the world left many Americans with a bad taste in their mouths. The uncertain role of the United States in the world did not have the same immediacy for most Americans as did the more pressing concerns of the culture wars and domestic politics, but it was one more haunting problem with no obvious solution.

While America's uncertain role in the world was disquieting and the often harsh and divisive struggles over equality, inclusivity, and cultural standards were a part of the atmospherics, affecting how Americans responded to the Iranian hostage crisis, Americans in every income bracket in the late 1970s were far more anxious about economic issues. Here is where the larger crisis in American society lay. In America, people had come to expect that each generation would do better than the one that preceded it. The economic pie was supposed to increase every year so that everyone's piece of the American dream got at least a little bigger. But in the 1970s the dream looked like a fool's fantasy. The economy wasn't working. Prices were increasing, income was stagnating, personal debt was exploding, foreign goods were flooding the American marketplace, and third-world nations had organized cartels to put the squeeze on the United States. Americans looked outward at their newly fierce economic competitors like Japan and Germany and at the evermore powerful petroleum exporting countries such as Saudi Arabia, Kuwait, Iraq, and Iran with escalating fears and simmering hostility. More than anything, Americans felt betrayed by the nation's economic reversals.

Even here, however, it's imperative to see the totality of the picture. In 1979 the United States was a very wealthy nation. Nobody outside the nation's borders looked at America with pity. Throughout the 1970s, even during the periods of economic downturn, America's extraordinary wage scale drew in immigrants from around the world, especially those from nations just south of the United States. At the end of the decade, U.S. households ranked in the bottom 20 percent had an average annual income of $15,374, more money than the richest 20 percent earned in all but a few countries in the world. From 1969 to 1979 the percentage of people in poverty declined in the United States, the number of Americans who went to college increased, the percentage who owned automobiles rose, and life expectancy lengthened. By world scales and historic comparisons, America was—as a nation—doing extraordinarily well. And with the great benefit of hindsight, we know today that in the two decades that followed the Iran hostage crisis American wealth would, with a hitch or two, explode upward, blowing ahead of even the most optimistic projections of 1970s era economists, pundits, and campaigning politicians.[6]

Of course, such long-term trends about aggregate national wealth and a few cherry-picked statistics tell little about how it felt to be an American in 1979 and 1980. After the long economic boom of the postwar years, roughly 1945 to 1971, the 1970s (and, in fact, even more so the early 1980s) were a period of slow or negative growth. Wages were stuck throughout most of the late 1970s and sharply declined in the election year of 1980. Working-class Americans were particularly hard hit. Under intense pressure from international competition, factories closed in the Northeast and Midwest, "dislocating," as the jargon of the times put it, hundreds of thousands of industrial, unionized workers and producing a downward economic spiral that affected millions of Americans and crushed numerous communities. In Youngstown, Ohio, so many people were out of work that the town had been forced to close the decaying bridges over the Mahoning River because there was no money to fix them. In Aurora, Minnesota, a town dependent on mining the iron ore no longer needed to feed America's dying steel industry, people desperately tried to sell their houses so they could start over somewhere else—but there were no takers. The American dream of owning one's own home had become, in Aurora, a millstone around the necks of desperate people.[7] Those companies that fled high-wage, regulatory-oriented states like Michigan, Pennsylvania, Ohio, and New Jersey and reopened their plants in the South and the West almost always paid lower wages with fewer benefits to a non-unionized workforce. The movement and growth of businesses into what came to be called the "Sunbelt" contributed to a sharp reduction of Southern poverty (the South was the poorest region in the nation), but the Northeast, in turn, saw its poverty rates creep upward and unemployment boom.

Even in those parts of the nation that did well in the late 1970s, such as oil-producing Texas, uncertainty and even a certain pessimism about the economic future shadowed most American homes. In the 1970s, America was becoming a different kind of economic nation. People talked about the rise of a "service economy." So called "Rust-Belt" industries like steel making, appliance manufacturing, and textiles, which had long been at the heart of the American economy, were hemorrhaging jobs. While new hi-tech companies that would eventually lead to economic renaissance were starting up in the late 1970s, few Americans saw their potential and they employed a relative handful of people. Almost nobody knew what was next. Even people with good jobs were scared. By the end of the decade only 12 percent of Americans told pollsters that they were satisfied with the "state of the country"; 84 percent grimly stated that they were dissatisfied.[8]

Two seemingly intractable problems fueled people's economic distress. The first was an unrelenting inflationary spiral that had begun at the tail end of the 1960s. Prices in the 1970s skyrocketed. The cost of the humble hamburger more than doubled; the price of coffee more than tripled.[9] In a country used to cheap food it was like a slap in the face. With prices sometimes jumping more than 15 percent a year, the cost of credit raced to stay ahead of the declining buying power of the dollar. By the end of the decade interest rates for home mortgages and car loans hit 17 percent. That meant that the monthly payment on a thirty-year $100,000 home mortgage was $1,425 and the total amount in interest the holder of that mortgage would pay the bank by the time he or she owned that house free and clear was $413,243. A generation earlier people had paid as little as $421 a month on the same $100,000 mortgage, with a total of only $51,177 in interest over the course of the loan. Millions of people couldn't afford home mortgages in the 1970s.

Young people's dreams of becoming home owners were crushed; elderly people on fixed incomes watched their standard of living decline month in and month out; and people who needed to borrow money to invest in new businesses that could provide work for the growing number of unemployed were stopped in their tracks by sky-high loan rates.

The causes of inflation were complicated. Economists argued with each other about its primary causes, but most agreed that inflation had been unleashed when President Lyndon Johnson had pushed the federal budget into deficit by insisting on "guns and butter"—an expensive war in Vietnam and expansive social programs—without a balancing tax hike. And there was no doubt that Nixon had made the problem worse by refusing to make unpopular budget cuts and by not pushing for a tight monetary policy that would have slowed down the economy and, thereby, reduce price and wage increases.

Other factors played in: Americans were buying huge quantities of foreign-made goods, which meant that they were sending more and more dollars overseas, creating in 1971 (and then for most of the rest of the decade), for the first time since the late nineteenth century, a trade deficit. And because corporate America refused to invest sufficiently in new technology and facilities, productivity (the measure of output per worker) was on the decline, even as wages (slowly) increased. There was more to the story but few Americans understood why the price of consumer goods kept rising faster than their wages. Most economists, too, were perplexed: price inflation was not supposed to occur when economic growth was slow or negative. A new term, "stagflation," was coined to describe the arresting phenomenon. Except for a few economics professors intrigued by the intellectual puzzle, nobody took pleasure in this unusual confluence of economic stagnation and price inflation. People just wanted the job market to get better, prices to stop climbing, the dollar to stop losing value, and interest rates to decline so that they could afford a home mortgage and car payments.

President Carter had taken office in January 1977 pledging to tackle the inflationary spiral. At the end of 1979, his efforts had come to nothing. When Iranian militants grabbed American hostages in Tehran, inflation in the United States was racing along at a 17 percent annual rate.

Inflation and its evil cousin, stagflation, were bad enough. Just as destructive to the national spirit was the energy crisis that both contributed to the inflationary spiral and exacerbated Americans' sense that they had lost control of their national economic destiny to foreigners who competed unfairly and conspired against them. And while language about conspiracies sounds suspiciously like a kind of paranoia, in the 1970s conspiracy-spouting Americans were not exhibiting signs of stress-induced mental instability. They were right.

Spiking oil prices and gasoline shortages plagued the United States in the 1970s. This crisis had a villain Americans could identify: the Organization of the Petroleum Exporting Countries, better known as OPEC. Iran was in the thick of what many Americans considered this den of thieves.

Americans' exuberant use of cheap petroleum had helped fuel the fantastic economic growth of the post–World War II years. The great land yachts of the late 1950s and early 1960s, gaudily tail finned, chromed, and 1,000 pounds heavier than they had been just a decade earlier, symbolized American prosperity. They also exacerbated Americans' great and growing dependence on refined oil. The average family auto in the early 1960s got about 12 miles per gallon of gas; by 1973 Americans had put a man on the moon but passenger cars averaged only 13.4 miles to the gallon. Gasoline consumption in the United States more than doubled between 1950 and 1970. By 1979 Americans, constituting less than 6 percent of the world's population, sucked up almost 30% of the world's oil production. As American oil demand increased, more and more of the petroleum Americans needed was imported. In 1969, the United States was still a net exporter of oil. By 1970 the scale had tipped, and between January 1973 and January 1977 alone, oil imports had shot up from 35 percent to 50 percent of domestic consumption. In large part, until the 1970s Americans could afford to ignore their growing oil habit because oil was so cheap that profligate use caused no pain. In January 1971 a barrel of oil imported from Saudi Arabia cost all of $1.80.[10]

The first oil crisis came in October 1973 at the tail end of the Israeli-Arab Yom Kippur War. Arab nations launched an oil embargo to punish the United States for providing Israel, hard-pressed by Egyptian and Syrian forces, with military equipment in the middle of the conflict. By year's end the price of a barrel of oil had risen to $12. President Nixon had called for voluntary rationing and limited sales at gas stations. Instead, nervous car owners lined up at the pumps to "top off" their gas tanks in case supplies dried up. The "oil panic" temporarily tripled the price of gasoline, sending prices from around thirty-four cents a gallon to over a dollar, compounding inflationary pressures. Government attempts to address the exploding costs and shortages seemed only to make things worse. By February 1974, motorists in some states routinely waited in line two or three hours to fill their tanks. Fights broke out in gas station lines. Truck drivers, angry over poorly handled emergency gas rationing, struck.

Americans did make some half-hearted responses to the soaring price of oil. For a while at least, Americans began buying more fuel-efficient Japanese-made cars: little, boxy Toyotas and Datsuns. (This helped with energy consumption and saved money for individual drivers. However, rising purchases of foreign-made cars worsened the trade deficit and hurt the American auto industry, which was vital to the American economy.) Responding to the crisis, Congress mandated that car manufacturers make more energy-efficient autos and passed the 1974 Emergency Highway Energy Conservation Act, which set a maximum national highway speed limit of fifty-five miles per hour. In general, Americans felt like they had lost what many considered their birthright: cheap gas, high speeds, and plush rides.

The Arab nations that led OPEC—Saudi Arabia, Kuwait, and Iraq—took great satisfaction in their successful action. OPEC had been founded in the early 1960s but had, up until 1973, failed in lining up member nations to act as a price-setting cartel. Their anger at the United States for aiding Israel, however, had unified them. And the embargo proved how vulnerable the industrialized nations of the world were to the oil producers. OPEC was, suddenly, a force in the world. The oil-consuming nations would have to meet the cartel's price. The Shah of Iran, though not directly involved in the decision to embargo oil, did take pleasure in admonishing the United States and other energy guzzling nations: "The industrial world will have to realize that the era of their terrific progress and even more terrific income and wealth based on cheap fuel is finished. They will have to find new sources of energy and tighten their belts."[11] The OPEC nations had learned how to run a cartel and Americans could only watch, seething with resentment.

Between the spring of 1974 and the last days of 1977, OPEC successfully stabilized oil prices at record levels. Americans, rather than radically overhaul their energy patterns, essentially accepted the new terms. Americans spent three times as much as they once had on gasoline, heating oil, and other petroleum products—sending billions of dollars to the oil-producing nations. (Of course, many billions of dollars simply moved within the United States from non-oil-producing regions to those states, such as Texas and Oklahoma, blessed with the "black gold." During the mid-1970s, particularly frigid winters hit the Northeast, and many residents sought help from the federal government to pay the high cost of heating their homes; a popular bumper sticker in Texas offered a different solution: "Let 'Em Shiver in the Dark.") The high cost of energy and the gleeful avarice of oil producers, both foreign and domestic, were, in the middle 1970s, just two more indignities most Americans felt forced to accept. People were angry but they also felt impotent.

Given Americans' grumpy resignation about the situation, Jimmy Carter had not headlined energy issues when he ran for the presidency in 1976. However, after being elected but even before taking office, Carter was confronted by another kind of energy shortage—this time natural gas—and he decided to put America's dependence on imported oil and its wasteful energy habits at the top of his White House agenda.

Carter, in his inaugural address, had hinted at a new spirit of sacrifice. In the best remembered passages of the somewhat lackluster speech he suggested: "We have learned that 'more' is not necessarily 'better,' that even our great Nation has its recognized limits, and that we can neither answer all questions nor solve all problems. We cannot afford to do everything, nor can we afford to lack boldness as we meet the future. So, together, in a spirit of individual sacrifice for the common good, we must simply do our best." These honest but not particularly inspiring words set the tone for the Carter presidency. They were a far cry from John Kennedy's limitless New Frontier or Lyndon Johnson's passionate Great Society. America had entered a new era and it took an unusual kind of American to feel good about it.

In his first major policy address, April 18, 1977, the president honed in on the particular sacrifices he had in mind. Without histrionics or much dramatic appeal at all, Carter called the energy crisis "the moral equivalent of war" (wags took note of the initials and immediately called Carter's energy campaign "MEOW"). The president went on: oil and natural gas were becoming ever scarcer and Americans had to learn how to conserve. People had to stop buying gas-guzzling cars and, to help them do the right thing, Carter proposed a heavy tax on such vehicles. New government regulations would force manufacturers to make more energy-efficient electric appliances. Oil and gas prices would be deregulated, allowing prices to go even higher, thus providing consumers with an incentive to use less oil and gas. The government would subsidize research into alternative energy sources and provide tax credits for solar energy and home insulation. Altogether, Carter's energy plan contained 113 proposals. The National Energy Plan was officially known by the acronym NEP; the Carter administration hoped that no one would compare it to the original NEP devised by Lenin to bring economic reform to the Soviet Union in the 1920s.

NEP would wend its way through Congress over the next eighteen months. Most of the more dramatic proposals were compromised away as the auto industry, utility companies, and the Senate's general aversion to passing any kind of tax increase in an election year exacted a heavy toll on Carter's vision. What Carter's growing number of critics, as well as his dwindling number of supporters, took away from the speech, the long congressional debate, and the eventual legislation was that things were worse than they once were. For reasons that seemed to run the gamut from inevitable planetary shortages of natural resources to the villainous activities of sheiks and other oil barons, Americans were going to have to pay more to have less. It was bad news.[12]

Americans' forced engagement with energy policy and OPEC's oligopolists took a decided turn for the worse in 1979. Almost exactly two years after his first big energy talk, Carter was forced to go back to the American people and tell them: "Our nation's energy problem is serious—and it's getting worse."[13] In December 1978, OPEC had taken advantage of supply disruptions caused by anti-Shah strikes in the Iranian oil fields to announce that the price of petroleum would have to increase. As OPEC intended, oil prices skyrocketed, doubling in less than six months. The deliberate cut in production also squeezed world oil supplies. In the United States, gas stations could not get enough gasoline to meet American drivers' demands.

On the second day of summer, more than half the gas stations in the United States had no gas to sell. Those that had gas charged 50 percent more for it than they had at the end of 1978. The political journalist Nicholas Lemann remembers, "The automotive equivalent of the Depression's bank runs began. Everybody considered the possibilities of not being able to get gas, panicked, and went off to fill the tank; the result was hours-long lines at gas stations all over the country." In the middle of the mess Lemann himself ran out of gas on the Central Expressway in Dallas: "[T]he people driving by looked at me without surprise, no doubt thinking, 'Poor bastard, it could have happened to me just as easily.'"[14] It was some solace to people that everybody was in it together but that didn't change the bottom line: OPEC had America by the throat and neither President Carter nor anybody else in charge seemed to know what to do about it.

By time the second round of the energy crisis hit in early 1979, Jimmy Carter did know that his presidency was in trouble. To some extent, this was nothing new. The Carter presidency had gotten off to a rocky start and had never fully gained stable footing. Jimmy

Carter had beaten long odds in becoming president of the United States, and the American people had gambled in electing him. Carter had run for office as an outsider, a man whose main credential was his self-proclaimed lack of experience. In his early stump speeches he invariably proclaimed in his soft, Georgia drawl: "I'm not a lawyer, I'm not a member of Congress, and I've never served in Washington."[15] Only one other man who had become president in the twentieth century before Carter could have made that claim, but that one exception was Dwight D. Eisenhower, whose resumé did include being Supreme Commander of the Allied troops in Europe during World War II.

In 1976, Carter's lack of national political experience was a decided advantage. The Watergate scandal had driven a stake into the heart of traditional national politics. Richard Nixon's main defense against charges that he had committed perjury, obstructed justice, sicced the IRS on his enemies, misappropriated government money for his personal use, and, in general, just behaved badly had been that he was far from the first president to do as he had done. While Americans overwhelmingly decided that his offensive defense was insufficient to save him from impeachment, they did tend to believe him. Nixon managed to demean the office of the president, even as he brought down his own presidency.

Other prominent public servants had contributed to Americans' distrust of the traditional circle of national political leadership. Senator Edward Kennedy, probably the best-known Democratic politician in the nation before Carter's rise, had demonstrated that conservatives like Nixon had no corner on bad behavior. The last living Kennedy brother had ended the 1960s, notoriously, by driving a car off a bridge on Chappaquiddick Island. His passenger, a twenty-eight-year-old woman, drowned. Kennedy failed to call the police for many hours and had a difficult time keeping his story straight regarding the accident and the events leading up to and after it. Kennedy was Carter's main rival within the Democratic Party.

Thus, Carter's gamble and the American people's wager. In an era during which too many national politicians, to say it most gently, seemed to have discarded a simple virtue like honesty, Carter appeared as a man of heroic character. Presidential skills like foreign policy experience, knowledge of Congress, and familiarity with the major players in the American economy that had seemed de rigeur since the days of Franklin Roosevelt were not what Americans were demanding in 1976.

Upon taking office, Carter proved as good as his word. He really did have contempt for much of official Washington. Some of his early actions aimed at the symbols of pomposity with which Richard Nixon had bedecked the presidency. No more bands playing "Hail to the Chief" every time the president appeared. No more Prussian-style uniforms for White House guards. After giving his short inaugural address, Carter eschewed the presidential limo and walked down Pennsylvania Avenue with his wife and daughter, waving happily to the crowds lining the street. People liked it.

The problems came with the more substantive parts of the job. Carter had made it plain during the campaign that a Carter presidency would not be "business as usual." The iron triangle of congressional committees, executive branch agencies, and special interest lobbyists would not set policy in a Carter White House. Carter proclaimed for all to hear: "I owe the special interests nothing. I owe the people everything."[16] Chris Matthews, the acerbic-tongued pundit and one-time speechwriter for both House Speaker Tip O'Neill and Carter himself, was appalled by the new president's approach to governance: "Carter's decision to 'run against Washington' was a brilliant bit of political positioning. . . . But his mistake was to allow this anti-Washington posture, so formidable out in the country, to hinder his effectiveness once in the capital. . . . 'People don't do their best work while they're being pissed on,' an old Washington hand once remarked to me."[17] Matthews was right on both scores: Carter's genuine scorn for Washington got him elected, but his inability or disinclination to disguise his disdain made him many political enemies. Those enemies helped make it difficult for him to get anything done in Congress.

Carter's problem with Congress was not just personal. Since the New Deal, members of Congress understood that their power had declined relative to the executive branch. The growth of the national security state during the cold war had intensified that relative loss of power. After the Vietnam debacle and the Watergate fiasco, federal legislators saw their chance to reign in the so-called imperial presidency and return their branch of government to a coequal role in federal policymaking. Both houses of Congress passed legislation aimed at limiting presidential power and instituted internal reforms that strengthened Capitol Hill's legislative and oversight capacities. In part, Congress simply gave itself the right to hire more people to staff more subcommittees and congressional agencies to combat the immense growth in the executive branch that had given the president a formidable capacity to push around Congress and make and implement policy as he saw fit.

As a result, by 1977 when Carter took over the presidency, Congress had both the power and the predilection to contest his leadership. Political scientist Sidney Milkis believes that by the late 1970s "a strong anti-bureaucratic, anti-institutional ethos" prevailed in the newly revitalized Congress and no president elected in 1976 would have had an easy time telling Congress what to do.[18] Carter, because he had run for office with little support from his own Democratic Party and because he had made his disdain for Congress and other insiders a central aspect of his campaign, was even more vulnerable to Congress's new assertiveness. The result was that now familiar American frustration: legislative gridlock. Carter's lack of support in Congress also made it hard for him to find political cover when he most needed it. Ergo, when trouble came—and in 1979 it was coming from several directions—Carter could not count on even his fellow Democrats to give him the time he needed to quietly and patiently work through the various political and governmental messes.

The public attacks on Carter started to come in waves in the spring of 1979. The timing was terrible; the nation was facing an escalating energy crisis. Carter was struggling to find the gift of leadership that would enable him to help the American people overcome it.

Carter took his first hit from one of his own men. It was a classic stab in the back. In a May 1979 kiss-and-tell piece for the *Atlantic*

Monthly, James Fallows, who had recently stepped down as Carter's chief speechwriter, excoriated the president. Fallows described Carter as a man who did not know his limits and who did not know how to listen to people who could help him govern. In a damning phrase that would resonate in the historical record, he wrote: "I came to think that Carter believes fifty things, but no one thing." Fallows coolly observed: "Carter needed the insiders' wisdom about the power game if he was to succeed in office—but he needed to remember why he, instead of one of them, had been elected. Maintaining this balance required a keen awareness of how much he needed to acquire, and an even keener sense of what he needed to avoid. The tragedy of Jimmy Carter was that he knew neither." Worse, Fallows maintained, "Carter and those closest to him to him took office in profound ignorance of their jobs. They were ignorant of the possibilities and the most likely pitfalls. They fell prey to predictable dangers and squandered precious time. . . . Carter often seemed more concerned with taking the correct position than with learning how to turn that position into results."[19] While Fallows may have caricatured his subject at times, Americans recognized the pen portrait.

Mainstream political pundits, suspicious of the anti-establishment Carter from the start, used Fallows's piece to rip the president apart. In the *New York Times*, William Safire snorted: "He offered apparent goodness without effectiveness; the secret of Carter is that he wanted, above all, to be President, and he had no clear idea of what he wanted to *do* as President." *Washington Post* columnist Joseph Kraft concurred: "The case of Mr. Carter demonstrates that good intentions are almost irrelevant and perhaps even downright harmful." *Newsweek*'s Peter Goldman reported that Carter and his men were objects of scorn in Congress, especially among their fellow Democrats: "[Carter's] own political gifts are held in light regard in Congress. Respect for his staff is low and sliding: [Speaker of the House] O'Neill has lately reverted to his old habit of calling Carter's man, Hamilton Jordan, 'whatzisname—Hannibal Jerkins.' "[20] Not unlike the newly feisty Congress, the post-Watergate mass media felt itself under no patriotic obligation to give any benefit of the doubt to the nation's elected leader. The mass media attack was ugly.

More problematically for Carter, all but the president's most stalwart supporters were cheering on the media. Carter's public opinion poll tracking showed him in danger of dropping into uncharted territory. A mid-summer poll showed only 25 percent of Americans willing to give their president a rating of good or excellent. Carter was about as popular as Richard Nixon was just prior to his resignation.

In June 1979 OPEC contributed to the nation's foul mood and Carter's misfortunes by decreeing that oil prices would, alas, have to rise again. Americans, who had already been banging their fists on steering wheels at the outrageous cost of a gallon of gas and occasionally throwing a punch at one another while waiting in long lines at short-supplied gas stations, were apoplectic. At the time of the OPEC announcement, Carter was at an economic summit in Tokyo, focused on energy issues. His aides suggested, strongly, that he not take a planned vacation in Hawaii and, instead, get himself immediately back to Washington.

The plan was for President Carter to appear July 5 on national television and take on the energy crisis. It was a daunting task and not just because nobody in the Carter administration knew what to do about rising gasoline and oil prices. The bigger problem was that Carter was in danger of losing his ability to lead the American people. The energy riptide was part of it. So was runaway inflation, which Carter had not been able to control. The media attacks gave voice to the public discontent. Stupid, little things contributed: the president's brother, in the long tradition of presidential ne'er-do-well siblings, had taken large sums of money from the terrorist-sponsoring nation of Libya and then defended himself by assuring the American people that a "heap of governments support terrorists and [Libya] at least admitted it."[21] Just thirty hours before Carter was scheduled to give his national energy address, his staff called the networks and canceled. Rosalyn Carter, who was probably the most able woman to hold down the odd post of First Lady since Eleanor Roosevelt, had read two pages of the speech and had bluntly told her husband, "Nobody wants to hear it."[22] She was right; nobody in the White House knew what to tell the American people.

Following the cancellation, Carter undertook a remarkable adventure in presidential leadership. He holed up in Camp David, the rustic presidential retreat in Maryland. He had with him a lengthy memo his pollster, Pat Caddell, had prepared for him. Caddell argued that Americans needed more than another laundry list of energy programs. The president had been down that path four times already. Caddell argued that "Americans were rapidly losing faith in themselves and in their country." The president had to restore that lost faith.[23]

Carter, the first born-again Christian in the White House, accepted the mission. And he pursued the idea with his usual intensity and zest for hard work. In the eleven days Carter spent at Camp David, he brought in carloads of politicians, theologians, businessmen, professors, and several of the gray eminences of insider Washington, seeking their advice. While Vice President Fritz Mondale, an old Washington hand himself, recoiled at what he considered a waste of time and a political mistake, the president listened to his guests. In ways both gentle and rough, they told him that he was failing to lead the country. Bill Clinton, then a thirty-two-year-old first-term governor from the troubled state of Arkansas, watched the action from a distance and told the press that Jimmy Carter talked to the American people like a "17th century New England Puritan [rather] than a 20th century Southern Baptist." (He would never make that particular mistake.) Carter, to his credit, sat there and took it; he tried to figure out how to take the barbs and turn them into a national balm.[24]

On July 15, President Carter made a remarkable speech to the nation. As usual, Carter's delivery was not exactly made for prime time: he was stiff and he rarely reached beyond a monotone. But the words were interesting and they were certainly provocative. In part he offered a history lesson: "We were sure that ours was a nation of the ballot, not the bullet, until the murders of John Kennedy, Robert Kennedy, and Martin Luther King, Jr. We were taught that our armies were always invincible and our causes always just, only to suffer the agony of Vietnam. We respected the Presidency as a place of honor, until the shock of Watergate." After that cavalcade of despair, he hit the crux of his speech: the nation faced more than a tough few years and a difficult economy. Starting straight at the camera, unblinking, he stated that Americans faced "a crisis of confidence. It is a crisis that strikes at the very heart and soul and spirit of our national will. We see this crisis in the growing doubt about the meaning of our own lives and in the loss of unity of purpose for our Nation."[25]

Carter followed up his jeremiad by asking his entire cabinet to submit letters of resignation. He accepted five resignations and asked his long-time right-hand man, Hamilton Jordan (a.k.a. "Hannibal Jerkins"), to reorganize the White House staff. Carter hoped he could shake up his administration and find a path to presidential leadership that had so far eluded him.

The day after Carter's big speech, Jordan laid out the situation. In an amazingly frank memo, he listed for Carter "negative perceptions about your presidency": "Carter is not in charge of his government," "Carter is not tough," "Carter is managing, not leading," "Carter has forgotten who elected him," and "Carter listens to a small group of Georgians and does not reach out for advice and different opinions." He told the president that people saw him, Jordan, as weak on details, not tough, and an "'unsubstantial' person" (the last charge, he felt, was unfair). The senior staff was widely seen as "all from Georgia, that we don't go out socially enough, that we have disdain for the Congress." For himself, he promised to try harder with Congress, to socialize and seek out Washington's major players, and to . . . dress better. Carter's senior aides were infamous for their casual appearance and for their less than strictly upright behavior; a rumor of cocaine use among senior staff prompted Carter, at one point, to tell them confidentially: "I am deeply concerned over recent reports that some members of the White House staff are using illegal drugs. . . . Whether you agree with the law or whether or not others obey the law is totally irrelevant. You will obey it, or you will seek employment elsewhere."[26]

Substantively, Jordan stepped up to become chief of staff. Until then, Carter had refused to have a chief of staff because he didn't want anyone to stand between him and key members of the administration. Carter did not want to become another Nixon, alone and cut off in the White House. By late 1979, almost all White House observers believed that Carter's good intentions had backfired. With no clear organizational hierarchy and Carter's propensity to micromanage, everything turned up on his desk—including the White House tennis court reservation schedule.[27] Besides elevating Jordan's status and responsibilities, Carter aimed to get out in front of America's troubles. He vowed to spend less time on paperwork, bring in new advisors, and reconnect with the American people.[28]

Unfortunately, outside the White House, most Americans were unconvinced. Many got exactly the wrong idea from the president's actions. Carter, for example, believed that by shaking up his cabinet, he would show Americans that he was a tough leader who demanded results. What a large majority of Americans instead perceived was that in the midst of runaway inflation, an energy crisis, and what the president himself described as a "crisis of confidence," the government was falling apart at the seams.

Carter's "crisis of confidence" speech and the subsequent administrative reshuffling and rethinking took place in July and early August 1979. By that time events in Iran had, from the American government's perspective, spun out of control. While the president and his men were well aware of how bad the situation was in Iran, publicly little was being said about it. What was the point? Events had moved far faster than anybody in the U.S. government had predicted.

THE SHAH, KHOMEINI, AND THE "GREAT SATAN"

When David Rockefeller, grandson of John D. Rockefeller and presi-dent of Chase Manhattan Bank, arrived in Tehran in May 1970, he barely knew Muhammad Reza Pahlavi, the Shah of Shahs. The two men had met briefly in Tehran in 1965 and then again in Cambridge, Massachusetts, at a dinner in 1968 when the regents of Harvard Uni-versity, for reasons of their own, had chosen to present the Shah with an honorary degree. The Chase Bank had strong links with the fabulously wealthy Pahlavi regime, and bank business took Rockefel-ler to Iran.

Rockefeller was in Tehran as co-convener of the Tehran Investment Seminar. The seminar brought thirty-five American businessmen, very big businessmen—Don Kendall of Pepsi, H. J. Heinz of H. J. Heinz, Don Burnham, chairman of Westinghouse, James A. Linen of Time, Inc., and Fred Bissinger, president of Allied Chemical, to name only a few—to Iran to stake out investment opportunities. The Americans met with the cordial Shah and his political and economic allies, the super-elite of

Iran. Over fine French wines and exquisite meals they learned from their hosts that they were welcome in Iran and that their partnership was eagerly sought in enterprises of all kinds. With strong support from the president of the United States, Richard Nixon, and the blessings of the Shah, direct American investment in Iran was taking what both sides hoped was a quiet step forward.

While the Iranian political and economic elite saw profit and promise in American investment, many outside the magic circle saw things differently. Nationalists, both secular and religious, did not want the Americans and American money to come to Iran. They called the investment seminar the "Conference of Imperialists" or "Rockefeller's Conference." (Because of the Rockefeller family's extensive global investments, the name "Rockefeller" was then synonymous in much of the world, unfairly or not, with avaricious economic exploitation.)

A few people even risked arrest by publicly protesting against the presence of the American investors. Demonstrators attacked the offices of the Iran-America Society in Tehran. Ayatollah Khomeini, the Shah's greatest detractor, supported the protests from exile in neighboring Iraq: "Any agreement that is concluded with these American capitalists and other imperialists is contrary to the will of the people and the ordinances of Islam."

Inside Iran, one of Khomeini's followers, Muhammad Reza Sa'idi, dared to speak out against the visiting Americans. Echoing his revered leader, he accused the Shah of selling the nation's patrimony to American imperialists. The forty-one-year-old cleric had challenged the Shah's regime before and, as a result, had been arrested several times by SAVAK (Sazman-i Ittili'at va Amniyat-i Kishvar; in English, National Security and Information Organization), the Shah's security force. This time the hard men who kept the Shah's order in Iran had no intention of just teaching Sa'idi a lesson and letting him go. On June 10, 1970, they tortured him to death.

During Sa'idi's torment, people say, he looked into the eyes of his torturers and told them: "I swear to God if you kill me, in every drop of my blood you can see the holy name of Khomeini." Sa'idi's body was buried in the holy city of Qom. His friends and fellow followers of the Ayatollah promised that his martyrdom would be avenged.[1]

IN THE 1970s, for Iranians across the political spectrum, the United States figured as a kind of deus ex machina in the drama of their national life; it was an outside force that intervened as it wished, often without regard for the desires or even well-being of the Iranian people. American power appeared full force in the form of military might, weapons sales, and capital investment; it was delivered more subtly in daily television programming (*Dallas* and *Wheel of Fortune* were particularly popular in the late 1970s) and it operated clandestinely in U.S. intelligence operations that darkened the political imagination of the Iranian people. While few Americans before the revolution and hostage crisis paid any serious attention to Iran (Gary Sick, the National Security Council staffer responsible for Iran in the Carter White House, wrote: "[I]t is not an exaggeration to say that America approached Iran from a position of almost unrelieved ignorance"[2]), Iranians, whether friends or foes of the American government, had no choice but to reckon with the power of the United States. The asymmetry of the relationship created, at best, ambivalence: "I want to beat you and be you, simultaneously," is how Iranian expert Marvin Zonis describes Iranian attitudes toward the United States.[3] At worst, Iranians believed American influence and power made a mockery of their national autonomy and desecrated their religious beliefs.

Iranians' perception of American power was based on real events, above all the regime-changing events of 1953. The Shah himself told the CIA's Kermit Roosevelt, "I owe my throne to God, my people, my army—and to you!"[4] The Shah's growing number of opponents believed that the United States continued to play a fundamental role in maintaining the Shah in power and in determining Iran's destiny. Clerics in the Islamic stronghold city of Isfahan, for example, wrote President Carter soon after he took office, reprimanding him but also asking for help. Six of their number, they told him, were to be executed by the Shah's security forces.

The American government could and must stop this deadly repression: "Mr. President: You are certainly aware of the heavy responsibility that the United States government undertook by the coup d'état which was engineered by the CIA. . . . From that day on the United States government has supported the present regime by every conceivable means."[5] (The Department of State ruled that no reply would be sent to this letter and President Carter himself never received the plea for help.[6]) Multitudes of Iranians saw the United States as the ghost in the machine, present even when it was absent, pulling strings, making secret deals, changing lives, bestowing boons, and providing cover for corrupt and even murderous acts.

All over the developing world in the 1960s and 1970s revolutionaries, reactionaries, and some people just caught in the middle castigated the United States for using its economic and military might to control other nations' destinies in its relentless pursuit of wealth and power. The charges had some truth to them. The U.S. government really had tried to assassinate Cuban leader Fidel Castro; it had backed the overthrow of the Guatemalan government and supported a murderous military regime; it had done the same in Chile. In Iran, the United States had made a deal with the devil, working closely with the Shah's fearsome state torturers, SAVAK; the list went on and on. In 1975 a former CIA agent, Philip Agee, published *Inside the Company*, an unauthorized exposé of American covert intelligence operations all over the world. (Agee also unmasked many covert CIA operatives; Congress responded by making the release of covert CIA operatives' identities illegal.) Bitterly, Agee concluded: "[W]e justified our penetration, disruption and sabotage . . . because we felt morality changed on crossing national frontiers."[7] In those parts of the world where the rule of law was weak and ineffective or where U.S. government officials perceived communist, anti-American forces at work, high-minded principles had, at times, been laid aside in the name of national security or to further American economic interests. At least some of the people in those countries that had been penetrated, disrupted, and sabotaged, not surprisingly, viewed the United States as a brutal nation.

In the United States in the immediate post-Vietnam era, with charges about CIA misdeeds in the third world headline news, politicians on both the left and right castigated American foreign policy. Ronald Reagan, widely perceived at the time as an ultra-conservative, attempted to take away the 1976 Republican Party presidential nomination from incumbent Gerald Ford not by condemning CIA activities but by charging the president and Secretary of State Henry Kissinger with pursuing an amoral foreign policy that was soft on communism. Détente with the Soviet Union, Reagan scoffed, was "a foreign policy whose principal accomplishment seems to be our acquisition of the right to sell Pepsi-Cola in Siberia."[8] Though Reagan failed to defeat Ford, he and his supporters successfully amended the 1976 Republican Party platform to call for "Morality in Foreign Policy." The amendment essentially chastised Ford for failing to treat the Soviet Union as an evil empire and called on the American government to fight, not cozy up to, the communist threat. This honorable battle, Reagan told his fellow conservatives, would once again give the American people "a sense of mission and greatness."[9] The cold war was heating up in the Republican Party.

Jimmy Carter, during his run for the presidency, also attacked the Ford-Kissinger foreign policy of realpolitik but from a different direction. After the bloody failure in Vietnam and the information made public by Senator Frank Church, investigative reporters, and various writers about CIA-sponsored coups and other covert acts that had resulted in assassinations, violent mayhem, death, and torture all over the third world, a majority of the American electorate, Carter believed, wanted American foreign policy to champion virtue, not narrow self-interest.

When Carter ran for president he promised that if he were elected the United States would pursue foreign policies commensurate with the nation's highest ideals. In campaign speeches, he was blunt: "Our people have learned the folly of our trying to inject our power into the internal affairs of other nations. It is time that our government learned that lesson too." And, he said, "Never again should our country become militarily involved in the internal affairs of another country unless there is a direct and obvious threat to the security of the United States or its people. We must not use the CIA or other covert means to effect violent change in any government or government policy. . . . The CIA must operate within the law." Adherence to American principles, not narrow self-interest, Carter explained, would best serve the global mission of the United States: "Over the years, our greatest source of strength has come from those basic, priceless values which are embodied in our Declaration of Independence, our Constitution, and our Bill of Rights: our belief in freedom of religion—our belief in freedom of expression—our belief in human dignity. . . . These principles have made us great, and unless our foreign policy reflects them, we make a mockery of all those values."[10] Carter's warm sentiments bathed the American public in feelings of righteousness. Whether such noble and decent thoughts could become effective foreign policy practices was yet to be seen.

Jimmy Carter was a relative latecomer to foreign policy concerns. He had grown up far from the elite universe of East Coast prep schools, Ivy League colleges, cushy jobs on Wall Street, and well-placed connections. Plains, Georgia, where Jimmy was raised in the 1930s and 1940s as the son of a relatively successful small-town businessman and a registered nurse, had about five hundred people. He had little opportunity to hear sophisticated people debate the great international issues of the day. At Georgia Southwestern College, the Georgia Institute of Technology, and then the U.S. Naval Academy, Carter trained to be an engineer. He spent seven years in the navy where he worked his way up to chief engineer of the *Seawolf*, a prototype nuclear submarine. When Carter's father died in 1953 he came home to Plains and took over the family peanut business. Achieving financial success (by Plains' standards), he became increasingly involved in local and then state politics. He lost the 1966 gubernatorial Democratic primary election to the arch-segregationist Lester Maddox (an Atlanta restaurant owner who had won the hearts of a majority of white Georgia voters by standing in the doorway of his restaurant, Pickrick, with an ax handle and refusing to admit black people). Carter came back in 1970 to run again. This time he hid his civil rights principles and pandered to white voters' segregationist sentiments. He won the governorship, replacing a man nationally regarded as a buffoon.

Carter's first forays into foreign policy and international relations came soon after he decided to run for president. He made the decision after he had been governor of Georgia for just two years. In those two years he had surprised a lot of people. First, despite the "seg" rhetoric he had deployed during his campaign, once elected he proved to be a strong, heartfelt supporter, in word and deed, of African American equality. In the deep South of the early 1970s that was big news—and it was courageous, if also smart politics for a man with national ambitions. Carter had also demonstrated his keen engineer's intelligence by reorganizing the ineptly run Georgia state government and making it both more efficient and more economical. While far from a household name outside of his home state, people in the political know were aware of the aggressive, talented "New South" governor. Supported by his youthful right-hand man, Hamilton Jordan, and practically nobody else, Carter thought that the 1976 Democratic presidential primary was going to be wide open and ripe for a new, outsider candidate: him.

Carter also understood that his foreign policy inexperience could be costly to his presidential-candidate credibility. The last governor to be president had been Franklin Roosevelt—but Roosevelt had also served Woodrow Wilson during World War I as assistant secretary of the navy. Carter was in relatively uncharted political territory. So, when an opportunity to gain a foreign policy credential came his way in late 1973, Carter took it.

Governor Carter's introduction to the world of big-time international relations came by way of the Trilateral Commission. Carter was invited to join the exclusive, members-only group by its director, Zbigniew Brzezinski, who saw something special—intelligence, high ambition, and political savvy—in the governor. The Trilateral Commission was, then, a very new organization. Its avowed purpose was simple: "Japan, Western Europe, and North America, in view of their great weight in the world economy and their massive relations with one another, bear a special responsibility for developing effective cooperation. . . . They must make concerted efforts to deal with the challenge of interdependence they cannot manage separately." In other words, the commission formed so that leading businessmen, politicians, and intellectuals from Japan, Western Europe, and the United States could meet together to identify international problems and their likely solutions. The body would be extra-governmental, its only power derived from the influence, connections, and mutually reinforcing convictions of its invited members. The Trilateral Commission quickly came to figure strongly in the fevered imagination of zealots—some would say crackpots—of both the far right and far left wings of American politics, who saw it as a cabal of "one-world government" conspirators. Fueling such fears, David Rockefeller was the "principal founder" of the Trilateral Commission.[11]

By the time Carter was running for the presidency he was well versed in foreign affairs. Whatever else, Carter was a voracious student. He later stated: "Those Trilateral Commission meetings for me were like classes in foreign policy—reading papers produced on every conceivable subject, hearing experienced leaders debate international issues and problems and meeting the big names."[12] Carter first met most of the men who would lead his White House foreign policy and national security policy at those meetings. Most critically, he picked up a first-class policy advisor for his presidential run, the Trilateral Commission director, Zbigniew Brzezinski.

Dr. Brzezinski was a foreign policy prodigy and a kind of rival-twin to Henry Kissinger. Like Kissinger, Brzezinski was an émigré. Kissinger was fifteen in 1938 when his family fled the Nazis; Brzezinski's family fled Poland a few years later to escape the communists. Though five years younger, Brzezinski overlapped with Kissinger at Harvard, where they both earned doctorates in the government department. Each man insists that the other created a competitive rivalry (and each insists that he had no real feelings about the other man). While Kissinger went on to become a Harvard professor, Brzezinski went off to earn tenure at Columbia University. He and Kissinger, at the same time, dazzled their way into the foreign policy "Establishment." Kissinger was on the faster track, supported by Nelson Rockefeller, the moderate Republican governor of New York and brother of David Rockefeller. Brzezinski, only slightly less successfully, worked on the moderate Democratic Party side. In 1960, "Zbig" advised John F. Kennedy on East-West relations. He worked for the Council of Foreign Relations and then took a position in the Johnson administration with the prestigious State Department Policy Planning Council. When Hubert Humphrey made his run for the presidency in 1968, Brzezinski was his foreign policy advisor. When Nixon defeated Humphrey and appointed Kissinger assistant for national security, Brzezinski took off for Asia and spent a good long while thinking about how Japan fit into the U.S.-Soviet rivalry and the emerging global economy. That line of thinking led to the Trilateral Commission, which put him into contact with the unlikely presidential contender, James Earl Carter.[13]

When Brzezinski was appointed national security advisor by Carter he brought a fully developed agenda to the job. Little on his list had anything directly to do with honoring international "human rights" or establishing American foreign policy as a simple reflection of America's "basic, priceless values." In most respects, Brzezinski was as hardheaded a realist as Henry Kissinger. He had even less trust and even more disgust for the leading communist powers in the world. He believed that the totalitarian governments of the Soviet Union and China had to be fiercely restrained and countered at every turn. And he had little faith that the communists had respect for anything but unmatchable military power. Unlike Kissinger and his old boss, Richard Nixon, Brzezinski did believe that the United States had to work more closely and energetically with its key allies, especially the Japanese and Western European nations. Kissinger, he believed, loved headline-grabbing one-man policy adventures too much and thought too little about creating a durable foreign policy "architecture" that could create long-term solutions to global problems. Brzezinski also believed that the Nixon administration had exercised ad hoc, knee-jerk responses to problems in the developing world too often. North-south relations, he argued, had to take greater prominence in America's long-term foreign policy strategy.

Brzezinski, who had opportunities to work with many of the leading Democrats contending for the 1976 presidential nomination, chose to align himself with Carter. Burnishing his own analytic ability, Brzezinski notes in his memoirs that he joined Carter's efforts when the Georgia governor's "national recognition factor in public opinion polls was less than 2 percent!"[14] Carter appreciated the trust and paid it back in full after winning the presidency. He selected Brzezinski as his national security advisor and guaranteed him direct access to the Oval Office. The hardheaded, fiercely anti-communist Brzezinksi, more than any other individual, guided President Carter through the labyrinths of national security and international diplomacy.

Brzezinski was not the only man advising the president on global affairs. To run the State Department, Carter picked Cyrus Roberts Vance. As his name might indicate, Vance was about as far from the inner circle of Georgians, such as Hamilton Jordan, who had run Carter's campaign and then staffed his White House, as was possible. Vance was a bona fide member of the "Eastern Establishment." He attended the Kent School in Connecticut and then Yale, where he received his undergraduate and law degrees. After honorable service in the navy during World War II, Vance joined the politically well-connected Wall Street law firm of Simpson, Thacher and Bartlett. Well-positioned in every possible way, Vance almost immediately began his distinguished career in public service. In 1960 he took his first major position in government, general counsel for the Department of Defense. Two years later, President Kennedy made him secretary of the army. Shortly after President Kennedy's assassination, Lyndon B. Johnson asked him to serve as deputy secretary of defense. Vance was, by the mid-1960s and in the parlance of the 1960s, a central figure in the "Establishment." Like almost all of the men associated with it (the notable exception being the iconoclastic insider, George W. Ball), Vance enthusiastically supported American military intervention in Vietnam. Likewise, by 1968 he and almost all of his peers realized that they had made a monumental mistake and counseled President Johnson to negotiate a peace settlement with the North Vietnamese communists (negotiations, in Paris, in which Vance played a central role).[15]

For Vance, Nixon's 1968 victory mandated a return to his law practice. He remained active in the foreign policy circuit, traveling widely and maintaining contact with key people in many parts of the world. During the 1976 fight for the Democratic presidential nomination, Vance was closely allied with his old Yale friend Sargent Shriver, an "old school" liberal who had been George McGovern's vice presidential running mate in the 1972 loss to Richard Nixon and Spiro Agnew. When Shriver withdrew from the race, Carter personally called Vance and asked him to join his foreign policy advising team. Vance had only met Carter a couple of times through the Trilateral Commission so he at first demurred, but after examining Carter's stated positions and his surprisingly good chances of winning the presidency, Vance signed on.

Vance's foreign policy views were not, at first glance, much different from Brzezinski's. He, too, supported a tough-minded approach to the Soviet Union, though one tempered by the need to reduce cold war tensions. He also advocated greater attention to problems of the developing world. Like Brzezinski he believed that the Kissinger approach had been too oriented toward crisis management and not enough focused on long-term problem solving. He was sympathetic to Carter's oft-stated concerns about applying American moral principles to foreign policy but, again like Brzezinski, was not sure that a concern for foreigners' human rights could come before America's more immediate national interests.

In a campaign advisory memo he wrote for Carter, Vance tried to outline a rhetorical middle ground. The memo is worth quoting at length: "The United States will continue in international forums its unwavering stand in favor of the rights of free men and, without unrealistically inserting itself into the internal operations of other governments, to give important weight to those considerations in selecting foreign policy positions in the interests of the United States."[16] Vance believed that Carter's idealism, which he respected, would have to be anchored to the day-in and day-out practical realities of "hard choices," the apt title of his memoir of service during the Carter years. Here is where Vance differed from Brzezinski, not so much in policy views as in temperament. Brzezinski was a hard-charger; Vance was a cautious player in world affairs. His background and his experience had taught him to move carefully, to operate in measured fashion, and to remain calm in the midst of seeming crisis. Vance believed that America's immense power and wealth were rarely served by risky acts or disruptive behavior.

Some of Jimmy Carter's inner circle looked with equal suspicion at Carter's two foreign policy campaign advisors. The "outsiders" from Georgia, disgusted with "the best and the brightest" who had led the United States into the Vietnam War, wanted their boss to look beyond the "East Coast Establishment" in selecting his national security and State Department appointees. During the interregnum, after Carter had won the election but before he was sworn in as president, Hamilton Jordan made his feelings clear: "[I]f, after the inauguration, you find a Cy Vance as secretary of state and Zbigniew Brzezinski as head of National Security, then I'd say we failed. And I'd quit."[17] Jordan's bluff was called. Carter appointed Vance and Brzezinski. Jordan did not quit. Vance and Brzezinski, both of whom had played hardball with much tougher customers, found Jordan's comments more amusing than anything else.[18]

Jimmy Carter had tremendous respect for his own intelligence. A happy outcome of that self-confidence was a willingness to surround himself with highly capable people, especially in the foreign policy–national security arena. In addition to his appointments of Brzezinski and Vance, Carter selected Harold Brown, president of the California Institute of Technology, longtime high-ranking government advisor and bureaucrat, as well as a nuclear weapons specialist, to be secretary of defense. The president counted on these three highly accomplished, seasoned professionals to keep the United States strong, safe, and a force for good in the world. *Newsweek* magazine reflected contemporary conventional wisdom by praising Carter's choices as "a safe-and-sane technocracy with button downs under its denims and moderation on its mind."[19] Carter never doubted that his hired experts worked for him, that he would be their boss, and that they would follow his lead. As a result, for the first years of the Carter administration, the president's human-rights-and-American-principles-first took rhetorical priority even as Brzezinski, Vance, and others worked the harder territory of national security interests and various bilateral diplomatic relations. Sometimes the dueling sets of concerns clashed. They did in Iran.

Iran was not supposed to be a focal point of Jimmy Carter's presidency. It was not supposed to be a place about which the American people had to worry. When Carter took office in January 1977 Iran and the United States were relatively trouble-free allies. The relationship was fairly new and had not developed without tensions but, from the American perspective, Iran and the United States were strong partners. Together, they were dedicated to open access to Persian Gulf oil, economic development of the region, anti-communism, and geopolitical stability in the Near and Middle East.

While the United States had played small and sporadic roles in Iran before World War II, the relationship between the two nations had really only begun at the onset of the cold war. Prior to World War II, the United States had been, essentially, shut out of Persian affairs. For more than a century, Iran had been a pawn in the "great Game" Russia and Great Britain had played throughout Southwest Asia and the Near East. Both imperial nations had fought to dominate the region and at every opportunity had run roughshod over the aspirations and, usually, the interests of the people who lived there. While not completely indifferent to the plight of the peoples of the region, few Americans saw any purpose in involving their nation in such a faraway part of the world.

During the latter half of the 1930s, as a result of decades of unwanted attention from both England and Russia, Iranians openly, even enthusiastically, sympathized with the Nazis' challenge to Soviet power and British imperialism. Hitler played to these sentiments by granting "Aryan" status to all Persian people. As a result, to keep Iranian oil fields out of the hands of the Germans during

World War II, both England and the Soviets invaded the country and quickly dispatched the poorly equipped Iranian military.

The ruler of Iran, Reza Pahlavi, father to Reza Muhammad Pahlavi, wrote President Roosevelt in 1941, asking for American help: "I consider it my duty, on the basis of the declarations of which Your Excellency has made several times regarding the necessity of defending principles of international justice and the rights of people to liberty. . . . to put an end to these acts of aggression."[20] Roosevelt, champion of national self-determination, agreed with the Shah that the occupation was wrong. But there was, Roosevelt believed, nothing he could yet do about the situation: defeating Germany came before all else. Shah Reza Pahlavi was forced into African exile where he died in 1944. The occupiers seated his twenty-one-year-old son, Muhammad, on the Peacock Throne. He ruled in name only; Great Britain and the Soviet Union controlled Iran.

In December 1943, the Big Three—Roosevelt, Winston Churchill, and Joseph Stalin—met in Tehran to begin working out the postwar settlement. Among other grander concerns, at Roosevelt's insistence, the Allied powers formally agreed to leave Iran no later than six months after the war's end, maintain the country's territorial integrity, and give postwar Iran national autonomy. President Roosevelt had begun a new relationship between Iran and the United States. The United States had become, Iranians believed, their protector.[21]

When the war finally ended, Great Britain did as it had agreed. It withdrew its troops from Iran. The Soviets did not. For roughly one hundred years, when the Russians committed an act of aggression in the Near East, England had responded. But England, after the war, was giving up on empire. It had lost the desire, the will, and the resources necessary for international primacy. Its imperial presence was fast fading from the Near and Middle East. The United States, haphazardly and with a different agenda, was just as quickly stepping into the breach. Iran, which had been for so long dominated by England, was one of the first nations in the region to receive critical American attention. In 1946, in step with Roosevelt's pledges and Americans' heightened fears about

Soviet communist global aggression, the Truman administration (coupled with Machiavellian diplomacy on the part of the Iranians) successfully pressured the Soviet Union to withdraw its troops from northern Iran.

In the next few years, American fears that the Soviets might invade or subvert Iran further linked the two nations. While cool heads in the State Department, including President Truman's secretary of state, Dean Acheson, warned against seeing Iran too narrowly through the lens of anti-communism, American preoccupation with battling the Soviet Union overshadowed all other considerations. In order to stabilize Iran's fragile government and prevent internal communist groups, in particular the Tudeh Party, from gaining strength, the United States began to modestly aid the government that was led by the still young Shah.

The Shah wanted the United States to supply Iran with a modern military capable of fending off a Soviet attack. American Ambassador John Wiley warned his colleagues that the Shah's "thinking (in) this regard is strictly in never never land." Secretary of State Acheson added that the Shah was a "very impractical young man . . . full of grandiose ideas; he fancied himself a great military leader."[22] Those Americans who were paying attention to Iran believed that economic and political reform were more important to the stability of Iran than was an expensive, modern military. A communist takeover of Iran, America's diplomats believed, was less likely to come from a Soviet military invasion than from an internal revolutionary movement that promised greater economic opportunities and an equitable sharing of the nation's wealth.

By 1953 Americans' fears about Iranian internal subversion—that's how they would have seen it at the time—had been proven correct. For several years, the United States had been supplying Iran with small amounts of military aid and assistance (a pittance compared to what the Shah requested), as well as economic development loans. This limited support had little impact on Iran's precarious economy. Iran remained a poor nation filled with angry, sometimes desperate people.

In the early 1950s, the obvious source of Iranian economic development funds was the "black gold" that had been first developed north of the Persian Gulf in the early years of the twentieth century. Iranians, however, had a problem: the British, through the Anglo-Iranian Oil Company, controlled "their" oil. Fifty-one percent of the company's shares were owned directly by the British government, the rest by private shareholders. Between 1945 and 1950, even as their military power collapsed and their empire rapidly receded, the British managed to earn some 250 million pounds from their Iranian oil holdings. During those same years, Iran received only 90 million pounds in royalty. For Iranian nationalists, British control of Iran's oil wealth was intolerable.[23]

By 1950 the Anglo-Iranian Oil Company was *the* political issue in Iran. Nationalist firebrands of all political persuasions demanded that British exploitation of Iranian oil be stopped. These Iranians were well aware that all around the world, in the mercurial political climate that followed the end of World War II and the beginning of the fierce Soviet-American rivalry, poor nations with large oil reserves were forcing rich oil corporations to renegotiate old agreements. Venezuela had led the way, successfully winning a 50–50 revenue-sharing agreement with its foreign oil producers, the most important of which was the American giant, Standard Oil of New Jersey. By 1948 Venezuela's oil income was six times higher than it had been in 1942. Venezuela did not hide its light under a bushel. In a show of solidarity with other producers—and to ensure that lower oil-producing costs elsewhere did not cause widespread corporate disinvestment in Venezuela's oil fields—Venezuelan officials translated their agreement into Arabic and urged Middle Eastern nations to gain similar concessions from their foreign corporate producers. In 1950 Saudi Arabia and Kuwait achieved the same 50–50 split. The U.S. government, seeking political stability that would safeguard anti-communist governments in both Latin America and the Middle East, as well as guarantee continued access to the increasingly necessary foreign oil reserves, strongly supported the renegotiated agreements.

Iranians wanted, at least, the same 50–50 split; some wanted much more. British investors who controlled the Iranian oil concession, not surprisingly, did not want to give away any more of their revenues than was absolutely necessary to appease Iranian demands. As they saw it, the British, not the Iranians, had taken the risks, raised the necessary capital, and created the business. To put the legal point to it, the British corporation had a contract signed by the proper Iranian authorities. Sir William Fraser, the fierce Scotsman who ran Anglo-Iranian, was loathe to offer anything additional to the Iranians, whom he viewed as a nation of corrupt ingrates. When U.S. Assistant Secretary of State George McGhee suggested to Fraser that the Iranian position was not unreasonable, he snorted, "One penny more and the company goes broke." Nonetheless, under ever increasing political pressure that was creating sporadic violence and promised to make Iran a very unpleasant business environment, the British were ready to sign off on the new going rate of a 50–50 split.[24]

It was too late. Nationalists in Iran perceived the Anglo-Iranian Oil Company as the paramount symbol of Western exploitation, responsible for their economic misery and disrespectful of their culture and religion. Muhammad Mossadegh, a wealthy, cosmopolitan man who despised the British and who had been jailed by the elder Reza Shah in the 1920s for demanding a more open political system, led the fight against any compromise agreement with Anglo-Iranian. At the Majlis, Iran's erratic parliament, Mossadegh spoke for many when he declaimed: "The source of all the misfortunes of this tortured nation is only the oil company." In language even more heated, he later privately explained his visceral hatred of the British to a bemused Averell Harriman, the eminent American businessman and diplomat: "You do not know how crafty they are. You do not know how evil they are. You do not know how they sully everything they touch." On March 3, 1951, Iran's prime minister, Ali Razmara, an army general strongly supported by the American diplomatic community in Iran, spoke out against those who wanted to throw out the British altogether and nationalize the Anglo-Iranian company. Four days later he was assassinated by a young man under the influence of Islamic fundamentalists, who were the most fiercely anti-British force operating in Iran. The members of the Majlis voted to nationalize the oil company and to make their champion, Mossadegh, the new prime minister. Under tremendous public pressure, the uncertain young Shah agreed to everything.[25]

Mossadegh quickly became the most powerful individual in Iran. Still, his position was far from secure. Iran was riven by factions and by regional rivalries. Islam unified the country but Islamic groups, ranging from modernist reformers to fundamentalists opposed to all forms of secular authority, vied with one another, as well as with more secular forces, for power and influence. Iran's neighbor, the Soviet Union, threatened and pressured from the north while supporting communist elements within Iran. The rule of law was little observed and corruption was commonplace. Ancient Persia had been a mighty civilization for millennia but modern Iran was a nation still searching for its identity and its role in the world. Further complicating Mossadegh's predicament, the British by no means intended to go quietly into the night. They wanted the oil back and they made no secret of it.

Mossadegh did his best to stay in front of the roiling tides of chaos, confrontation, and crisis. He tried to appease everyone by saying whatever he hoped they wanted to hear. He seemed not to care that he constantly contradicted himself, sometimes even when talking to the same person. His habit of holding meetings with high-powered foreign dignitaries while wearing his pajamas, sprawled on his unmade bed, further confused the situation.

In response to the abrogation of their contract and the nationalization of their property, the British organized a boycott of Iranian oil. Overwhelmingly, the world fell in line, including the United States. American oil companies strongly backed the British position. They wanted to send a clear message to other oil-rich nations: if you nationalized the property of foreign corporations or broke legal contracts you would be held accountable. President Truman, in his typical plainspoken style, was ambivalent about the whole thing, telling newspaperman Arthur Krock that "foreign oil countries have a good case against some groups of foreign capital. . . . [B]ut it was regarded as 'treason' to say so."[26] Quietly, the British planned a military attack. Iran was in deep trouble.

The Truman administration strongly opposed Great Britain's plan to invade Iran. State Department officials feared that a British imperialist invasion would push Iranians, and possibly others in the region, into the welcoming arms of the Soviet Union. Secretary of State Dean Acheson sent man-of-the-world Averell Harriman and two expert assistants to broker a deal. Harriman spent several weeks in Iran trying to involve Prime Minister Mossadegh in a rational conversation about the oil business and international relations. The slippery prime minister was far more worried about maintaining his leadership in the face of very real internal threats of assassination. Rather than respond directly to the Americans' thoughtful comments on macroeconomics, corporate law, and the art of negotiation, Mossadegh gave his American brokers a lesson in revolutionary politics. He asked them what they thought would have happened if some wise and well-meaning Persian gentlemen had shown up in Boston Harbor in the middle of the Boston Tea Party and asked the American colonists to be reasonable and stop throwing perfectly good British tea into the sea?

Harriman's mission failed but he insightfully concluded, "Any settlement of the dispute would end his [Mossadegh's] political career." Mossadegh's hold on power depended not on working out balanced agreements with foreign corporations but on his ability to unify Iranians through their hatred of a common enemy: foreign exploiters. In the years ahead, other Iranian leaders, including the Ayatollah Khomeini, would remember this lesson. Not long after Harriman's retreat from Iran, a leading Islamic cleric, Ayatollah Kashani, announced a new national holiday, "a day of hatred against the British Government."[27]

When President Eisenhower took over the presidency in January 1953, Iran was a mess. The country was in financial ruin due to the successful British-led boycott. The streets were alive with agitation and rival groups fought for power. The communist Tudeh Party was gaining strength and had become a key supporter of

Prime Minister Mossadegh. For several years the United States had, with no success, attempted to work with the British and the Iranians to find a peaceful solution to the impasse. That failed policy changed when the new administration took power.

By 1953, the American government was reeling from the Korean War stalemate, the ever-more successful communist-led Vietnamese struggle to end French control of their country, Soviet nuclear arms development, the discovery of communist spies in the United States, and the hysterical charges by Senator Joseph McCarthy of an internal plot by communists to take over the American government. Iranians' seizure and nationalization of the British oil company's private property and Prime Minister Mossadegh's anti-Western rhetoric struck many influential Americans as direct proof of the communist nature of the Mossadegh regime. Two years earlier, in March 1951, *Time* magazine had warned that the Mossadegh regime was "one of the worst calamities to the anti-Communist world since the Red conquest of China."[28] And in January 1952, *Time* had surprised its readers by naming Mossadegh "Man of the Year." He was, the magazine warned, the most dangerous representative of a new kind of communistic threat: "[H]e gabbled a defiant challenge that sprang out of a hatred and envy almost incomprehensible in the West."[29] While no one in 1953, not even the editors of the unrelentingly anti-communist *Time* magazine, accused Mossadegh, himself, of actually *being* a communist, key Americans believed that his extreme nationalism would pave the way for a communist takeover of Iran and, possibly, other major oil-producing nations of the Near and Middle East. Cold war fears of communist control of the world's largest oil reserves, more than the details surrounding any specific oil profit-sharing agreement, were beginning to rule American policymakers' perceptions of the Iranian imbroglio.

When President Eisenhower took office in January 1953 he shared his predecessor's hardnosed anti-communism. In the 1952 campaign, Eisenhower had suggested going even further than Truman by rolling back the communist tide. But Eisenhower, a frugal fiscal conservative, worried that Truman's fight to contain the global communist threat was going to bankrupt the American people. An April 1950 secret National Security Council strategy-setting document, known as NSC 68, had insisted that the American government must be prepared to spend whatever amount of money it took to block Soviet global threats. Truman had acted accordingly and under his direction the American military budget had skyrocketed. Ike dissented from that new conventional wisdom. He argued that ever-escalating military budgets would create "a permanent state of mobilization" in which "our whole democratic way of life would be destroyed."[30]

Eisenhower developed an alternative, less expensive strategy for winning the cold war. Instead of building up a massive, quite expensive conventional military force, President Eisenhower got a bigger—much bigger—bang for the buck by investing heavily in America's relatively cheap nuclear weapons and by making it painfully clear to the Soviets that the United States would be quite willing to use them if threatened. He also strongly supported the increased use of the CIA in fighting America's enemies covertly. Bribes, subversion, and sabotage, he believed, were cost-effective alternatives to conventional military operations. Better, they risked no American lives and "plausible deniability" allowed the U.S. government to lose little, if any, international respect if a mission failed or, for that matter, if it succeeded through the premature death of anti-American foreign individuals. Best of all, the operations could proceed without any public scrutiny whatsoever; neither Congress nor the press nor any group of agitated citizens need be appeased or consulted or won over to the cause. The president and his men could do as they wished without interference. Eisenhower did not seem to believe that covert ops aimed at overthrowing foreign governments carried out without the knowledge—let alone approval—of Congress or the American people posed a threat to domestic democratic decision making.

Iran became Eisenhower's covert operations test case. Like Truman, Eisenhower rejected a British or a combined Anglo-American direct military overthrow of Mossadegh. Preemptive military strikes against other people's countries were likely to draw the wrath of nations the Americans hoped not to lose to Soviet influence. Instead, President Eisenhower's team decided to see if a covert operation could, on the cheap, take out the communist-influenced threat and replace it with a pro-West, pro-American ruler.

The British had first come up with the secret plan to depose Mossadegh. In November 1952, right before the American presidential election, British intelligence operatives discussed their scheme, code-named Operation Ajax, in London with the CIA's Kermit Roosevelt. He immediately passed along the details to CIA Deputy Director Allen Dulles. Dulles, however, knew that Truman's secretary of state, Dean Acheson, opposed all such covert operations. So Dulles waited for Acheson's replacement. After Eisenhower's victory, Allen Dulles became director of the CIA and his brother John Foster Dulles replaced Acheson as secretary of state. Both men, as it happened, had previously worked for the high-powered Wall Street law firm of Sullivan and Cromwell, which represented many oil companies, including the Anglo-Iranian Oil Company. They very much believed that Mossadegh had to go. In accord with the Eisenhower administration's new strategic orientation, the covert operation (planned by the British but to be carried out by the American intelligence community) was, suddenly, on.

It was quite an adventure for the operation's leader, Kermit Roosevelt. The plan was simple. "Kim" Roosevelt, a quiet, unassuming upper-class sort of fellow who spoke no Farsi or any other Middle Eastern languages, would find useful elements within the Iranian army, cobble together the appearance of an anti-Mossadegh, pro-Shah popular force, and convince the Shah, himself, to take firm control of the country once the contrived popular street protests and Iranian military forces moved against Mossadegh. The CIA budgeted one million dollars cash for the operation which, when converted into Iranian rial, created a bit of a logistics challenge; the largest rial note was worth only $7.50 and a million dollars' worth of rials made for an immense, bulky pile of paper money.

Roosevelt, with help from the British and the CIA's limited Iranian resources, pulled it off. For the bargain price of $100,000 he hired large numbers of weightlifters, wrestlers, burly thugs, and assorted tough guys ready to take to the streets to act as protesters at the appropriate time. He convinced key Iranian military leaders, fed up with Mossadegh's incompetence, communist leanings, and the chaotic state of Iran's economy and society, to sign up as well. On August 1, several months after the operation had begun, Roosevelt brought the most important element of the plan onboard. The CIA's man in Tehran snuck into the Shah's palace and explained the operation to the still young, titular head of Iran. For several years the Shah had been trying, often in a desultory and painfully uncertain fashion, to regain the power Mossadegh and others had steadily taken from him since the Anglo-Iranian Oil Company crisis had begun in 1950. While quite nervous, the Shah agreed to go along with the CIA plan.

In mid-August 1953 the operation to overthrow Mossadegh and put the Shah in control of Iran began. As historian Barry Rubin observes, "All in all, only five Americans, with a half-dozen Iranian contacts had organized the entire uprising."[31] At first, it looked like the seat-of-the-pants operation would enjoy as much success as it seemed to have deserved.

Just as the overthrow was to begin, a key member of the Iranian team was betrayed and arrested. Other arrests quickly followed. Radio Tehran warned the public of a coup attempt and rumors of American involvement were everywhere. Demonstrators took to the streets, chanting "Yankee go home," while communist Tudeh Party members smashed statues of the Shah and made power grabs of their own. The Shah thought he saw the writing on the wall. Unceremoniously, he grabbed what he could and fled to Italy. In Rome, the Shah mulled over his fate. He told his wife that they had little money, maybe just enough to buy a farm. The United States, he told her hopelessly, looked like their best bet.[32]

Roosevelt was less worried. His paid-for mobs and the army had yet to appear. The army took to the stage first and quickly brought order to the streets. A majority of rank-and-file soldiers, who had no contact with the American operation, proved to be anti-communist royalists, loyal to the Shah. Roosevelt's hired mobs came out the next day and took the offensive, destroying the pro-Mossadegh Tehran newspaper offices and hunting down communist Tudeh Party members. The army let them do their work. Soon, tens of thousands of Iranians, sick of the chaos Mossadegh had brought Iran, joined the pro-Shah forces. One step ahead of the violent-minded mobs, Mossadegh fled Tehran. Several hundred people had been killed, most of them by mob violence. After more than three years of economic hard times and political turmoil many people in Iran were ready for order and hoped the Shah could bring it. On August 22, 1953, the Shah came home from Italy. He immediately began to restore full authority to the Peacock Throne.

Operation Ajax had supplied the spark—and Roosevelt the money—that ignited the overthrow of Mossadegh, but the erratic, pajama-wearing prime minister had already lost much of his public support by mid-1953. The Shah was seen by many in Iran as their best hope. Iran expert Barry Rubin judges that the CIA operation "had been like pushing on an already-opened door."[33] Still, the CIA had been integral to the restoration of the Shah's power and the Shah's enemies would never forget the role the United States had so casually played in their nation.[34]

In the United States no newspaper or radio station or fledgling television evening news show (in 1953 the evening news played for all of fifteen minutes, including commercials, on the three national networks) mentioned the role the CIA had played in Iran even though it is likely that a few reporters had wind of the story. In those days national security concerns overrode reporters' and editors' professional desire or duty to tell the American people what their government was covertly doing in their name. Overwhelmingly, journalists operated according to war standards of reporting—even if the war was a "cold" one. The *New York Times* reported the story according to the conventional wisdom of the time, explaining the return of the Shah to power as a homegrown, popular revolt against a failed dictator. Mossadegh, the paper reported, had "flirt[ed] with Russia," and the Shah, while not perfect, was a "moderating influence" who stood the best chance of bringing reform and economic stability to the unfortunate people of

Iran.[35] Some twenty-five years later, after the failed war in Vietnam and Watergate changed all the rules regarding the press's coverage of the presidency, President Jimmy Carter could only wish for so compliant and un-curious a mass media.

Quickly and with little difficulty the United States, England, and the new regime in Iran worked out the oil problem. In essence, the 50–50 revenue-sharing deal that had been on the table back in 1950 was implemented. To save face for the Shah, the new contract formally maintained the nationalization of Iranian oil but foreigners were given contracts to manage and refine the oil. And the refined oil was to be sold to a consortium of foreign oil companies that would control its sale and distribution. One other rather important change also was agreed to by the British: American oil companies would have a 40 percent interest in the foreign consortium that would run the Iranian oil business (as part of the deal both the Iranian government and the new foreign partners paid a large cash settlement to the old Anglo-Iranian Oil Company, which retained a 40 percent share in the enterprise).

The United States also became a partner in building a more stable Iran. The Eisenhower administration ponied up over a billion dollars in economic and military aid between 1953 and 1960. American financial, industrial, and construction companies flocked to Iran to help spend American foreign aid money and Iran's burgeoning oil riches. The number of American government officials in Iran boomed, with technical advisors alone jumping from some 26 in 1952, before the overthrow of Mossadegh, to 207 in January 1956. The U.S. embassy rapidly expanded in size and became a beehive of activity in central Tehran. The CIA and other U.S. intelligence-gathering services made Iran a strategic center for monitoring Soviet activities and for operating against regional enemies; they worked closely with the Shah's cooperative security forces. When President Eisenhower, in early 1957, declared that the United States was prepared to use military force throughout the Middle East to protect the region from Soviet communist threats, the Shah enthusiastically and publicly supported this new "Eisenhower doctrine." The United States and Iran had become strong allies in an unstable part of the world that contained the largest portion of the world's known oil reserves.

The Shah used American assistance and his nation's oil wealth to consolidate his power. Immediately after the Shah's return in late August 1953, Mossadegh was found and imprisoned; he lived out his last few years under house arrest. The communist Tudeh Party, which had sided with Mossadegh against the Shah, was destroyed and communists were hunted down, imprisoned, and sometimes killed. The Shah rewarded the army officers who had restored him to the throne by making them rich, powerful, and, thus, loyal. In 1957, the Shah, with help from the CIA, formally created his own national security force, SAVAK. SAVAK's purpose was to keep the Shah's order but it quickly became a power base unto itself, and even the Shah had to be wary of its chief, General Teymour Bakhtiar.[36] SAVAK would became internationally infamous for the brutality, cruelty, and macabre creativity of its torturers. Backed by the Americans, protected by SAVAK and the military, and ever wealthier due to his direct control of Iranian oil, the Shah became more secure in his reign.

Still, into the early 1960s, the Shah's control over Iran was openly challenged. A "National Front" composed of students, intellectuals, and urban bourgeoisie espoused a kind of liberal or leftist Islam and agitated for a constitutional government with greater political openness, democratic participation, and economic equality. While the organized communist movement had been driven underground, workers, peasants, and poor Iranians resented the great economic inequities of the Shah's regime and struggled to find the political means for expressing their frustrations. Large landholders and tribal leaders challenged his authority at the local level, insisting on their traditional rights to autonomy. Merchants in Iran's traditional marketplaces, the bazaars, deplored the Shah's plans to modernize the economy and make them marginal or even obsolete. Most important, traditional Islamic clergymen deeply opposed the Shah's secular modernization plans and agitated for an Islamic state in which they would control education and law making (which, they believed, should strictly follow the Koran). The

Shah's hold was further weakened by Iranians' widespread perception that the Shah was beholden to the Americans who had secured his throne.

In 1961, violent (if small-scale) political turmoil broke out in Iran. And though the Shah was able to shut down the protests by unleashing SAVAK and imprisoning dissidents, Soviet Premier Nikita Khrushchev told American pundit Walter Lippman that the anti-communist Shah would soon fall like a "ripe apple."[37] The Kennedy administration feared Soviet intrigue in the Persian Gulf and worried, in particular, that homegrown communism was regaining a strong following in Iran. Administration officials urged the Shah to do something to manage the unrest before it became widespread. In fact, the Kennedy administration, hand-fed intelligence by SAVAK, whose leaders knew that the Kennedy administration was always ready to provide aid to fight communism, was misguided about the nature of the danger; communists were not the greatest threat to the Shah's regime. Islamic traditionalists led the struggle against the Shah and his dream of a powerful, modern Iran.[38]

Shah Muhammad Reza Pahlavi, of course, considered himself a good Muslim. But like his father before him, he distrusted the Islamic clergy and saw them as the major impediment to his plans for Iran. He chastised them as "a stupid and reactionary bunch whose brains have not moved . . . for a thousand years." His sonorous label for the Islamic forces was the "black reaction."[39] The Shah wanted to modernize Iran. He wanted to institute secular schools, strictly limit the judicial role of the clergy, improve the status of women, equalize the role of non-Muslims in public life, and bring Western management and distribution systems to the Iranian economy. The Shah looked to Europe and the United States, not to the Islamic Arab world, for ideas, programs, and plans that would make Iran a successful nation. The Islamic clergy, whose power would be drastically limited by the Shah's reforms and who believed, not without reason, that the Shah rejected the sovereignty of Islamic law, refused to be silent in the face of such a threat to their status and their beliefs.

The Shah's father, Reza Shah, had tried to move in a similar direction in the late 1920s and early 1930s. He had been impressed and excited by what the Turks were doing in the post-World War I years in modernizing their Islamic nation. After meeting Turkey's leader, the "Young Turk" firebrand Kamal Ataturk, he announced: "We must bring our people to the same level of development and progress as his." A fierce military man with little feel for politics or concern about the sensitivities of his people, Reza Shah began his modernization campaign somewhat quixotically by ordering all men immediately to begin wearing Western-style hats and suits. Compliance was mixed. Later, and far more controversially, he decreed that all women must stop veiling their faces and covering their heads. Some women welcomed the mandated change; most did not.[40]

The Shah proceeded with greater logic and political care than his headstrong father. Adding to his motivation, in the early 1960s the new Kennedy administration was pushing him hard to institute economic reform measures that would help to reduce the poverty of the great majority of his people. The Kennedy people believed the battle against "third-world" communist insurgency needed an economic element and they meant to tie U.S. aid in Iran to targeted reforms. The Shah was not blind to such a need and believed that carefully managed economic reforms could expand his support within Iran and strengthen his country overall. In 1963, the Shah's desire to follow in his beloved father's footsteps, to control internal unrest, and to meet American pressures resulted in the "White Revolution."

The Shah meant for his "White Revolution" to appease and, in some cases, remove his domestic political critics. To win the support of Iran's many poor rural people and at the same time limit the power of large landowners, he promised land reform. For the urban poor, he offered an industrial profit-sharing plan. To modernize (and break the authority of the clergy), he instituted a national literacy corps and women's suffrage. To control corruption and create economic growth he moved to privatize state-owned enterprises while at the same time nationalizing Iran's forests. While not all aspects of the "White Revolution" fully succeeded—

land reform was, in fact, quite limited—overall the Shah's multifaceted plan gained him greater support within Iran and the enthusiastic regard of his American allies. But it also infuriated his greatest enemy, the force of Islamic traditionalism within Iran.

In 1963, Ayatollah Ruhollah Khomeini was the most visible leader of the Islamic resistance movement. The ayatollah was already nearly sixty-one years old. An outstanding student of Islam, he had trained in a seminary in the holy city of Qom and at the remarkably early age of thirty-two was deemed by his teachers to be a *mojtahed*, a clergyman capable of interpreting Islamic law in all areas of human life. He became known as an *ayatollah al-ozma* (literally, "grand sign of God"), an honorific that became widely used in the 1920s in Iran to honor especially learned religious leaders. Unusual for a Shi'ite Islamic leader, the Ayatollah Khomeini combined his steely and learned interpretations of the Koran with a love of traditional Persian poetry and a fervent mysticism that demanded not just knowledge of Islam but an emotional experience of God's being. This combination of religious wisdom, cultural passion, and spiritual transcendence enabled Khomeini to become a man of great power in Iran. In the United States, the term *charisma* has become an overused word applied casually to movie stars and sports figures. Khomeini was what the phrase *charismatic leadership* at least as it was defined by German social theorist Max Weber, was meant to explain. With his burning eyes, clenched fists, and long white beard, the Ayatollah Khomeini exuded a captivating moral urgency and prophetic power that pulled at the hearts of a great many Iranians who felt spiritually torn by political strife, economic corruption, and the powerful allure of non-Islamic, Western culture.[41]

Khomeini believed that only in Islam could the Iranian people find their destiny and the Iranian state its political legitimacy. The attempts of Reza Shah and then his son to use secular, Western methods to advance Iran's development infuriated Khomeini. In 1942, he anonymously published *Kashf al-Asar* (The discovery of secrets), in which he lambasted Reza Shah as an "illiterate soldier" and proclaimed that "only the law of God will always stay valid

63

and immutable."[42] Mostly, though, through the 1940s and 1950s, Khomeini carefully hid his scorn for the Pahlavis, avoiding the Shah's security forces and waiting for a time when the people would have, as he saw it, the courage and the strength to stop the forces of secularization.

Finally, in 1963 the ayatollah's scorn overflowed and, ready or not, he spoke directly to the people about the need to resist the Shah's westward turn. Openly and uncompromisingly, he attacked the Shah's "White Revolution" as an anti-Islamic sacrilege aimed at destroying the role of the clergy in Iran. On June 3, 1963, he spoke before a crowd of thousands in the holy city of Qom: "O Mr. Shah, dear Mr. Shah, abandon these improper acts. I don't want people to offer thanks should your masters decide that you must leave. . . . Listen to my advice, listen to the clergy's advice, not to that of Israel. That would not help you. You wretched, miserable man."[43] Inspired by Khomeini, as well as other mullahs (religious leaders), tens of thousands of people took to the streets, rioting and protesting. The Shah and his men were caught completely off guard by the rebellion. The police, SAVAK, the military, and gangland thugs (including the aptly named Sha'ban the Brainless) who had long been paid enforcers of the Shah's order were sent into action and attacked the crowds. SAVAK agents arrested Khomeini, and the Shah's men stated that all the instigators of the riots would be executed. Khomeini's followers feared that the Ayatollah would be singled out for retribution. People took to the streets chanting, "Khomeini or death!" and throughout Iran, bazaars shut down in protest. Hundreds of protesters were shot dead as martial law was declared.

The time for an Islamic revolution had not arrived. Many supported the Shah's "White Revolution." The fury of SAVAK and the loyalty of the army repressed the dissenters. The ayatollah was not made a martyr by the Shah's regime but was simply imprisoned for ten months until the streets quieted. The Shah had weathered the first great storm of his rule.

The ayatollah was not cowed by his imprisonment. When released from jail in early 1964 he began to think more strategically, more politically, about how to increase the forces aligned against the Shah by including secular nationalists, communists, and left-wing Islamists. In autumn 1964, he saw an opportunity.

The United States had asked the Shah to provide American military advisors and military personnel in Iran immunity against local prosecution. American military lawbreakers would, instead, be brought to justice through American military courts. The United States had similar agreements with most of the other nations in which the United States had troops stationed. In 1964 hundreds of thousands of American troops were based in Europe, Korea, Japan, Vietnam, and elsewhere in the world, even though just twenty-five years earlier the United States had no troops stationed outside its own borders and territories. The Shah readily, if secretly, agreed to the American request.

Khomeini received word of the secret agreement and immediately saw the political possibility the agreement provided him. He told his compatriots: "They can no longer call us reactionary. The point is that we are fighting against the America [*sic*]. All the world's freedom fighters will support us on this issue. We must use it as a weapon to attack the regime so that the whole nation will realize that this Shah is an American agent and this is an American plot."[44] It was October 1964. The United States had been involved in a covert war against Cuba, creating great enmity among many people in the developing world, especially throughout Latin America. President Johnson, just three months earlier, had gotten Congress to approve the Gulf of Tonkin resolution that had put the United States on the road to a war against nationalist—and communist—forces in Vietnam. Leaders in India, Indonesia, and other Asian countries had recently condemned the United States for seeking to bully third-world nations into compliance with American desires. Khomeini sensed that the Shah's alliance with—and dependence on—the United States was a weakness he could use to unify disparate Iranian groups, both secular and religious, against the Shah's regime. The American military immunity agreement was the stick he would use to beat the Shah.

In late October 1964, before a great crowd that had gathered in Qom to hear the ayatollah speak on the religiously fraught occasion of the birthday of Fatimah (Muhammad's daughter), Khomeini ripped into the Shah, chastising him for his subservience to the Americans. "Since the day I heard of the latest developments affecting Iran, I have barely slept," he told the crowd mournfully. "With sorrowful heart, I count the days until death shall come and deliver me. . . . They have sold us, they have sold our independence. . . . reduced us to the level of a colony, and made the Muslim nation of Iran appear more backward than savages in the eyes of the world." He then offered an alternative vision of Iran: "If the religious leaders have influence, they will not permit this nation to be the slaves of Britain one day, and America the next. If the religious leaders have influence they will not permit Israel to take over the Iranian economy. . . . If the religious leaders have influence they will not permit people's innocent daughters to be under young men at school. . . . If the religious leaders have influence, they strike this government in the mouth. . . . [T]hey will not permit America to carry out these scandalous deeds, they will throw him out of Iran." While not forgetting to condemn the Shah's generally open relation with the Jewish state of Israel, the ayatollah reserved his greatest contempt for the United States: "Let the American president know that in the eyes of the Iranian people he is the most repulsive member of the human race. . . . Let the American government know that its name has been ruined and disgraced in Iran."[45] Over the next fifteen years, Khomeini relentlessly attacked the Shah as a pawn of the non-Islamic, secular, and evil American superpower.

Key figures in the American government were not completely unaware of the contempt some of Iran's traditional clergy had for the Shah and, more specifically, for the Shah's greatest international ally, the United States. During this period of unrest, a fairly rare National Security Council overview report on Iran did note that the "fanatical clergy" opposed the Shah's "White Revolution." But the report concluded that these clerics were not likely to be able to instigate a successful "country-wide rising of tribal and urban elements." The Shah's military and security forces, NSC staffers believed, should be strong enough to put down any rebellion and suppress all serious dissident elements. They were, for the moment, correct.[46]

SAVAK agents arrested Khomeini a few days after his jeremiad. This time they took him to the Tehran airport and informed him that he was no longer welcome in Iran. He was shipped off to Turkey. In October 1965, after much agitation among his followers in Iran and international pressure from human rights groups, he was allowed to continue his exile in the Shi'i city of Najaf in Iraq. There he would stay for the next thirteen years, expanding his contacts among anti-Shah groups both inside and outside Iran, lecturing on Islamic theology, the moral degeneration of society, and the need for an Islamic state. He waited for events to bring him home.

A little more than a decade after the CIA-inspired coup that had restored his power, the Shah seemingly had triumphed over his internal enemies. During the 1960s and early 1970s his hold on power grew more secure as his wealth skyrocketed. In October 1971, the Shah celebrated his thirtieth year in power (he did not count British and Soviet occupation or the Mossadegh usurpation against his reign) and the 2,500th anniversary of the founding of the Persian Empire by Cyrus the Great with one of the most expensive parties the world had ever seen. Kings, emperors, princes, presidents, sheiks, sultans, and hundreds of immensely wealthy jet-setters came to a tent city the Shah had built on the ruins of Persepolis. They drank Dom Perignon Rose 1959 and Chateau Lafite Rothschild 1945 from specially designed Baccarat crystal goblets while they supped on poached quails eggs stuffed with caviar, crayfish mousse, roast peacock stuffed with foie gras, and other delicacies prepared by Maxim's of Paris. The Shah's shindig cost the Iranian people, a majority of whom lived in poverty, some $200 million.

A few well-placed Americans were disgusted by the Shah's garish extravagance. George Ball, whose titles included American ambassador to the United Nations, acidly observed: "The son of a colonel in a Persian Cossack regiment play-acting as the emperor of a country with an average per capita income of $250 per year. . . . The world was either too polite or too humorless to laugh."[47] Such derision, outside Iran, was rare. Inside Iran it was dangerous; a small group of students who dared to protest the extravaganza were badly beaten by the Shah's security force. When Khomeini, in Iraq, spoke out in support of the students and intoned, "we do not want you to celebrate over our people's corpses," the Shah airily dismissed his old enemy. He explained: "The Iranian people have nothing but scorn for a man like Khomeini. . . . [S]ome say he is a paid agent of the British." The super-rich Shah, toasted by the world's elite, would not let anything bother him; he had a grand time at his party.[48]

During the Nixon years relations between Iran and the United States grew much closer. President Nixon perceived the Shah as a useful ally in the dangerous thickets of Middle East politics and an oil-rich friend during a time of OPEC-inspired crises. Nixon, as usual, had a plan and it had every appearance of brilliance.

By May 1972 the United States was navigating troubled international waters. The direct American military involvement in the Vietnam War was in its last desperate months. The United States was going to be forced to accept defeat, no matter how the terms were dressed up by Nixon and his men. The American people were fed up with military intervention and wanted no part in new foreign commitments. At the same time, the world remained a dangerous place. In particular, the Middle East was a cauldron of discontent, Soviet intrigue, and virulent bellicosity aimed at Israel. It was also the home, as cannot be repeated enough times, of the world's greatest known oil reserves. Europe, North America, and Japan needed that oil to maintain their pleasant way of life. These two realities—the Middle East was a tinderbox and Middle East oil had to be kept flowing—were given another twist by the British decision to bail out altogether from the region, a course of action they announced in 1968 and completed in 1971. (Britain's last vestiges of imperial military power had been focused on the Persian Gulf and Suez Canal—and the British presence had mostly been a stabilizing force for the region.) With no domestic support for a new costly international commitment, Nixon knew that he had to come up with something different to protect America's interests in the

Persian Gulf. Whatever else can be said about Mr. Nixon, he was an innovative practitioner of global hardball.

On May 30 and 31, 1972, President Nixon, accompanied by his redoubtable national security advisor, Henry Kissinger, came to Tehran to court the Shah. Nixon had just pulled off a series of world-changing diplomatic coups. In February he had journeyed to Beijing, met with Mao Zedong, and began the process by which the "Running Dogs of Capitalism" and the "Red Chinese" would learn to get along and even cooperate when it was mutually beneficial. In late May, Nixon and Kissinger flew to Moscow where the nervous Soviets, fearful of whatever devilry Nixon had gotten up with the Chinese (who had no love for their communist neighbors), agreed to an arms control treaty and promised to pursue a more friendly set of relations with their longtime American foes. Nixon and Kissinger, eager to pull off one more master stroke, flew directly from Moscow to Tehran.[49]

In Tehran, Nixon asked the Shah to become the military guarantor of stability in the Persian Gulf. Nixon's meaning was clear: the Shah was to be the protector of American interests in the region. Supposedly, during the meeting Nixon looked the Shah in the eye and humbly beseeched him, "Protect me."[50]

The strategic background to this proposal was the Nixon doctrine. In June 1969, just five months after becoming president, Nixon had outlined a simple proposition: the United States would fight direct Soviet military attacks wherever they occurred but any other kind of aggression, even by communist forces on allied nations, would not be automatically countered by the U.S. military. Instead, the United States would offer its friends the military equipment and, if necessary, the funds needed to wage war. The Vietnam War had taught Nixon this lesson. And though Nixon was no ancient history buff, the policy also resembled the strategy the Roman Empire had used in protecting friendly or allied peoples outside of its immediate interest. The Shah was to be the single most important exemplar of the Nixon doctrine.

As regional-power designate, under the imprimatur of the United States, the Shah began a monumental military shopping spree.

Back in the late 1940s, American officials had mocked his desire to lead a world-class army. Suddenly, he was America's darling and Nixon administration officials cheered on his grand (grandiose?) plans. While Pentagon officials wrung their hands and wrote memos suggesting that selling the Shah state-of-the-art American weapons might not be in the U.S. national interest, the White House gave the Shah an unblinking green light.

The Shah, who studied military weapons catalogs and defense trade journals like some men flipped through *Playboy*, spent some $12.1 billion between 1971 and 1976. He wanted all the good stuff and he got it: F-14 Tom Cats, then F-16 and F-18 fighter planes, C-130 transport planes, helicopter gunships, and on and on. It was a dream come true for American weapons manufacturers, who not only sold the equipment but also spare parts and then arranged for technical training and maintenance contracts. Bribery, in Iran, was a way of life and American corporations parceled out millions of dollars to high-ranking military officers and government officials to secure deals, making the Shah's most trusted men wealthy (or wealthier). Tens of thousands of American technicians, mechanics, and weapons trainers flocked to Iran where they quickly learned to live like rich men, surrounded by servants in guarded expatriate enclaves well removed from the grinding poverty that made up everyday life for most Iranians. While few Americans paid close attention to the local folks, religious Iranians watched the hard-drinking, fun-loving expatriates with less than perfect equanimity.[51]

The Shah paid for his weapons with oil revenues. The 1970s were the glory years for OPEC and the Shah was instrumental in engineering the price hikes that brought previously unimagined riches to the Persian Gulf. Because of huge increases in global oil demand produced by international economic development the oil producers had an unprecedented opportunity to squeeze their customers, as well as the giant oil companies that operated the production and distribution systems. In 1971 the Shah brought the OPEC Gulf committee together with the leading international oil companies and won a bigger share of the profits and a higher per barrel price for petroleum. An OPEC official stated, "After the Tehran

Agreement, OPEC got muscles." The Shah pushed as hard as anyone, gaining far greater control of Iranian oil by pushing aside the
international consortium that had been set up after the 1953 coup
and replacing it with the National Iranian Oil Company. The Shah
crowed: "Finally I won out. . . . Seventy-two years of foreign control of the operations of our industry was ended." The OPEC Decade was in full bloom.[52]

The OPEC cartel forced the oil-guzzling world to accept price
hike after price hike. The 1973 oil embargo revealed just how vulnerable most of the industrial world was to OPEC. Few people, at
least in the short run, saw any alternative to base obeisance to the
oil producers' demands. During this era of "oil shock," the Shah
showed his new muscle but he also demonstrated an allegiance to
his American ally. Throughout the oil embargo that followed the
October 1973 Arab-Israeli Yom Kippur War, the Shah continued to
sell oil to the United States and, more surprisingly, to Israel—which
had been an unwavering, longtime supporter of the Shah and his
security forces. Such welcome assistance aside, no one pushed
harder for higher oil prices than the Shah. In private correspondence, President Nixon tried to convince the Shah to slow down his
price demands. The Shah was unrepentant: "We are conscious of
the importance of this source of Energy to the prosperity and stability of the international economy but we also know that for us this
source of wealth might be finished in thirty years." The once anxious leader-in-name-only of Iran took to lecturing the people of Europe and North America, telling them that "they will need to tighten
their belts. . . . [T]hey will have to work harder. . . . Your young
boys and young girls who receive so much money from their fathers
will also have to think that they must earn their living somehow."[53]

The Shah was in the driver's seat and the United States depended
on their best friend in the Persian Gulf to spend billions of his new
petro-dollars in the United States, combat Soviet communist influence in the region, and act as a force of stabilization, Westerniza-
tion, and modernization in the Islamic world. During those fateful
days in August 1953, President Eisenhower had created the special
relationship with the Shah. Kennedy and Johnson had maintained

it, and Richard Nixon had cemented the friendship and dramatically increased the ties that bound the United States to the Shah's Iran. The caretaker president, Gerald Ford, kept most of Nixon's national security team and over his two years in office continued Nixon's policies. When James Earl Carter was sworn into office on January 20, 1977, the American-Iran alliance was the bedrock of U.S. policy in the Persian Gulf. Despite concerns raised in the State Department and by a few members of Congress about the Shah's repressive regime, President Carter had no plans to challenge that policy. The United States needed the Shah. President Carter believed that the special relationship would continue as a strong, enduring, and vital friendship.

TAKEOVER IN TEHRAN

After the 1953 coup, when Muhammad Mossadegh was thrown out of power, his nephew (and supporter) Prince Mozaffar Firouz had ended up in Paris. Iranians from all the anti-Shah factions turned up in Paris. They opened shops or lived on the money they had been able to take with them. They plotted. Firouz, often enough, found a role in such intrigues; in the mid-1960s he had acted as middleman between Saddam Hussein and the Ayatollah Khomeini, using one of his ubiquitous cousins to carry messages. In the late 1970s, the prince was still in Paris and still pursuing intrigues against the Shah.

Long before, he had been a minister in the Iranian government. He had also been the Iranian ambassador to the Soviet Union. And he had been at Mossadegh's side while the old man—his uncle—had fenced with the British, the Americans, and the Soviets. The Americans had pegged Firouz as a communist. He was not but he had allowed certain people, including his friends in the Soviet Union, to believe that he was at least a little bit of a communist.

Firouz believed the Shah to be a usurper brought to power by "foreign bayonets," a "valet" who dutifully served his masters. Decades earlier, the Shah's father had ordered the assassination of the prince's father who had, Firouz believed, more rights to the throne of Iran than did any member of the parvenu Pahlavi family.

Life, the prince believed, was "a question of being a man of action."[1] So, in 1977, when he got word of a visit by the Shah to the White House, he took the opportunity to try to interject himself back into the tides of history.

He wrote the new American president, warning Carter that the CIA and the State Department had lied to him about Iran. The ex-president, Nixon, and the ex-ambassador to Iran, the CIA spymaster Richard Helms, had worked against America's long-term interest in Iran. The Shah had corrupted them. American support of the Shah, he told Carter, was leading to disaster.

Firouz thought he knew something of American politics. He pursued a parallel avenue, sending the same message to the new American ambassador to the United Nations, Andrew Young, a man known to side with the underdog. From Young he received a short but polite letter; a sure sign of support, he believed. But nothing changed.

In December 1978, with Iran in turmoil, Firouz wrote again to the president. He generously absolved Carter of blame for past American policy. But, he warned, "everyone in the world knows that the Shah can only remain as a result of U.S. protection and complicity." Then he asked how a man such as Carter, committed to the "defense of human rights and the respect of peoples," can allow "during his presidency a daily massacre of the Iranian people . . . carried out with U.S. arms and American military complicity?" He concluded: "We therefore ask you Mr. President, for God's sake to act without delay, to avoid further bloodshed in Iran and put and end to a situation . . . for which the policy of the U.S. during the past years is responsible."[2]

Jimmy Carter never saw the letter. Somebody at the NSC glanced at it, filed it, and forgot it. No action was taken. What could be done? The Shah was falling. Iran was alive with intrigues that American intelligence agents, diplomats, and Persian Gulf experts could follow only dimly. Everyone, it seemed, had something to hide, something to gain *or to lose. Was Firouz offering himself as an alternative to the Shah? What did he want? He wasn't even in the game anymore. There were too many players already. The problem for Carter, Brzezinski, Vance, and the rest of the men charged with salvaging the wreckage of U.S.-Iran relations was that at the end of 1978 no good policy alternative to the Shah existed. No one in Washington knew whom in Iran to trust. Things were out of control and nothing good was likely to come out of the chaos.*

NOT EVERYBODY in the United States loved the Shah of Iran. In the mid-1970s, before Jimmy Carter took on the presidency, a number of liberal Democrats and moderate Republicans in Congress had made the Shah one of their favorite targets. Senator Ted Kennedy attacked the Shah and the Ford administration for the billion-dollar arms deals that were sending more fighter planes to Iran than the Iranians could man and maintain. The money, Kennedy argued, could better be used to educate and uplift Iran's impoverished masses. In the House of Representatives, Congressman Donald Fraser exposed SAVAK brutality and asked why the United States embraced a regime that used torture to maintain power. On university campuses all over the United States, Iranian students set up card tables and passed out leaflets to their generally indifferent peers decrying the Shah's murderous repression.

When Jimmy Carter ran for president in 1976 he, too, spoke out against the profligate Iranian arms deals and the miserable human rights record of America's best friend in the Persian Gulf. And just a few weeks after Carter's inaugural, Americans' favorite television show, *60 Minutes*, ran an exposé on SAVAK agents brazenly operating against Iranian dissidents inside the United States.[3] None of the American critics, however, had any idea that their attacks were aimed at a failing regime run by a sick man who would soon learn that he was dying. The Iranian students attending American universities knew nothing of the Shah's physical condition. They saw the ill health of the regime. None, however, could have predicted how quickly the Shah would fall nor what world-shaking power their student counterparts in Iran would claim when they captured the U.S. embassy in Tehran.

Most influential Americans believed in the Shah, and even those who questioned his policies assumed he was firmly in control of his nation. In 1977, when Jimmy Carter took office, the Shah appeared robust and took every opportunity to lecture the world about Iranian progress and the West's need for reforms.

Privately, the Shah was not particularly pleased about the 1976 U.S. presidential election. He had known all the presidents from Roosevelt onward. Nixon was his favorite, a man he had known since the year of the anti-Mossadegh uprising. And he understood that Ford, guided by Kissinger, was a stand-in for Nixon. Carter was a man he did not know and who had spoken out against him. Still, words were not the same as deeds. The Shah himself had been indulging in anti-American rhetoric in Iran in order to distance himself from his unpopular ally and to co-opt his domestic enemies' attacks on him.

The new American president was not focused on the Shah's machinations or Iran's internal problems in the early months of his administration. Carter was taking a political beating and mostly from his own party. The Democratic Speaker of the House, Tip O'Neill, did not like Carter though he was trying to support his president. But the House Democrats were not interested in falling into lockstep with their self-proclaimed anti-Washington, outsider president. The Democrats were a disorderly bunch, divided into a conservative Southern faction, an old-school northeastern and midwestern urban liberal group, a recently elected do-gooder, anti-corruption suburban-based cohort, and a constellation of solo acts and self-promoters. In the cliché-driven world of politics, it was like herding cats. And Carter and his Georgia boys were not very good with the lasso. They were inexperienced, they didn't have a clear set of legislative priorities, and from the top down they failed to show individual members of Congress the respect they demanded. Early on, Carter's congressional relations team warned the president that the administration was "viewed merely as another 'interest group' " by Capitol Hill, "not unlike organized labor, business or environmentalists." The president later wrote that he enjoyed no more than a "one week honeymoon" with Congress.[4]

In record time, Carter had both alienated and lost the respect of Congress.[5] Still, Carter was not a man of small plans. He entered the presidency believing he could restore Americans' trust in the presidency, persuade Americans to conserve energy, stimulate the economy, balance the federal budget, stop or at least limit congressional pork-barrel spending, get a handle on runaway health costs, and, front and center, turn around American foreign policy. He meant to make good on his agenda. As a result, he pursued a multifront legislative and administrative battle plan.

Carter's early emphasis on foreign policy surprised most pundits. They figured the former Georgia governor with no obvious background in international relations would be uncomfortable negotiating with world leaders and formulating sophisticated strategic plans about the shape of the world. They assumed his experienced foreign policy team, led by Secretary of State Cyrus Vance and NSC Advisor Zbigniew Brzezinski, would carry the international relations portfolio. They did not yet understand James Earl Carter.

Carter laid out the general terrain of his foreign policy in his inaugural address. Above all, Carter promised, "Our commitment to human rights must be absolute." Idealistically, he also assured Americans, "We will not behave in foreign places so as to violate our rules and standards here at home." Finally, he stated, "We pledge perseverance and wisdom in our efforts to limit the world's armaments to those necessary for each nation's own domestic safety."[6] These three goals—defending human rights, exhibiting principled behavior abroad, and limiting world armaments—not always on easy terms with one another, framed the president's activist foreign policy. At least as importantly, Carter's three principles gave Americans an idealized, if inaccurate, vision of who they were as a people in the world.

Pragmatically, as was true for the six presidents before him, Carter saw the Soviet Union as the greatest threat to the United States and to world peace. While Carter entered the White House committed to maintaining the Nixon-era policy of détente and even improving relations between the Soviet Union and the United States, he had been tutored on the evils of the Soviet regime by Zbigniew Brzezinski and he held no love for the Kremlin. He aimed his human rights rhetoric squarely at Moscow. Unlike Nixon and Ford, who had usually looked the other way while the Soviet government crushed domestic dissent and individual freedoms, Carter publicly damned the Soviets for their relentless campaigns of repression. The Soviets, to Carter's surprise, were furious with him for saying the obvious. Despite the mutual disregard and the continuing war of words, Carter simultaneously pursued his other primary foreign policy goal: U.S.-USSR nuclear arms limitations. Throughout Carter's presidency, as energy crises, economic maelstroms, and all the other horror shows of the late 1970s plagued the United States, he relentlessly struggled to sign and ratify a major arms treaty with the Soviets in order to reduce the risk of nuclear annihilation. (Although he eventually reached agreement with the Soviets, the unfriendly Senate blocked the president by refusing to ratify the agreement.) Carter was genuinely committed to a new foreign policy focused on human rights, but like the cold war presidents who preceded him, he saw world events primarily through a lens that was colored Red and focused on the Soviet Union. Given Soviet power and policy, he would have been foolish not to have paid close attention to Soviet acts and intentions.[7]

Still, much more than his immediate predecessors, Carter had other priorities that broadened his global perspective to include not just East-West relations but also a north-south orientation. Carter believed that the Nixon administration's wholesale support of brutal dictators in Latin America had hurt American credibility there and in much of the developing world. As both a symbol and practical step in mending relations, Carter spent a great deal of political capital pushing through an agreement that gave the Panama Canal to the Panamanian government. Ronald Reagan, who had lost his bid for the Republican presidential nomination in 1976 but who remained a vital public voice, was among the most outspoken opponents of the "giveaway." He argued that the canal was America's—"we paid for it, it's ours"—and that U.S. national security could be harmed by Panamanian control of the vital waterway. Many Americans found Reagan's argument compelling and people paid attention to the issue. Senators in politically contested states who supported Carter's position faced murderous political attack ads from conservative groups. Carter won the canal vote but eighteen senators who supported him lost their reelection bids in 1978 or 1980. The canal agreement strengthened U.S. relations throughout Latin America—and in the long term proved to be a wise move—but politically, at home, it was a loser.[8]

Carter, most famously, also succeeded in transforming Arab-Israeli relations in the Middle East. In his memoirs, he writes, "[C]onstantly the work for peace in the Middle East was on my agenda, and on my mind."[9] In perhaps the greatest coup of his presidency, Carter convinced Egyptian President Anwar el-Sadat and Israeli Prime Minister Menachim Begin to meet with him at Camp David in Maryland for thirteen straight days in September 1978. Carter then engaged in shuttle diplomacy to Cairo and Jerusalem in March 1979. Through his tenacity and skill, and the political courage of Sadat and Begin, Israel and Egypt agreed to historic peace terms, still in effect today.

The long drawn-out, successful U.S.-Egypt-Israel negotiations were exactly of the sort modern American presidents dream: through personal diplomacy, tough-minded men work out seemingly intractable problems for the greater good of their respective nations and the world. Through much of late 1978 and early 1979, while Iran was imploding, Carter and Secretary of State Vance were deeply engaged in the Egypt-Israel peace negotiations. Later, at the end of 1979, when the U.S. embassy was overrun and Americans were held hostage, Carter and his men assumed that a model of rational negotiation, backed with as much economic pressure as was needed, would likewise work in resolving the unexpected difficulties between the United States and Iran.

During the first two years of the Carter administration, the president's foreign policy focused on Arabs and Israelis, the aggressive

Soviets, and Latin American crises. The Carter administration did not ignore Iran during this period but it was not perceived as a hot spot. It was supposed to be stable, a source of security, and the Shah was supposed to be a friendly face in an often hostile part of the world.

The Shah certainly expected to be America's friend. That is why he took offense at the various accusations made by American congressmen. And he was worried about Carter's human rights talk and Carter's vows to reduce American arms sales overseas. In response, soon after Carter took office, the Shah had made some small efforts to curb SAVAK brutality and to offer his people limited civil liberties. By American standards his liberalization measures were meager fare but compared to the men who ran neighboring regimes, such as Iraq and the Soviet Union, he was a genuine reformer. More annoyingly from the Shah's perspective, the new American administration was second-guessing his every arms purchase. Carter's Iranian ambassador, William Sullivan, had the effrontery to tell the Shah to his face that his weapons purchases seemed a waste of Iran's resources.

Secretary of State Cyrus Vance called on the Shah in Tehran in May 1977 both to reassure the Shah of America's deep commitment to friendship and, gently, to introduce ideas for reform in Iran. First were two carrots for the Shah: Vance asked the Shah if he and his wife might not like to make a state visit to the White House in November. He also assured the Shah that President Carter would honor the already agreed to sale of 160 F-16 jet fighter planes to Iran and would support the Shah's desire for state-of-the-art airborne warning and control (AWAC) aircraft. Then, Secretary Vance asked the Shah to please address his human rights record in Iran. Not surprisingly, the Shah was disturbed by Vance's admonitions. He defended himself as a fierce anti-communist. Vance must understand that Iran had to take all necessary measures to protect itself and the region against Soviet aggression. Cyrus the Great was referenced. The genteel, cautious secretary of state and the imperious if often fatalistic Shah did not have a perfect meeting of minds.[10]

Despite the tensions, the Shah and the Shahbanou came to Washington in November 1977. Carter, over fierce objections from members of Congress over the AWAC deal, had made good on Vance's assurances. Despite Carter's efforts, however, the Shah was not mollified. During the open congressional fight over supplying the AWACs to Iran, charges of human rights abuses had been levied against the Shah, embarrassing him. Worse, Carter had issued a policy directive stating that arms transfers would, hereafter, be only used as an "exceptional" means of foreign policy, and written exceptions were made for most of America's close allies but not for Iran. Still, the Shah came and he came with gifts.

Upon arrival at the White House, the Shah presented the Carters with a spectacular tapestry depicting George Washington. Weavers in Isfahan had spent two years making it. That the leading clergymen in Isfahan, only six months earlier, had written President Carter, asking him to intercede with the Shah to prevent the execution of six local clergymen by the state security forces seems to have gone unremarked upon. By all accounts the visit had went quite well except for one unfortunate and prophetic moment. During the outdoor welcoming ceremonies at the White House, a surprising number of unruly anti-Shah demonstrators, almost all of them Iranian students studying in the United States, massed outside the gates chanting slogans such as "Death to the Shah!"—slogans that would in a short time become quite familiar to Americans. They tussled with a smaller group of Shah supporters and order was restored only after police deployed copious quantities of tear gas. As the various dignitaries, including the Shah and the president, made their remarks, tears rolled down their checks. The Shah, underlining why he was not an ally to be trifled with, capped off the visit by telling the president that he would do his best to prevent any increase in the price of oil over the next year. The Shah was greatly pleased by the respect Vice President Walter Mondale and the president had shown him. Carter was reassured and charmed by the Shah's reasoned responses to his concerns about Iranian human rights violations. Everyone was happy.[11]

A few weeks later, at the very end of 1977, the Shah hosted the president in Tehran. Carter was in the midst of one of those presidential whirlwind tours of Europe and Asia. He and Mrs. Carter were only in Tehran for a couple of days but for the Carters it would be, alas, a memorable time.

As the Dom Perignon flowed, poured by liveried waiters in the spectacular surroundings of the Shah's palace, President Carter stood and made a remarkable New Year's Eve toast to his host. Given what was to happen soon enough thereafter, the toast best be quoted at length:

> Iran, because of the great leadership of the Shah, is an island of stability in one of the more troubled areas of the world.
>
> This is a great tribute to you, Your Majesty, and to your leadership and the respect and the admiration and love which your people give to you. . . .
>
> As I drove through the beautiful streets of Tehran today with the Shah, we saw literally thousands of Iranian citizens, standing beside the street with a friendly attitude, expressing their welcome to me. And I also saw hundreds, perhaps even thousands of American citizens who stood there welcoming their President to a nation which had taken them to heart and made them feel at home. . . .
>
> We have no other nation on Earth who is closer to us in planning for our mutual security. . . . And there is no leader with whom I have a deeper sense of personal gratitude and personal friendship.[12]

Carter knew more about the Shah's situation than his words suggest. Just before the president left for his foreign travels, the NSC's Iranian expert, Gary Sick, had warned his boss, Zbigniew Brzezinski, about fierce anti-Shah demonstrations in Iran. He wrote, "[O]pposition to the Shah's regime runs deeper than one would suspect. Perhaps the Shah is truly running scared."[13] Carter knew of the Shah's ongoing problems—he had been thoroughly briefed—when he rose to make his prepared remarks. Still, Carter believed the grandiloquent toast to be a useful sop to an important ally who, he knew, fed on praise from his American friends. Soon enough, President Carter would have to eat his fulsome words.[14]

In 1978, very few people in the United States cared about Iran or the Shah. Mostly, they worried about inflation, which, mid-year, was merrily ripping along at a life-altering annual rate of 10 percent, and about the unemployment rate, which remained stuck at around 6 percent. The biggest public policy story of the year came not from the Carter White House but from California. A longtime political gadfly named Howard Jarvis had successfully led a right-wing populist revolt against local and state tax rates. By a two-to-one ratio, Californian voters passed the Jarvis referendum, Proposition 13, which took some $7 billion in property taxes away from the state government and put it back into the pockets of California property owners. Too many people just did not trust the government to spend their money wisely. Soon, local taxpayers around the country joined the anti-tax, anti-government-spending bandwagon (an issue Ronald Reagan would champion in the 1980 presidential campaign).

On the domestic front, Carter accomplished little other than alienating traditional Democratic Party constituencies. He wanted to reduce federal spending to slow down the inflation rate. They wanted more federal money spent on education, urban problems, and a comprehensive national health insurance program. In August 1978, 69 percent of Americans told pollsters that President Carter was not doing a good job. After the Begin-Sadat agreements were announced in the early fall, Carter's approval ratings approached 50 percent. For Carter, that was about as good as it was going to get.[15]

While most of the nation worried about inflation and groused about high taxes, a few interested parties were keeping an eye on Iran. Carter had, more or less, made his peace both with the Shah's human rights record and his seemingly insatiable need for expensive weapons systems. Others, in Congress and in the State Department, had not. Carter in this case was placing, as he saw it, national interests above national principles. But he remained ambivalent.

The Iranian arms issue came to a head in the summer of 1978. The Shah continued to want many American weapons. The State Department, led by Cyrus Vance, felt that the weapons sales should

83

be reduced and the Shah induced to pay more attention to the economic needs and increasingly heated political demands of his people. The NSC's Zbigniew Brzezinski believed Vance had the wrong priorities. As he succinctly wrote in his memoirs, he and his NSC team "focused on the central importance of Iran to the safeguarding of the American and, more generally, Western interests in the oil region of the Persian Gulf." Vance and his people, "while certainly not inclined to reject that view, were much more preoccupied with the goal of promoting the democratization of Iran."[16] While Carter tried to weigh the competing and increasingly rancorous advice of his chief international relations advisors, other concerns about the weapons issue actually ranked higher in his thoughts. Democrats in Congress, taking the president at his earlier word about the need to reduce international arms and to not reward human-rights-abusing regimes, were lined up against selling Iran more weapons. Hamilton Jordan reported: "We do not have the political capital to expend on another controversial foreign policy issue right now. To do so would be at the expense of other things [domestic policies] more important to us."[17] Carter agreed.

The Shah was sorely agitated by the Americans' public debates about his right to purchase weapons and then their refusal to comply with his needs. Secretary of State Vance told the president that the Shah had been "surprised and distressed" by the unexpected difficulties, in particular the rejection of his request for FG Wild Weasel missiles. Vance dutifully reported that the disappointed Shah had asked if he could, at least, instead have 1,000 SHRIKE missiles. All through 1978, as Iran began to slide ever more quickly into revolutionary chaos, the Shah continued his relentless campaign to buy expensive weapons.[18]

For Americans who wanted to know what was happening in Iran in 1978 it was difficult but not impossible to follow the story. By far the best widely available source on events was the good gray lady of American journalism: the *New York Times*. Throughout the year stories popped up in the paper. On March 5, 1978, the *New York Times* entered the roiling waters of Iranian politics warily: "Violence over the emancipation of women, among the religious conservatives, may have been caused by political opposition to the Shah's efforts to modernize the country." By May 18, the newspaper was willing more directly to dismiss the Iranian regime's usual claims that communists and foreign elements were behind the anti-Shah protests, stating instead that the main dissidents were "Muslim traditionalists loyal to the Ayatollah Mohammed [sic] Khomeini." The story's sub-headline suggested that no need for alarm yet existed: "Ruler Appears Unworried by Riots and Demands for Reform." A couple of weeks later, with protests escalating, the New York Times offered a more in-depth and astute analysis: "A battle line is drawn in Iran. On one side is the autocratic monarch, Shah Mohammed Reza Pahlavi, with his old money, American support and the army behind him. On the other side is a weak federation of unlikely bedfellows, including intellectuals, merchants, Marxists, and students who have allied themselves with the clergy of the conservative Muslim sect that dominates Iran."[19]

For those Americans who did not choose to wade through the New York Times every morning (it was possible but not always easy to buy the paper in much of the country), Iranian news was hard to come by. Judging by congressional correspondence to the White House the only Americans following the Iranian situation closely were weapons manufacturers, pushing hard to sell more arms, and people of Iranian descent living in the United States—most of whom seemed opposed to Carter's close relations with the Shah.[20] CNN had yet to make its debut, network television rarely gave over its few precious minutes to troubled Iran, and local newspapers—then still a rich source for news, at least for Americans over forty—tended to have extremely limited coverage of international events. Most Americans did not care much about foreign news. Not unreasonably, for them, international events got interesting only when they directly affected Americans. For many months the deepening crisis in Iran had only a limited impact on Americans.

In Iran, during 1978, the story was quite different. Many Iranians, including the Shah and the Ayatollah Khomeini, read tremendous importance into every American action that affected, even tangentially, Iran. In a society where the rule of law had only minor impact on social relations and in which conspiracy, subterfuge, personal relations, and the rule of powerful men dominated everyday life, the United States was widely perceived as the master string-puller. While almost no one in the United States knew the truth about the 1953 coup that restored the Shah's power, most everyone in Iran knew what role the CIA had played and—they were sure—continued to play in their nation. So, as forces in Iran began to mobilize in earnest against the Shah, everyone there watched the United States to see what, as they saw it, the giant bully would do next.

In early 1978, the Ayatollah Khomeini, still in Iraqi exile, followed the political logic he had begun in 1964. He cast his baleful gaze on the United States. Carter, he said, bore responsibility for the Shah's murderous regime: "[H]e uses the logic of bandits. . . . 'We have military bases in Iran; we can't talk about human rights there.' "[21] America, Khomeini exhorted, propped up the Shah, demonstrating the cynical hypocrisy of a nation that claimed to champion freedom but supported only repression. To destroy the Shah's credibility, Khomeini tarred Reza Pahlavi as an American stooge. The charge had just enough truth to weaken the Shah and to demonize the United States in Iran.

The Shah was baffled by the roaring surge of protests that swept up his people. His confusion was not simply a character flaw or an indicator of his relative isolation from his own people, though neither was irrelevant. The causes of the escalating crisis were not easy to follow and they were multiple. Iranian expert James Bill, one of the very few people in the United States to have accurately called the Iranian revolution as it was unfolding, lists several key factors. First, Iran's oil-based hyper-economic growth of 1973–1975, based on OPEC-driven price revisions (a nice name for price gouging), had slowed dramatically. Little of the new revenues had trickled down to the Iranian masses. Instead, they watched the Shah amass a world-class military and invest in nuclear power plants, heart transplant centers, and a variety of other boondoggles that meant nothing to the Iranian masses. Worse, Bill explains, as rapid economic growth stopped, those at the top of the economic scale continued their corrupt kleptocratic ways: embezzling, taking bribes, and sucking up whatever revenues they could get their hands on. The Shah did nothing to stop the corruption that was, after all, largely benefitting his cronies, supporters, and extended family. Instead, the Shah permitted an escalating anti-price-gouging campaign to continue against bazaar merchants, who saw themselves as scapegoats for the regime's bad economic policies. The Shah also continued his modernization and secularization campaigns aimed at the power of the Islamic religious establishment, thus further politicizing this explosive force in Iranian society. The combined weight of these economic grievances and religious antipathies, combined with the simple fact that the Shah's regime offered people few conventional political avenues to pursue their interests, greeting dissent instead with death and torture, had created a powder keg.[22]

Lighting that powder keg was a mass movement that social and political theorists at the time had not anticipated. In Iran, millions of people were turning away from secularism and modernism, at least selectively, and looking to their religious traditions for answers to life's riddles. Traditional Islam in Iran in the 1970s was massively resurgent. Here's an irony worth underlining: something of the same phenomenon was occurring in the United States at the same time. Millions of Americans were turning away from "watered-down" Christianity or godless secularism and embracing a traditional (well, traditional circa 1920) evangelical or fundamentalist Christianity. Both of these traditional religious revivals have continued ever since. Now is not the time to explain the American side of the story, but the Islamic resurgence does demand an explanation.

One woman's story—an extreme version, admittedly—explains something of the path taken by so many in 1970s Iran (and throughout much of the Islamic world in the years that followed) to what most in the West call fundamentalist Islam. Massoumeh Ebtekar was one of the young student leaders who seized the U.S.

embassy and guarded the hostages. Though her path to radical Islam does not exemplify the lives of the overwhelming majority of people who pursue a traditional Islamic life, it does connect to the life story of many of those who, sometimes only briefly, become radical anti-Western activists—or even terrorists.

When Ebtekar was three years old she moved with her family to the United States. While her father earned a Ph.D. in mechanical engineering from the prestigious University of Pennsylvania, Massoumeh went to the local public school. Several years later, when her family returned to Tehran, her American-accented English was better than her Farsi. Her parents enrolled her in an international high school run by Americans and based on Western educational standards. Ebtekar had the twin consciousness of someone who had spent her childhood in the United States but whose future, she believed, lay in Iran. In her senior year, she wrote a long essay on the existential philosophers Jean-Paul Sartre and Albert Camus. Like many well-educated teenagers in the West at that time, she bemoaned "the darkness of the world, the sense of nausea" that the existentialists identified at the core of modern, secular, morally relativistic existence. Rather than wear black clothes, smoke unfiltered cigarettes, drink bitter cups of coffee, and revel in teenage angst with a like-minded boyfriend, Ebtekar sought an alternative to the bleakness and moral uncertainty of modern thought (and it was not the even more ethically unanchored postmodernism a new wave of Parisian intellectuals provided her sophisticated peers in the West).

While still in high school, Ebtekar attended the wildly popular public lectures given by Dr. Ali Shari'ati at the Islamic religious center, Hosseiniyeh Ershad, in northern Tehran. Shari'ati aimed his lectures squarely at Iran's booming population of secularly educated students; in 1960 only 5,781 young people had been admitted to Iranian universities and just 15,924 students had graduated high school, whereas by the end of the 1970s, thanks to Iran's oil wealth and the Shah's modernization plan, the number of students had grown to 28,500 and 235,000, respectively.[23] Shari'ati, like Ebtekar, knew the ways of both the West and Iran. He had been a student in Paris, working toward a doctorate in sociology, at the time of the

Algerian revolution. Enthusiastically, he had participated in the radical politics of the day and had translated the writings of Che Guevara, Franz Fanon, and others into Farsi. Rather than embrace wholesale the materialist ideology of Marxism, Shari'ati argued that Islam was itself a revolutionary, liberatory set of beliefs that championed democracy and egalitarianism. Shari'ati, in the words of political theorist Daniel Brumberg, was adapting the "'Third Worldist' ideologies of the sixties, which held that liberation from imperialism required the politicization of native ideology. Armed with this idea . . . Shari-ati and others concluded that to capture the imagination of the masses they had to *create* a culturally 'authentic' Islamic radicalism."[24] Brumberg concludes that this inspirational mélange fit perfectly the spiritual and secular needs of Iran's first generation of relatively well-educated young people who struggled to "accommodate their traditional upbringing to the demands of the modern university" and Western-inspired urban life.[25]

Ebtekar had found a teacher. She writes: "In his lectures and essays, he led thousands of Iranian intellectuals who had become secularized back to Islam and persuaded them to accept the leadership of Imam Khomeini with courage and devotion. . . . Islam, he taught, could be a viable alternative to the ideologies of fatality and despair that emanated from the West." The Hosseiniyeh Ershad was shut down by SAVAK in November 1972, only three years after it had opened, and Shari'ati was jailed for two years and then exiled to England where he died in 1977. But for many young, well-educated people, including Massoumeh Ebtekar, Shari'ati had given expression and answers to the contradictions of their life experiences.

Ebtekar rebelled against the secular life her years in the United States and her American-run high school had attempted to instill in her. She embraced the order, the certainty, and the spiritual majesty Islam provided her. In particular, this teenage girl repudiated the sexual temptations "a Western-oriented lifestyle" seductively offered young people as "modern" and "natural." Ebtekar's personal rebellion in the mid-1970s had political saliency. The Shah's pro-Western policies, she observed, aimed "to take away our faith" and replace it with the banality of "consumerist attitudes." A serious person in a culture that respected spiritually charged introspection, Ebtekar took up the banner of Islam against the repressive, corrupt, secular regime of Reza Shah Pahlavi. She rejected not just the Shah but even the most idealistic promises of the West. She asked, "[C]ould liberalism, could democracy, could justice itself bring about all that human beings long for?" Her answer was no. Only faith in Allah could bring a yearning humanity what it most needed.[26]

Like any revolutionary movement, the forces lined up against the Shah in 1978 were motivated by a mélange of interests and principles. Middle-class pro-democracy activists worked with bearded Islamicists who embraced anti–big business bazaar merchants who made common cause with communist workers. Except for the communists, everyone was united in their anti-Shah politics by a common Islamic faith—even if for some Islam was less an absolute source of all truth than it was a cultural comfort. The multiconstituent base of the mass movement against the Shah made it hard for outsiders, including the diplomats and intelligence analysts who worked for the U.S. government, to get a handle on exactly what was happening in Iran.

In the late summer and fall of 1978, as protests and violence in Iran escalated, President Carter was kept abreast of the situation even as his attention and that of Secretary of State Vance were far more focused on the Israeli-Egypt peace talks. In August, the phlegmatic and imperturbable undersecretary of state, Warren Christopher, filling in for Vance who was busy with the Israeli-Egypt conundrum, warned the president in a classified memo: "It will be difficult for the Shah to maintain his course . . . [should] encourage him to persevere." A month later, Christopher had more bad news for the president: "[A]uthority was progressively slipping away from the government into the hands of religious leaders and street mobs. . . . The Shah seems depressed and undecided on how to proceed. . . . We recommend a message to the Shah to assure him of our continuing support." Five days later, on September 13, Christopher told the president, without comment, that the Iranian ambassador to the United States assured him that "communists" were behind the troubles and that the Shah's declaration of martial law would put a stop to the unrest. Christopher was a man of almost uncanny analytic power and the uncommented upon reference to "communists" being behind all the troubles spoke for itself. The Shah and his loyalists either were not facing up to the reality of their predicament or they were too scared to tell the Americans what they really knew—that an uncontrollable anti-Shah mass movement had erupted in Iran.[27]

By the early fall of 1978, the men surrounding Carter were divided over how to solve the Iranian predicament. The NSC's Gary Sick, who was in the middle of the policy debates, makes a telling comment in his own tough-minded account of the Iran debacle. He writes: "The classic model of foreign policy decision making is the chessboard. . . . The process is incremental, goal-oriented, competitive and fundamentally rational. . . . Governments are organized to deal with chesslike questions."[28] His point: in 1978 and early 1979, Iran was no chessboard. The most powerful anti-Shah forces were not interested in playing by the rules; many were not even interested in the game.

Throughout his reign, the Shah had fenced with pro-democracy, liberalizing forces within Iran. The Kennedy administration and then the Carter administration had pushed him in the same direction, pressuring him to open up his government and reform the Iranian economy. The Shah had, incrementally, complied with these reform pressures. Economic reforms, in particular, were in accord with his own long-term vision of a modern Iran. He had also periodically unleashed his security forces when he felt either threatened or powerful enough to crush his opponents. Throughout 1978, the Shah sought to play out this game. The problem he faced and the challenge his American friends pondered was what to do when the moves he had long used to maintain his dominant position were no longer effective. Making that challenge more difficult, neither the Shah nor his American supporters saw how dangerous Islamic forces had become to the Pahlavi regime.

The Shah's political problems were exacerbated by his personal concerns. Since 1973, the Shah had been battling lymphoma and by mid-1978 he was facing complications. He had kept his illness secret from his people and even his closest allies. In Iran, a sick man was a weak man and he feared that even his friends in the United States would desert him if they knew of his problem. By fall 1978 the Shah was depressed and lethargic. The U.S. diplomatic corps in Tehran warned Secretary of State Vance of the Shah's sour mood and he, in turn, told the president that the Shah seemed unable to act decisively.[29]

While the Shah worried, Iran was fast becoming a train wreck. Protesters were everywhere. Shouts of "Down with the Shah" thundered through Tehran, Isfahan, Tabriz, and almost every major city in Iran. Students at the nation's elite universities went on strike. Oil workers went on strike. As oil revenues plummeted the economy faltered. Islamic extremists began to attack symbols of the secular temptations the Shah had encouraged. In August, during Ramadan, the Muslim month-long period of fasting and prayer, they burned down movie theaters showing films they believed to be un-Islamic. On August 20, a crowded theater was torched; the fire department was slow to arrive, people were trapped, and 377 died. Rather than blame the extremists, the anti-Shah insurgents asserted that SAVAK agents had set the fire to discredit the forces of Islam. Barry Rubin writes, "[I]n a country with an almost unlimited belief in conspiracy," most Iranians seemed to accept this assertion.[30] The tragedy fueled further protests. The anti-Shah forces became increasingly brazen. By late 1978 Iran was in a state of chaos.

For at least a couple of years anti-Shah forces both inside Iran and out had painted the Shah as a brutal oppressor of the Iranian people. Now that all hell was breaking loose in Iran, the Shah seemed loathe to live up to such a portrait. State security forces did respond violently and murderously—but only episodically and indecisively. On September 8, soldiers fired on agitated demonstrators in Tehran's Jaleh Square, slaughtering at least 700 people and perhaps as many as 2,000. But the Shah did not give the word to SAVAK and the military to unleash their unmitigated fury on the masses of protesters. He was not sure what to do. He declared martial law. He opened discussions with more moderate forces within the opposition. His people pressured Iraq to force Khomeini out and remove him from the region, forcing the ayatollah to seek refuge in Paris. Plaintively, he asked his American and British allies for advice.

In late October, U.S. Ambassador William Sullivan was still urging the Shah to reform his government and provide "effective" economic and social measures "to show it [the government] can lead."[31] The Shah must have been hard-pressed to see how this advice had any relevance to the situation at hand. The Shah just seemed to become more depressed; his regime was paralyzed. Few among his loyalists had any inspirational thoughts. Even the heads of the security forces had no idea how to stop the revolutionary masses arrayed against the regime. As the troubles spun out of control, a former SAVAK director confronted a current leader of SAVAK and asked him how such instability could have come into existence: "What have you and the other generals been doing during all these years?" The answer he received seemed like a bad joke: "We have been doing real estate."[32] Some of these men, at least, had not been loyal to the Shah out of a sense of principle or some dedication to the national good. Their loyalty was based solely on venal self-interest. Corruption had helped precipitate the revolutionary forces arrayed against the Shah and corrupt inattention to duty—dastardly deadly duty that it was—would help to bring down his regime.

To President Carter, the catastrophic nature of the Iran crisis appeared to have erupted almost overnight. Even through the ugliness of the spring and summer protests, his key men had expressed faith in the stability of the Shah's regime. The CIA, overly dependent on intelligence it received from SAVAK, had been sanguine about the Shah's long-term rule, reporting to Carter in August that Iran "is not in a revolutionary or even pre-revolutionary situation."[33] The State Department, while well-aware of the troubles erupting throughout Iran, generally advocated continued support of the Shah and remained focused only on pressuring him to reform. Confident of the Shah's regime, State Department officials had quashed efforts in late September by moderate Iranian opposition leaders to meet with level-headed Vice President Walter Mondale. The moderates had pleaded for an "open channel" as "essential and desirable for establishment of good relations and future cooperation between Iranians and your government." Mondale had been firmly warned away from any such meeting: "[It] could be embarrassing in our relations with the Iranian government."[34] Mondale had complied and through 1978 no one in the highest reaches of the U.S. government had any line on the revolutionary forces in Iran.

Only at the end of 1978 did the president come to understand how grim events were in Iran. Vance told him on November 30 the British had given up on the Shah. On December 2, Vance told the president that mobs, at the urging of Islamic clergymen, were attacking American property. In Isfahan, where the city's clerics had beseeched Carter to stop the execution of their brethren, the homes of two Americans had been fire bombed and five American-owned vehicles destroyed. Only five days earlier, the Iranian ambassador to the United States, Ardeshir Zahedi, who kept Washington's political elite well supplied with caviar at his many lavish parties, had personally assured Secretary of State Vance that everything was going to be fine, that the protesters were "disorganized," and that rural Iranians remained steadfast supporters of the Shah.[35]

By the end of 1978, the Iranian revolution was news in the United States. Congress, the press, and interested parties of all kinds weighed in. On university campuses with large numbers of Iranian students, anti-Shah, pro-revolution protests took place. The Iranian Student Association and the Association of Iranian Moslems picketed in front of the White House. Congressmen sent the president letters; liberals urged him to remain neutral, while more conservative members insisted that he stand up for the Shah. Quietly, at the behest of the White House, the liberal 1972 Democratic candidate for president, Senator George McGovern, postponed planned hearings on human rights abuses committed by SAVAK. The White House feared the effect the hearings would have on American public opinion and on the wavering support of the Shah in the mass media and among the political elite. Brzezinski, already in public-opinion damage-control mode, let it be known to the press that he had not been well served by the CIA and an aide assured him that "word is getting out to the heartland" about "intelligence failure in Iran." The *New York Times* ran story after story, introducing the Ayatollah Khomeini to a segment of the American public, detailing the Shah's mishandling of the crisis, and explaining why Iran had geopolitical and economic meaning to the United States. Fundamentally, the explanation amounted to one word: oil.[36]

NSC Advisor Brzezinski believed that the United States, Japan, and Western Europe could not allow Persian Gulf oil to be jeopardized by a hostile takeover of Iran. The Soviets, he believed, would feast on the instability an Iranian revolution would produce and would see the Carter administration's inability to buck up a key ally as a powerful indicator of American weakness. If the Shah fell, the Soviets would push hard throughout the region, jeopardizing the West's access to oil and investment opportunities.

Brzezinski believed that the State Department was incapable of handling the Iranian crisis. The department's country director for Iran, Henry Precht, held out hope that moderate pro-democracy, secular elements could—and should—replace the Shah. Ambassador Sullivan seemed to be more caught up in fighting bureaucratic turf wars than he was in the perilous plight of Iran. His perspective, Brzezinski, later wrote, was that of a "Pollyanna." Brzezinski, supported by his Iranian point man, Gary Sick, believed that it would take firm measures to restore the Shah's authority. "Firm measures" was a euphemism for "bloodbath." The State Department abhorred this hard line. The NSC and the State Department were at loggerheads.[37]

Battling bouts of ennui and illness, the Shah was trying. In November he had gone before the people, speaking over the radio and on television. He promised open elections and social justice. Breaking precedent, he offered a halfway apology for "past mistakes, unlawful actions, oppression and corruption." He pleaded with religious leaders "to try to protect the only Shi-ite country in the world through their guidance and by inviting people to observe peace and order."[38] It was too late. Nobody was listening.

At the end of December, with the streets alive with protest and the country paralyzed by strikes, the Shah asked Ambassador Sullivan to meet with him. He wanted the United States to tell him what to do. Sullivan reported to Secretary Vance that the Shah asked him if the United States would support "a new hard line military government that would initiate a policy of 'brutal repression.' " Sullivan had told the Shah that the "United States could not make such a decision for the Shah."[39] The Shah, without explicit American support for such ferocity, could not make himself give the orders that would result in the deaths of so many of his people and turn him into an object of global horror. He had never, even through the years of SAVAK torture and mayhem, seen himself as the destroyer of the Iranian people.[40]

President Carter was caught between the rival camps of the NSC and the State Department. Secretary of the Treasury Michael Blumenthal recommended that Carter seek advice from the old Washington insider George Ball, the man who had prophetically told President Lyndon Johnson to get out of Vietnam before it destroyed his presidency. From November 30 to December 12 Ball studied the matter while Carter waited for his report. Ball, echoing the State Department perspective, came up with a complicated scheme that would ease out the Shah and create a transitional government: the "Council of Notables." It was a nice idea, not unlike what the Bush administration would orchestrate in Afghanistan in 2002, but without direct American intervention in Iran it had no chance of becoming a reality. Brzezinski was beside himself over the administration's waste of two critical weeks.[41]

It was nearly over. The Shah had lost control of the streets. Whether he retained command of his military was an open question. He was very sick and he knew he might die before too much longer.

Key Americans came flocking to Iran to judge events for themselves. Secretary of the Treasury Blumenthal showed up and departed grim-faced. The Shah had offered Blumenthal the refrain he had used so many times before to American and British officials: "I don't know what to do." Robert Bowie, the CIA's top analyst, quietly zipped in and out of Iran; he was dismayed at the Shah's loss of control. Senate Majority Leader Robert Byrd, the great champion of the legislative branch of government who had long before learned not to trust the spin he was fed by the executive branch, came to offer the Shah his personal support. Aside from his professional concerns, Byrd had a family interest in Iran in the form of a son-in-law of Iranian descent. According to the account provided by Ambassador Sullivan, Senator Byrd had been briefed on Iran prior to his visit by Zbig Brzezinski, who told him that the State Department was preventing the Shah from taking the strong measures needed to stop the dissidents. The West Virginia senator planned to stiffen the Shah's spine by telling him to use whatever means he thought necessary to curtail his enemies' actions. Ambassador Sullivan received his distinguished visitor before the senator could meet with the Shah; he heard out Byrd's plan. He then asked the senator, stone-faced, if "this message was intended to entail a United States encouragement for the shah to use force in order to kill the political opposition in the streets." Byrd seemingly had not understood that his words—and Brzezinski's advice—amounted to a turkey shoot of many, many Iranian men, women, and youths. After meeting with his son-in-law's Iranian relatives and then the deeply depressed Shah, Senator Byrd returned to the United States too aware that the Shah's days in power were numbered.[42]

The most controversial of the late-arriving American visitors was General Robert "Dutch" Huyser. Huyser had been drafted into the military during World War II as a private and through extraordinary ability had bootstrapped his way to four-star general. In the late 1970s he was Deputy Commander in Chief of the U.S. European Command and the military officer responsible for overseeing American military sales and assistance programs to forty-four nations, including Iran. In April 1978, even as the Iranian domestic situation was deteriorating, the Shah had requested that General Huyser assist him in reorganizing his military structure and doctrine. Huyser successfully fulfilled this mission, earning the Shah's trust. He was smart, can-do, and well aware of the intricacies of international relations. When he arrived in Tehran, at the express orders of President Carter, he knew personally the leaders of the Iranian military, as well as the Shah.

General Huyser's core mission was to meet with the top leaders of the Iranian military, assure them absolutely of continued American support, and convince them to stay in Iran in the event—the extremely likely event—that the Shah left. As Huyser's no-nonsense boss, General Alexander Haig, told Huyser at the time, the mission was dangerously ambiguous. It was not clear, Haig later wrote, if "his purpose was to make a military coup" or, as an after-the-fact "sensitive" but not "top secret" mission summary document reported, to work "toward continued Iranian support for the legitimate government in Iran."[43]

Huyser was not sure, either, of the parameters of his mission. Primarily, he sought to convince the dispirited and frightened leaders of the Iranian military to stay in Iran, even if the Shah left, and to make plans to restore order. He was shocked by what he found. Above all, the men feared for their lives if the Shah left. And most had convinced themselves that if the Shah left they must leave as well.

To a man, the military men were furious with the United States and with Great Britain. Why, they asked, did the United States not stop the BBC's Farsi-language service from broadcasting news reports that included speeches by Khomeini and other anti-Shah elements? Such reports, they felt, proved official British government—and perhaps American government—support for the anti-Shah forces. Certainly, they said, that is what the Shah's supporters in Iran, who listened zealously to such news, feared. In Iran no broadcasting of Khomeini's remarks was ever allowed. Huyser comprehended their anger but made no headway in explaining British and American ideas about balanced news coverage and freedom of the press. The cultural divide was unbridgeable.[44]

Huyser quickly understood that Iran's military leaders wanted the United States to somehow solve their problems. Why, they asked, had the Americans not simply "done something about Khomeini"?[45] Over and over again, Iran's highest ranking officers begged Huyser to tell them what to do. General A. Gharabaghi tried to explain to Huyser how people saw things in Iran: "[T]hings are very different from your country. If you expect an individual to accomplish something, you have to give him a specific order. . . . People of my country have been trained that way for hundreds of years."[46] For the hard-charging Huyser, who saw personal initiative in service to duty as a way of life, this approach was more than a little frustrating.

As the Shah's regime groaned through its last days, Major General Huyser met continually with the Shah's military men, trying to get them to do the right thing. He, himself, was not always sure what that right thing was supposed to be—though he certainly encouraged the generals' talk of pulling off a military coup. And he passed along to Washington the generals' half-hearted planning for a coup if events, in their minds, warranted it.[47]

Huyser's month-long presence in Iran, which was supposed to be secret, was carefully followed by the conspiracy-minded Iranian public. The dissident Iranian media, cheered on by the Soviets, spoke in the darkest possible tones about the threat of an American-sponsored coup to save the Shah, just like the CIA-led coup of 1953. In Moscow, *Pravda* reported: "General Huyser is carrying out the role of 'Governor-General' in Iran. In Washington it was said the General has 'successfully replaced the Shah.' "[48]

For months, Ambassador Sullivan had been urging the Shah to institute political reforms. That effort had clearly failed. Likewise for months, even years, the State Department had blocked all attempts to work with anti-Shah elements in or out of Iran, most especially the Ayatollah Khomeini. In December, the State Department had begun to reach out tentatively to some of the more pro-democratic anti-Shah forces. By early January, with the Shah's authority destroyed and his hand picked prime minister, the moderate, Western-educated Shahpour Bakhtiar, likely to last for a ridiculously short time, Sullivan vehemently argued that the American government policy had to turn 180 degrees.[49] In the strongest possible terms he urged Secretary of State Vance to open up lines of communication with Khomeini. In Washington, the State Department's Iranian expert, Henry Precht, had already reached the same conclusion. Indeed, he had been the first to consider reaching out to Khomeini, whom he hoped was more moderate and open to compromise than his fierce anti-American rhetoric suggested. General Huyser, who had witnessed the incredible popularity of the ayatollah in Iran, supported the Khomeini option as well. Secretary of Defense Brown, briefed by his man Huyser and though only tangentially involved with the Iranian policymaking, signed on to Sullivan and Huyser's assessment. Sullivan seemed to have won the day and a senior, Farsi-speaking State Department official had even been assigned to go to Paris and contact the ayatollah. On January 5, in the wee hours of the might, Sullivan was told that the president had decided not to pursue the Paris mission.[50]

Carter had lost faith in his ambassador to Iran. Sullivan, in Carter's view, seemed to have swung wildly from an unyielding support of the Shah to a nearly hysterical sense that only an overture to Khomeini could save American interests in Iran. Carter wanted to give the newly selected prime minister Bakhtiar a chance. In early January, Carter was working his way through the rapidly changing situation in Iran in the beautiful Carribean island of Guadeloupe, where he was meeting with the leaders of France, Great Britain, and West Germany. While he was being briefed he wrote the following notes to himself:

> Shah will leave Iran for US in a few days. . . . will leave constitutionally aware of coup group and plans—Set up at Shah's suggestion to support Baktiar [*sic*] will take over if Bak unsuccessful widespread rumors re coup should help Bak
>   Shah wants US coop [with] Coup
>   Public US expression "sensible move"
>   Coup groups will support Baktiar [*sic*]
>   Shah confirmed names of coup group
>   . . . minimize bloodshed—no guarantee[51]

The United States would stay the course with the Shah to the end. When the Shah left Iran, as everybody in the Carter administration agreed he must for order to be restored, the United States would then support the "legitimate government" of Iran in the form of the

Shah's handpicked successor, Prime Minister Bakhtiar. The Iranian military would supply the steel needed to keep the prime minister in power and if the military generals' direct control of Iran was necessary to maintain order then the United States would support their coup. The Shah might then return. In essence, Carter hoped that pro-Shah or, at least, Shah-linked moderate elements in Iran could pull their own chestnuts out of the fire. The United States would not directly intervene on their behalf. There would be no repeat of 1953. Nor would the U.S. government jump ship and support the Shah's avowed enemies.

When Ambassador Sullivan was told that the Khomeini mission had been scrapped he went ballistic. He tried for several days to convince his superiors to reconsider. He failed. On January 10 he discarded all diplomatic niceties and sent a blistering telegraph to Washington: "You should know that President has made gross and perhaps irretrievable mistake by failing to send emissary to Paris to see Khomeini. . . . I can not rpt not understand the rationale. . . . I urge you immediately to joint [sic] Harold Brown in this plea for sanity. . . . Failure to act immediately could permanently frustrate U.S. national interests in Iran."[52] Carter was appalled by Sullivan's outburst. While Cyrus Vance talked Carter out of recalling him immediately, the president no longer listened to almost anything he said.[53] The Carter White House, strongly bucked up by Brzezinski, was not ready to make overtures to the revolutionary Islamic forces led by the ayatollah. The same day Sullivan sent his intemperate telegram, Carter had read an NSC-supplied, translated version of an interview done with Khomeini in the Paris newspaper *Le Monde*. Before passing it back to Brzezinski, Carter had scrawled one word on the top of the paper, "Nutty."[54]

The Shah of Iran left his country on January 16. He flew away on a Boeing 707, proudly made in America, that he piloted himself. But where was he to go? And when would he be able to come home?

SHASLIK NERG BESSAWARI AZERBAIYAN OR "THE RED BLINDFOLD WOULD BE LOVELY"

On November 4, 1979, Robert Ode was on special short-term assignment at the U.S. embassy in Iran. He'd only been there for a couple of months. He was part of the skeleton crew operating the much-reduced U.S. Mission Tehran while the Iranian revolution sorted itself out. Sixty-five years old, he had retired from the foreign service in 1976. He'd put in thirty years all over the world. A steady, sure hand, he looked a decade younger than his age.

Ode's work at the embassy was routine. Mostly, he processed visa applications. Because of the chaos and anti-American hysteria, the U.S. government had stopped issuing visas for several months. Now there was a big backlog and visas to the United States were a hot commodity, especially for persecuted Iranian Jews and Ba'hai's, as well as for anybody associated in any way with the Shah's overthrown regime (and, revolution or no revolution, for the many young Iranians who still wished to study in American universities). The paperwork had overwhelmed the reduced regular staff.[1]

Ode's previous special assignment for the State Department had been well out of the ordinary. At the tail end of 1978, State had sent him to Guyana to help handle the fallout of the Jonestown horrors. The Reverend Jim Jones, leader of the 3,000-member People's Temple in San Francisco, had taken around 1,100 of his followers down to Guyana, on the northeast coast of South America, to build a socialist-religious utopian enclave. Jones had for all practical purposes gone insane—or further insane—and Jonestown had become an armed camp in which extreme loyalty to "Father" was paramount. In November 1978, an American delegation led by Congressman Leo Ryan arrived in Guyana to investigate charges that Jones was holding people against their will. Jones had the congressman and three staffers killed. In an apocalyptic paranoid fury, he then ordered his followers to drink cyanide-laced Kool-Aid, a task for which they had been rehearsing for some time. Most complied. Those that didn't were shot down by Jones loyalists. On November 18, 1978, while the Shah's regime crumbled, 913 Americans, including 276 children, died in Jonestown. Ode's job was to assist the 167 survivors and look after the repatriation of the corpses. In the late 1970s, "cults" (Hare Krishnas, "Moonies," the Children of God) and "cult" deprogramming were just part of the backdrop to the more general pandemonium and, in retrospect, it's amazing how calmly Americans treated the mass suicide and murders at Jonestown. Ode himself was a calm man and he had done his best to bracket the madness and do the job he had been assigned.[2]

After the horrors of Jonestown, Tehran had seemed like relatively light duty for Ode. Nightly gunfire, constant anti-American street protests, and shouts of "Marg bar Amrika" (Death to America) were unpleasant but seemed like manageable threats.

They were not. Robert Ode would become the oldest captive taken by the Iranian student revolutionaries. To the best of his ability, this veteran foreign service officer gave his youthful captors a very hard time for 444 days.

CONSIDERING THAT the Shah of Iran had been a strong American ally for a quarter of a century, the American press response to his regime's collapse was striking: almost every editorial cheered his fall. The *Chicago Tribune*, for years a conservative champion of the anti-communist cause, lambasted the Shah and mocked his handlers' statement that the Shah was just going on a temporary vacation: "[He should take] a vacation in the strictest sense of the word—he must vacate his throne, his country, and his power. He must get out." The liberal-oriented *Baltimore Sun* urged readers to see the Iranian debacle as a part of larger American foreign policy miscalculation: "Iran is the place where U.S. overseas policies for selling arms and purchasing oil finally collapsed in a wreckage of false assumptions and dangerous gambles." Presciently, the *Sun* editorial argued, "What we are seeing in the turmoil of Tehran is the reckless futility of making U.S. security hostage to unstable regimes."

Only the *Los Angeles Times* issued a different kind of warning. Taking note of the violent anti-Shah protests occurring in Los Angeles, the paper's editorial observed: "The Iranian protesters claim that they want democracy in their homeland. Their behavior here indicates that they have yet to comprehend the meaning of the word."[3] The editorial had a point: what was going to replace the Shah's regime? Almost no one in the United States prayed for the return of SAVAK torture chambers. But few, including the Carter White House, know what to expect from the Iranian revolution. No one really imagined Iran would be ruled by fundamentalist Islamic theocrats who allowed the American diplomatic mission in Tehran to be held hostage for 444 days while enraged mobs burned American flags and chanted, "Marg bar Amrika!" The American people, with few exceptions, simply could not imagine, let alone understand, the hostility so many Iranians felt toward the United States. The Islamic revolution in Iran was terra incognita for the Carter administration and the American public.

In Iran, the revolution appeared to be cause for nationwide celebration and the Ayatollah Khomeini's return from exile created joyous pandemonium on the streets of Tehran. The ayatollah came home on February 1, 1979, in a chartered Air France jumbo jet. The ayatollah's retinue revealed their ability to work well in the nonspiritual world; they sold the remaining seats on the Paris-to-Tehran flight to journalists, covering the cost of the charter. A journalist who flew on the plane with Khomeini wrote: "I have never met anyone who made so great an impression as this man to whom the nuances and compromises of the twentieth century were, it seemed, of as little lasting significance as the snow that fell that winter."[4] Khomeini was seventy-six years old. But his extraordinary mind remained nimble and his iron will was fixed on creating an Islamic government based solely on *shari'a* (Islamic law).

As Khomeini made his way into Tehran (in a Chevy Blazer) millions upon millions of Iranians lined the streets. They chanted, "Khomeini, O Imam!" In Iran, among Shi'ite Muslims, the title "Imam" carries powerful connotations of semi-divine authority. In a nation in crisis and chaos, it seemed that a solid majority of Iranians hoped that Khomeini, incorruptible and devout beyond all other considerations, could lead them forward to a just, moral, and spiritually uplifting future. He was a national symbol of anti-Shah unity. But as well as any of the other men and women who had fought to bring down the Shah and who competed to control the revolutionary fervor of the streets, Khomeini knew that the nature of the government that was to come was far from a fixed certainty. Factions that ranged from liberal pro-democracy forces to pro-Soviet groups to Islamic fundamentalists all sought to shape the revolution in their own images. No one ruled Iran when the ayatollah came home from exile.

Within twenty-four hours of Khomeini's return to Iran, Zbigniew Brzezinski sent a top secret briefing paper focused on Islamic fundamentalism—NSC Weekly Report #87—to President Carter. He, better than anyone else in a leadership position in government, had begun honing in on the implications of Islamic rule in Iran. Referring to "Ayatollah Khomeini's remarkable political victory over the Shah," he generally soft-pedaled the specific threat of "Islamic fundamentalism" to American interests, concluding that "the foreign policy consequences for the U.S. of a strengthening of Islamic sentiment are rather mixed." He underlined that "Islam is a very 'political' religion . . . [with] no clear demarcation between church and state." And he made sure that his boss understood that "Iranian Shiism is quite different from the Sunni rite of Islam found elsewhere in the Middle East. It is more populist and oppositionist for doctrinal and historical reasons."

The president received a separate paper explaining the history of the Islamic schism. The Shi'a faction of Islam formed in the seventh century after the death of the Prophet Muhammad in a dispute over leadership succession. The Shi'a argued that leadership should descend through the Prophet's family while the Sunni stated that leadership would be chosen by the departed Prophet's close circle and wise religious leaders. In 680 A.D. the grandson of the Prophet, Hosain, sought to regain rule; his group of 72 men, women, and children were slaughtered by soldiers of the Umayyad dynasty, establishing a vital Shi'a principle; better to die a martyr to righteousness than to live meekly under injustice. Of equal importance, Shi'i doctrine emphasizes more than does Sunni the importance of obeying a learned religious authority, the *ulema*, capable of explaining religious law to the rest of the community. Ideally, one learned man embodies this authority but since no structure akin to the Roman Catholic Church exists among the Shi'i for selecting such a man, several learned figures usually vie for leadership.[5]

Brzezinski predicted that the force of Islamic revolution in Iran—and elsewhere—would not become a major, institutionalized political power: "religious institutions rarely succeed in dominating the political systems of Moslem countries." He argued that the Islamic leaders "have no experience of running a government and will find it necessary to rely on technicians and experts. The experience of power is likely to tarnish the purity of the fundamentalist movements which have thrived on their opposition to authority." As to whether this turn to "technicians and experts" and the tarnishing of the "purity" of the "fundamentalist movement" would be a short-, medium-, or long-term process, Brzezinski remained mute.

Brzezinski concluded his analysis of Islamic fundamentalism with an evocative observation on U.S. relations with the Islamic world. He wrote Carter: "We will clearly have to continue to pursue our relations with individual Muslim countries on the basis of shared interests, but our emphasis on moral as well as material values, our support for a world of diversity, and our commitment to social justice should place us in a strong position to deepen our dialogue with the Muslim world."[6] This practical and hopeful vision, with its balanced attention to national self-interest and shared principles would, to a large extent, fall prey in Iran to the vehemence and political utility of longstanding anti-Americanism among the Iranian revolutionaries, the Carter administration's ambivalent attachment to the Shah, and, most explosively, the hostage crisis. In the rest of the Islamic world the American government's strong support of successive Israeli governments in their struggles with Palestinian nationalism was a virtually insurmountable problem creating a major divide between the United States and most Islamic people in the region.

Brzezinski had made an excellent start in rethinking American relations with the Islamic world. While his concerns about Soviet influence in the broader region—specifically what he referred to as "the arc of instability" (a.k.a., "the crescent of crisis") running from Afghanistan to Yemen to the Horn of Africa—remained a top priority and focus, he understood that the United States needed to consider how to address, in its own right, the "strengthening of Islamic sentiment" in the area. It was a potential breakthrough moment. No one in the Carter administration, including the NSC advisor, or any of the four presidencies that followed, seems to have worked Brzezinski's pithy thoughts into a new paradigm or action plan before the September 11, 2001, attack. The moment was lost and Brzezinski's insights buried under the ensuing hostage crisis. Rather than "deepen our dialogue with the Muslim world" based on shared moral and spiritual concerns, the dominant discourse through which a great many Americans understood Islam would soon enough center on iterations of the word terrorism.[7]

On the ground in Iran, after so many years of willfully ignoring all forces other than the Pahlavi regime and its SAVAK henchmen, the State Department and the Central Intelligence Agency could offer President Carter little advice on the internal workings of the key revolutionary factions vying for control. As a result, in the first months of the Iranian revolution, the U.S. government essentially played a watch-and-wait game. Shah or no Shah, the United States had critical interests in Iran. First of all, not only had Iran faithfully—if expensively—supplied oil to the United States and its allies; it also had helped stabilize the entire oil-rich Persian Gulf region.

Less publicly, the United States had sited a number of intelligence-gathering listening posts along Iran's northern border with the Soviet Union and whatever else Khomeini and the other mullahs believed in, they were not communist sympathizers. Finally, the Shah's massive militarization and economic modernization policies had resulted in many lucrative contracts for American corporations and financial institutions—who were more than willing to continue doing business with whatever government took control of Iran. Most American political and economic elites hoped that regardless of who controlled Iran, both nations' interests would result in continuing relations.

So, while thousands of Americans had fled Iran's revolutionary uncertainties and dangerous anti-Americanism, in late January about ten thousand Americans remained, most of them involved in the oil business and military contracting. The U.S. embassy continued to operate amid all the uncertainty and its personnel, both overtly and covertly, tried their best to create relationships with Iran's new powerbrokers. Few of the revolutionaries, however, had any interest in making deals with the Americans, who had figured so strongly in the pre-revolution rhetoric as evildoers extraordinaire. And for those non-revolutionary Iranians, associating with Americans (especially Americans connected to the U.S. government) could be very dangerous, even deadly. Nobody in revolutionary Iran wanted to be perceived as a pro-Shah American agent.

On the other side of Iran's northern border, the Soviet government watched the revolutionary chaos with glee. Soviet officials saw the collapse of the Shah's regime as a punishing American loss and, therefore, a Soviet gain. In the cold war zero-sum game, few in the Soviet politburo seemed to have weighed the effects a fiercely politicized Islamic movement might have on their own regional allies or on the millions of Islamic people who lived unhappily within the Central Asian republics of the Soviet empire. That threat was still just over the horizon, unseen. In the immediate weeks after the Shah's departure, the Soviet-directed and based radio network, the National Voice of Iran, fired up anti-American hostility with sham news reports: "[U.S.] Embassy employees and 25,000 imperialist agents" were working overtime to restore the Shah to his throne, the network proclaimed. "We urge our fellow citizens to be alert and pay full attention to the activities of the U.S. embassy." Most Iranian revolutionaries did not need Soviet propaganda to fuel their fears of a U.S.-sponsored coup that would bring the Shah back to Iran. They remembered 1953. Khomeini himself warned the Iranian people, "We will not let the United States bring the shah back. . . . This is what the shah wants. Wake up. Watch out."[8]

The Shah, indeed, had not yet given up, at least not completely. Originally, he had planned to fly directly to the United States. He had even arranged to stay, with the Carter administration's blessings, at the luxurious Palm Springs digs of one of his super-rich American friends, Walter Annenberg, a Nixon crony and one-time ambassador to England. Instead he chose to go to Egypt where he had been invited by Anwar Sadat. Then, he had jetted over to Morocco, where King Hassan had offered him hospitality. Why exactly the Shah refrained from immediately traveling to the United States may never be known. But certainly some around the Shah still hoped he could ride a military coup back to power. The Shah's ambassador to the United States, Ardeshir Zahedi, had joined the Shah in Morocco and, according to British journalist and author William Shawcross, was urging him not to go to the United States because it would forever brand him in Iran as an American CIA puppet. He should instead wait in Muslim Morocco to see if the Iranian military, one way or the other, could pave a way for his return.[9]

It was not to be. Masses of soldiers, like their civilian counterparts, celebrated the return of Khomeini. By February 10 the Iranian air force was controlled by pro-Khomeini forces and was battling the remaining pro-Shah forces, the Imperial Guard. Overwhelmingly, the military office corps declined to carry on a civil war and declared itself loyal to the revolution. In just days, all organized pro-Shah forces had quit. The Shah's loyal, high-ranking military leaders, as well as the hard men who ran SAVAK, fled the country or were hunted down and often killed by the revolutionary forces. In Iran, in the early months of 1979, it was payback time. Revolutionary mobs meted out street justice and held kangaroo court trials, executing thousands.

In the United States in early 1979, Iran was in the news. Newspapers covered the chaos and the exodus of thousands of American expatriates from Iran. The Ayatollah Khomeini made his network debut on both ABC and NBC on November 3, 1978 and in early January the *CBS Evening News* had a five-minute feature on the ayatollah. The CBS feature included a well-spoken North Texas State Iranian student who pithily explained that the revolutionaries wanted an "Islamic government" and that in Islam there is "no difference in church and state." A good deal of network coverage focused on the Shah's travails.[10] His hard fall from power had a storybook quality to it that a good many Americans, generally fascinated by other countries' royal families (especially their troubles and scandals), enjoyed following. Despite the increase of mass media coverage, few people in the United States in January 1979 could have explained anything—or probably cared much, if at all—about the Iranian revolution. Exceptions to this general rule would include people who diligently perused the front section of the *New York Times*, which contained insightful coverage of the unfolding events.

Some latter-day critics of both American policy in the region and the American mass media suggest a deliberate effort by elites to keep Americans ignorant of the meaning of events in revolutionary Iran and of the reasons the United States was not beloved by the revolutionaries. A likelier explanation for the lack of focused coverage (by the television networks, at least) of the revolution and the U.S. government's complicity in the Shah's regime is less Machiavellian. Just three and a half years after the fall of South Vietnam and following multiple declarations by both President Ford and

President Carter that the United States needed to draw back from overseas military entanglements and stop its cynical, often covert interventions in other nations' affairs, Americans understood that U.S. foreign policy was, to put it generously, in transition. While some Americans had to be aware of the 1953 CIA action that had put the Shah in power (since television news coverage, for example, did occasionally refer to the coup), fewer still would have seen the salience of an event that had occurred over a quarter of a century ago during the administration of a president who had died nearly two decades earlier. The American public rarely exhibits the kind of haunting dark historical consciousness that pervades so many societies around the world—especially those places that have suffered indignities, horrors, and defeats at the hands of other peoples and nations. The "Lost Cause" culture of the old Confederate states, still wistfully maintained by some Southern whites, is a major American exception that proves the rule. Overwhelmingly, from the American perspective, the mess in Iran was just one more fiasco which, most Americans reasonably believed, had little to do with their everyday lives. With the "misery index" of inflation and unemployment soaring toward double digits, people had bigger, more immediate problems with which to contend.[11]

Still, some people in the United States did want notice taken of the Iran situation. But they were not the critics of America's long-standing relationship with the Shah's regime. The Shah's most ardent supporters began to surface, publicly attacking the Carter administration's policies and demanding that the Shah be treated as an old ally and deserving friend. They charged that a hapless president had lost Iran to America's enemies. The words echoed accusations that had been made when the communists had taken over China back in 1949 and when Cuba had fallen to Castro a decade later. The notion that Iran, like China and Cuba, was America's to lose revealed a good deal about the cold war ethos that still permeated much of America's foreign policy elite, even after the disaster of Vietnam.

Henry Kissinger, who had worked with President Nixon to make Iran a pillar of American security in the Persian Gulf, led the charge. In a widely reported and influential speech made before NBC radio affiliate station executives in late January, he blamed the Carter White House's human rights policies for weakening the Shah and slammed Carter and "congressional scrutiny" for contributing to the "disintegration of the Central Intelligence Agency," which further impeded American policy in Iran. (He chose not to mention the CIA's reckless reliance on SAVAK for insight into internal Iranian activities.) Finally, the real and perceived economic and political weakness of the United States since the end of the Vietnam War, Kissinger argued, provided a third American dagger stuck in the Shah's political corpse. Carter had allowed "a major setback for American security, the stability of the Middle East and the stability and security of international order in general." NSC staffers made sure that their boss, Zbigniew Brzezinski, got a copy of the wire service story on the Kissinger speech.[12]

It is easy to forget, given what happened on November 4, that the Iranian revolution was not only small potatoes for most Americans throughout most of 1979, it was also not the focus of the Carter administration, even in the foreign policy arena. At the end of 1978, while the Shah's regime crumbled, President Carter was celebrating one of his greatest foreign policy coups, the normalization of relations with the People's Republic of China. In late January 1979, as the Shah cooled his heels in Morocco, Vice Premier Deng Xiaoping came to the White House on a path-breaking, official state visit. Carter was thrilled by the breakthrough and charmed by the chain-smoking, diminutive Deng. He later wrote: "The Deng Xiaoping visit was one of the delightful experiences of my presidency. To me, everything went right."[13] Carter even got Deng to allow Bibles back into China, a cause dear to the president's heart. Compared to the importance of the Chinese diplomatic breakthrough, the fall of the Shah could, hopefully, be relegated by the Carter administration to a challenging turn of events rather than a foreign policy debacle.

On February 14, 1979, armed Iranians did their best to focus Americans' attention on their revolution. Spraying automatic weapon fire at the heavily outgunned Marine Corps guards, a group of militants, backed up by snipers lined up on neighboring rooftops, came over the U.S. embassy walls. Fearing a bloodbath that the heavily outnumbered Americans would lose, Ambassador Sullivan ordered the Marines not to fire back unless their lives were in immediate peril. Instead, they laid down a fog of tear gas to slow down the attack. In the embassy's vault, Ambassador Sullivan led an efficient team effort to destroy documents and equipment that could not fall into the revolutionaries' hands. The defense attaché, combat veteran Colonel Thomas Schaefer, stated, "I can honestly say the attack sounded worse than any firefight I ever heard in Vietnam."[14]

Ambassador Sullivan has, ever since the Shah's fall, received a fair amount of criticism for somehow not having done more to buck up the Shah and stop the revolution in Iran (as if he could have if only he had acted more wisely). Nobody, however, has ever faulted him for his courage. Once the militants had successfully taken over the embassy, they began threatening the ambassador with various deadly weapons and making fierce demands that did not bode well for the safety of the captured American personnel. Standing tall and never losing his cool, Sullivan kept the militants talking. As embassy army attaché Colonel Leland Holland reported with the brevity befitting a man accustomed to seeing men in dangerous situations: "In a crisis his feathers didn't ruffle."[15]

This embassy takeover was not *the* embassy takeover. Sullivan was hoping for a rescue. When the attack began, Colonel Holland, hunkered down in the ambassador's office, bullets whizzing everywhere, had called various phone numbers he had been given by an Iranian police general in case of an emergency. He had gotten through and, sure enough, a flying squad of equally well-armed militants, led by Ibrahim Yazdi of the Ayatolloh Khomeini's very own Revolutionary Council, arrived and began firing on the original group of revolutionary militants. They won; after taking casualties, the first group laid down their arms. According to the Farsi-speaking embassy press attaché, Barry Rosen, Yazdi apologized for the difficulties. He told Rosen, "In times of revolution mistakes occur. Right now it is impossible for the government to control every group in Iran. But the Provisional Government of Iran did not want this to happen. We will try to insure your safety."[16]

This embassy takeover was the model most everybody on the American side had in mind down the road. It had been scary and the embassy was shot up, but no American had been seriously injured. The Americans had been hostages for less than an hour. Khomeini's people, despite all their heated rhetoric about "Death to America," had worn the white hats and ridden in to the rescue. The Carter administration, glumly and with caution, would try to find a way to work with the new, still evolving Iranian regime while at the same time drastically reducing the number of Americans—targets—inside Iran. The most optimistic of Washington foreign policy savants, most especially the State Department's Iran expert, Henry Precht, hoped that the "moderates" within the revolutionary coalition would rise to the fore and reestablish working relations with the United States. Maybe it would all work out.

Between late February and late August 1979, President Carter and the American people had plenty to worry about aside from the Iranian revolution. While in the United States, Chinese leader Deng Xiaoping had told Jimmy Carter that China was going to punish Vietnam for invading Cambodia in order to end the genocidal rule of Pol Pot and the Khmer Rouge. Carter had tried to talk Deng out of the attack but the fierce Chinese leader (in 1989 he earned the nickname "butcher of Tiananmen Square" for issuing shoot-to-kill orders against peaceful demonstrators) had not come seeking advice. The attack on Vietnam came on schedule at the end of February. Since the United States had only just normalized relations with the supposedly peaceful Chinese government, the unilateral, preemptive, and punitive attack was not well received by those Americans who noted it. Several congressmen used the opportunity to attack Carter's general foreign policy as weak-willed and reactive. Leaders of the Soviet Union were more aggrieved; the United States, they sneered, was becoming China's cat's paw. Carter historian Burton Kaufman observes: "Rather than the United States playing its 'China card' [against the Soviet Union] . . . perhaps China had successfully played its 'American card' [against the Soviets]."[17]

Closer to home, the Carter administration was waffling over the ongoing Nicaraguan civil war. As in Iran, an old American friend, the dictator Anastasio Somoza, was under attack from revolutionary forces. Here, the insurgents were Che Guevara–loving, communistic, Cuban-backed guerrillas known as the Sandanistas. While only a true blackheart could find anything at all morally decent about the thuggish Somoza, he had been a strong anti-communist who welcomed American capitalists with open arms (and an open palm), and for better than thirty years that had been enough to keep him on the right side of cold war American policy. It was not clear how the administration hoped to "win" in Nicaragua.

Additionally, in the late summer of 1979, Senator Frank Church, scourge of the CIA and head of the Senate Foreign Relations Committee, looking to cover his political backside against an expected attack from conservatives in his 1980 reelection bid in Idaho, accused the Carter administration of being soft on the Soviet communist threat. Several thousand Soviet combat troops, Church warned, had moved into Cuba, just ninety miles off the coast of Florida, while Commander in Chief Jimmy Carter had watched impotently. In reality, the Soviets had kept armed troops in Cuba since President Kennedy had half-heartedly tried to overthrow Fidel Castro's Soviet-allied regime. And while the Soviets had increased the number of their troops stationed in Cuba, the escalation was, from every possible angle—except that of political perception—insignificant. But Church needed a "red-meat" issue and he was more than willing to lay into Carter, the supposed leader of Church's own Democratic Party, to get his headlines and prove his anti-communist mettle. While the president could point to the Egypt-Israeli negotiations to prove that he was not without his successes, a large majority of Americans, at least according to poll data, believed that Jimmy Carter did not know where he was leading the United States, globally or at home.[18]

By mid-1979, the United States was in bad shape. The Iranian revolution had caused oil prices—once again—to spike, driving millions of Americans to ponder the ego-punishing possibility that an uncomfortable, unattractive, and underpowered vehicle, likely made in Japan, was in their future. Inflation, America's number-one bête noire, was raging along at better than 12 percent per annum, chewing up Americans' savings and tearing at their hopes for a secure retirement. The president responded to the inflationary spiral by urging Congress to cut spending and produce an austere federal budget (conventional economic wisdom: starve inflation by cutting government spending and raising interest rates and feed a recession with increased government spending and/or tax cuts). While a slimmed-down federal budget was reasonable economic policy it was bad politics. The liberal wing of the Democratic Party attacked Carter as a right-wing tightwad indifferent to the plight of the poor and the unemployed who depended on government spending to ease their suffering during hard times. The fact that African American teenagers had an unemployment rate of 35.5 percent in 1979 fueled Democrats' insistence that the nation needed a jobs plan and not domestic program cutbacks. The liberals' liberal, Senator Ted Kennedy, was openly attacking the president and discussing the possibility of running against Carter for the 1980 Democratic Party presidential nomination. Carter's failures, he hoped, would be enough to make voters forget his own scandalous problems at Chappaquiddick.

Carter fought back in mid-July with his "malaise" speech, the honest but politically unwise speech in which he suggested that Americans' suffered from a "crisis of spirit." While few people really knew what Carter was getting at since he never defined his key term or explained what exactly Americans were supposed to do to make inflation go away and the energy crisis dissipate, poll numbers taken right after the speech suggested most people approved of the effort—at least Carter was trying to lead Americans . . . somewhere.

Carter had gained back some political ground with his speech but he could not hold it. Through the late spring and summer of 1979, more than policy predicaments and political calculations tore at Jimmy Carter. In August the *Washington Post*, which had only a few years earlier broken the Watergate scandal, ran a front-page story that signaled to savvy readers that the Carter presidency was in trouble. The story described an incident that had actually occurred several weeks earlier near Carter's home-town of Plains, Georgia, where the president was trying to relax by doing a little fishing. While Carter sat alone in his humble row-boat, rod and reel in hand, an aquatic rabbit, hissing in an obvi-ously ill-tempered way, bunny-paddled like mad right for him. The president was forced to take up an oar and beat back the bunny. Playing off the recent blockbuster film, *Jaws*, a cartoon titled "Paws" depicted the absurd scene. The *Post* seemed to suggest that not even a bunny rabbit was willing to take the president of the United States seriously.[19]

Shortly after the "Paws" incident made the national news, Zbig-niew Brzezinski tried to buck up the president. He sent Carter a bold foreign policy strategy report. The president, he wrote, for political and policy purposes, had to change how people in the United States and around the world viewed the Carter administra-tion's international leadership. For good reason, the September 13, 1979, document was copiously stamped "Top Secret."

Brzezinski told the president that he had two overarching foreign policy problems. First, the American people did not perceive Carter as having achieved anything important in the realm of foreign pol-icy. Politically, that judgment was not going to help the president in the upcoming presidential race. Second, he told the president, around the world, "notably in allied countries," the administration was dismissed as "the most timid since World War II." Brzezinski was no slouch in buttering up powerful men, and he assured the president that much of this criticism was inaccurate: "[T]he U.S. public is simply misinformed, because of the excessively critical and even prejudiced views of the Washington press corps . . . [which is] echoed by a mindless foreign press." Still, Brzezinski mournfully added, real problems did exist with Carter's foreign policy record.

As was his wont, Brzezinski zeroed in on the core cold war ri-valry. The fundamental problem, he wrote Carter, was "the in-creasingly pervasive feeling in the country and abroad that in the U.S.-Soviet relationship the Soviet side increasingly is the assertive party and the U.S. side is the more acquiescent. . . . [T]his is seen as especially true in relationship to the various trouble spots." Brzezinski then offered a list of hot spots where the Soviets pushed while the United States got shoved: "For better or for worse, we were passive in Iran; the Soviets were far from passive in Afghanistan. We pursued a diplomatically amiable policy in Africa; the Soviets relied on Cuban arms, not without some effect. In Latin America, and particularly in Central America, revolutionary fervor is on the rise, and we have not been able to give those who want to rely on us a sense of security." While too much the diplomat and the courtier to say it directly, Brzezinski was essentially calling the president a wimp.

Brzezinski insisted that Carter had to be a stronger international leader. He laid it on the line: "[B]oth in tone and occasionally in substance, we have been excessively acquiescent . . . the country craves, and our national security needs, both a more assertive tone and a more assertive substance to our foreign policy." He concluded: "I believe that both for international reasons as well as for domestic political reasons you ought to *deliberately toughen both the tone and substance of our foreign policy*. The country associates assertiveness with leadership, and the world at large expects American leadership."[20] Less than eight weeks before the Iran hostage crisis erupted, the Carter administration was thinking hard about how to show the American people and the world that the United States, not the Soviet Union, was the world's toughest superpower. Showing strength through patience and compromise was not in the cards.

Toward Iran, the general American policy of letting the revolution sort itself out while the United States just kind of muddled through was not working very well. The State Department's hope that a moderate element would slowly take control of the government was not panning out. Brzezinski's belief that over time experts and secularists of various stripes would replace Islamic fundamentalists in key decision-making posts was clearly not happening, at least in the short term. (And some twenty-five years later it has not come to pass, either—though powerful tensions between the theocrats and secular elements in Iran have existed for several years.) The best hopes for a restored relationship—or at least a working relationship—were coming through military-to-military channels.

The Iranian armed forces needed ongoing shipments of American military parts and supplies to keep themselves operational. This need was made pressing by a war that had broken out between autonomy-seeking Kurds living in northern Iran and the Khomeini-led central government. The Carter administration, while not unsympathetic to the Kurds' desires, saw the military's needs for renewed U.S. supplies as an opening wedge in normalizing relations with revolutionary Iran. (The Kurds, throughout the region, have for decades always enjoyed official American sympathy. Nonetheless, their enemies—whether the governments of Turkey, Iran, or Iraq—have slaughtered the independence-seeking Kurds while the United States—at least until the 2003 Iraq War—for geopolitical reasons, either looked the other way or supplied weapons to the killers.)[21]

In early October 1979, the Iranians and American government officials met in New York City in an attempt to work out a deal. The American side was eager to move forward. Restored relations with Iran, even on less than ideal terms, would prove that Carter had not "lost" Iran. Instead, the Carter administration could demonstrate that it had weathered the crisis and come out, if not ahead, at least in a position that would secure a working relationship in which oil would flow and American interests in the region could be maintained.

Ibrahim Yazdi—the same man who had led the February 14 embassy rescue mission—headed the Iranian delegation in New York for the opening session of the United Nations. He met with a slew of top Carter officials, including Secretary of State Vance. Yazdi made it clear that he did not trust the Carter administration and insisted that American officials demonstrate, concretely, that they had no intention of seeking the overthrow of the Khomeini-led government and that they fully accepted the revolution. Yazdi stated that proof positive of American intentions could only be demonstrated by extraditing back to Iran the many high-level Shah-loyalist "criminals" who had made their way to the United States. This was a problem: no one doubted that returning such men to Iran amounted to death sentences for them all. Yazdi also insisted that the United States must return all monetary assets of the Iranian people kept in the United States—he meant the Shah's money.

Despite this impasse, conversations continued. The State Department's Iran country director, Henry Precht, went to Iran in late October to continue negotiating (he flew home well before November 4). And on November 1, Zbigniew Brzezinski had a meeting with Yazdi, the new Iranian defense minister, Mustapha Ali Chamran, and the relatively moderate Iranian prime minister, Mehdi Bazargan. All were in Algiers to honor the twenty-fifth anniversary of another successful revolution, the Algerian people's overthrow of French imperialist rule. Brzezinski was pleasantly surprised by the competence and the intelligence of the Iranian leaders and returned to Washington somewhat optimistic that bilateral relations between the United States and Iran could be markedly improved. (Alas, just four days after this meeting, in part because of this meeting with the American NSC advisor, both Yazdi and Bazargan were removed from office by Khomeini's hard-line inner circle.) Brzezinski did note one major problem: the Iranians were extremely angry that the United States had allowed the biggest Iranian "criminal" of them all, the deposed Shah, to enter the United States.[22]

For many months the Shah had been looking for a refuge. After it had become clear that the Shah was not going to get back his Peacock Throne, King Hassan had told Mr. Pahlavi that he had to leave Morocco. The king, while quite popular with his people, had enough worries about agitating Islamic elements in Morocco without having the Shah as his guest. He told the Shah that, regrettably, he must leave by March 30 (Hassan wanted him out before the Islamic Conference—a high-level meeting of Islamic diplomats—began in Morocco in early April). The Shah contacted the U.S. ambassador to Morocco and informed him that he was now ready to make his home in America.

The Shah had waited too long. President Carter did not—very much did not—want the Shah to come to the United States at that moment. The Carter administration was hoping to restore normal relations with the new Iranian government. In addition, Ambassador Sullivan was secretly negotiating with the Iranian government to provide safe passage for a small group of Americans—probably involved in monitoring Soviet activities—trapped in northern Iran. And after the February 14 embassy takeover ruckus nobody wanted to incite the Iranian revolutionaries—except, it seems, Brzezinski, who insisted that the United States owed the Shah asylum and that the Iranian government would just have to accept the American decision.

The ambassador in Morocco, Richard Parker, was informed by his State Department superiors to stall for time. An American intelligence officer then met with the Shah in Marrakesh (in the early 1970s "jet-setters" had made the fabled city a major destination on their extravagant circuit) and tried to explain to him how risky it would be for the Shah to come to America; not only could such a visit harm American interests in Iran but, the officer pointed out, the Shah had no diplomatic immunity in the United States and he could be entangled in myriad legal battles and hounded by unfriendly congressional investigations. The Shah did not feel that he had a whole lot of choices and he reiterated his desire to travel to the United States.

President Carter was unmoved. He told Secretary of State Vance to "scout around to help find him [the Shah] a place to stay." Vance told David Newsom, the undersecretary of state for political affairs, to have someone more compelling—one of the Shah's American friends—tell the Shah that he really could not, at that point in time, come to America. Newsom asked Henry Kissinger for help. Kissinger was appalled by Carter's decision and said that the refusal to admit the Shah was "a national dishonor." He refused to be Carter's messenger. Newsom then tried David Rockefeller, whom he thought was the Shah's business associate in the United States. Newsom asked Mr. Rockefeller to fly to Morocco and personally explain the situation to the Shah. Rockefeller, whose Chase Manhattan Bank had billions of dollars in loans and accounts with the Pahlavi regime, told the undersecretary that he "refused to become complicit in the decision." Whether or not the undersecretary of state tried anybody else, in the end it became the unhappy task of the U.S. ambassador to Morocco—neither a jet-setter nor a friend of the Shah—to inform Reza Pahlavi that he could not come to the United States. He told the Shah that as far as the U.S. Department of State could determine after an exhaustive survey only two nations in the world would allow Mr. Pahlavi entrance: South Africa and Paraguay.

The Shah was not going to finish his days in African exile as had his father, and he was adamant that he would not disappear in Paraguay like some Nazi war criminal. His twin sister Princess Ashraf, a powerful and determined woman who might well have made a better (perhaps it should be said, more ruthless) leader of Iran than her emotional brother, took charge. Installed in a tony townhouse in Manhattan, she had David Rockefeller meet her at her home. Rockefeller, though worried about Chase's ongoing Iranian business, decided he would help.

It is not completely clear why Rockefeller made this decision or why he then threw himself so fully into it. Some have argued that Rockefeller was engineering a complex plot in which the Shah's admittance to the United States would result in some kind of outrageous Iranian response (like seizing American hostages) which, in turn, would cause the U.S. government to freeze all Iranian assets in American banks, most specifically the billions of Iranian assets kept in Rockefeller's Chase Manhattan Bank. This asset freeze would safeguard immense outstanding loans the Shah's regime had borrowed from Chase, loans that the new revolutionary regime in Iran might declare null and void due to certain irregularities taken by the Shah's men at the time of the agreement. A congressional committee would eventually investigate this scenario and find no proof of it; as former diplomat George Ball remarked, "Chase Manhattan Bank is not that smart." Still, Iranian expert James Bill in his masterful history of U.S.-Iranian relations, *The Eagle and the*

Lion, suggests the scenario is not unreasonable and offers some modest evidence to support it.

Certainly, in part, Rockefeller's decision was simply personal; while he was not, in fact, a close friend of the Shah's, his recently deceased brother Nelson Rockefeller, the ex-governor of New York and ex-vice president under Gerald Ford, had been, and his brother's widow, Happy, implored him to help. Also, David Rockefeller was a member of the same elite circle of the super-rich to which the Shah belonged and he sympathized with the Shah's predicament. Finally, Rockefeller was a man of certain principles. One of his beliefs was that you do not turn your back on a friend in need; the Shah had been America's friend. As he saw it, the United States owed him asylum.

Once Rockefeller decided to assist the Shah, he met with Henry Kissinger, longtime Rockefeller family advisor. Kissinger had already made it plain, in public and private, that he believed that the Carter administration had bungled every aspect of the Iranian situation. Since so much of Carter's "human rights" talk had been aimed at the cold-blooded realpolitik of the Kissinger-Nixon years, Kissinger felt no compunction about blasting the Carter White House over its failures. Refusing to admit one of America's most loyal allies in his hour of need, Kissinger believed, was indicative of the weak-kneed way the Carter administration approached international affairs; it sent a terrible message to the world.

Kissinger quickly revealed why he had become one of the highest paid international consultants in the world. He called someone in the Bahamain government and arranged asylum for the Shah. The Bahamas turned out to be a temporary solution—the Shah was mercilessly fleeced by corrupt Bahamians and felt himself to be in imminent danger of physical harm since the new government in Iran had made it clear that if they could not bring the Shah to justice in Iran, they would try to kill him wherever he was. In early June, Kissinger arranged for the president of Mexico to personally clear the way for the Shah to take up residence in a well-secured mansion in the resort town of Cuernavaca. For the next seven months, Kissinger, Rockefeller, and the Washington power broker extraordinaire John McCloy, whose law firm represented Chase Manhattan as well as major oil companies, pressured the Carter administration to let the Shah come to America.

Some highlights of their campaign: on April 9, Rockefeller met with Carter in the White House and gave him a one-page brief. Rockefeller informed the president that he had recently visited over twenty countries and that the leaders of these nations had expressed great concerns about the Carter administration's foreign policy, "which they perceive to be vacillating and lacking in an understandable global approach." In particular, after observing Carter's treatment of the Shah "they have questions about the dependability of the United States as a friend." John McCloy, who in his eighties was still the most influential of the cold war "Wise Men," having dueled with the Soviets on behalf of several presidents, was particularly relentless. He lobbied everyone from Cy Vance to Brzezinski to Carter; he even met personally with the relatively lowly NSC Iran expert Gary Sick. In an April 16 memo he sent to Vance's right-hand man, Warren Christopher, he laid out the case he would make repeatedly: for a quarter of a century, as six presidents had attested, the Shah had been America's strongest friend in a troubled region and the whole world so recognized this fact. Now that this friend needed help the United States must respond: "I very much fear that failure on our part to respond . . . would take the form of a conspicuous and perhaps historical example of the unwisdom of other leaders affiliating themselves with the United States interests. It could seriously impair our ability in the future to obtain the support of those of whom we might well stand in need."

Warren Christopher, the imperturbable voice of reason in the State Department and at the Carter White House, laid out the problem for McCloy. In deliberately bland prose that offered no room for argument, Christopher stated, "We are doing all we can to find a satisfactory resolution of this difficult problem, consistent with our obligations to the many persons in different places whose safety is or may be involved." Christopher believed that if the Shah was admitted to the United States, the Iranian revolutionaries would retaliate against Americans residing in Iran. It was that simple. So, despite the public and private pressure from some of the most powerful men in the United States, through the spring, summer, and into the fall, President Carter refused to allow the former Shah to enter the United States. Nobody in the White House was particularly proud of the decision and it wasn't pleasant to have conservative newspaper columnist George Will snidely declare, "It is so sad that an Administration that knows so much about morality has so little dignity." Prudence may not be the most heroic of characteristics but as Warren Christopher understood, it is often a sign of wisdom.[23]

By August, Carter officials were seriously divided over the Shah's request to come to America. Kissinger, Rockefeller, and McCloy had pressed hard and in all directions. Vice President Mondale had been won over and in a mid-July meeting he and Brzezinski laid out the pro-Shah case for the president. Carter was furious: "Fuck the Shah. I'm not going to welcome him when he has other places where he'll be safe." All he needed, Carter said, was the Shah "here playing tennis while Americans in Tehran were being kidnapped or even killed."[24]

The case took an unexpected turn when word of the Shah's deteriorating physical condition reached the White House. On August 10 the Shah's irrepressible sister wrote Carter about her brother's serious illness and demanded that he be admitted to the United States. Warren Christopher dutifully replied, noting that the president was, of course, concerned about the Shah's "well-being." Carter had little if any idea, however, that the Shah *was* in fact dangerously ill. By mid-October David Rockefeller's assistant, Joseph Reed, detailed for the State Department the dangerous state of the Shah's health: he had a voracious cancer and could only be treated in a state-of-the-art U.S. hospital.[25]

After having Christopher verify that the health situation was very real and then talking the matter over with Brzezinski by phone, Carter approved the Shah's asylum on emergency medical grounds. As Cy Vance said, it was simply a matter of "common decency." Chief of Staff Hamilton Jordan gave Carter the political spin: "[I]f the Shah dies in Mexico can you imagine the field day Kissinger will have with that? He'll say that first you caused the

Shah's downfall and now you've killed him." Carter had been softened up by the Kissinger-Rockefeller-McCloy treatment and by the arguments of several of his key advisors, Brzezinski and Mondale in particular. Given a new, pressing reason for changing his course, he took it. On October 22, the seriously ill Shah flew into New York City for medical treatment. Rockefeller aide Joseph Reed sent a memo to McCloy and other pro-Shah lobbyists that read, in part, "Our 'mission impossible' is completed. . . . My applause is like thunder."[26]

On diplomatic ground in Tehran, no one among the skeleton crew holding down the fort at the U.S. embassy in Iran would have voted to admit the Shah to the United States. Life was not very pleasant for Americans in Iran in late 1979 and they were extremely aware that any pro-Shah gesture on the part of the U.S. government would ignite anti-American activities. Back in May, Senator Jacob Javits had sponsored a Senate resolution condemning the revolutionary government in Iran for persecuting and, indeed, slaughtering Jews and Bahais, as well as political opponents. The resolution had created an outpouring of anti-American vitriol in Iran and was widely seen as proof positive of the Americans' plan to reinstate the Shah. Barry Rosen, at the embassy, closely followed the revolutionary press as it whipped up political zeal by demonizing the United States: Americans were blowing up railroads, killing villagers, aiding the Kurdish rebellion, and working with Iranian military leaders to bring back the Shah. Hating America and blaming America was a powerful glue holding together the disparate and often contentious strands of the Iranian revolution—which was, throughout 1979, still in great disorder and uncertainty. The only element more powerful in unifying Iran's revolutionary masses was an unrelenting hatred of the Shah. Painted everywhere on walls, chanted constantly in the myriad marches at and around the U.S. embassy, was the militants' favorite slogan: "Marg bar Shah!"—Death to the Shah.[27]

News that the Shah had been admitted to the United States flashed around Iran. The U.S. officials did try to manage the situation. Chargé d'affaires Bruce Laingen (Sullivan had been recalled and no new ambassador had yet been sent) informed the Iranian government that the Shah had a dire medical emergency and was being admitted to the United States for treatment. Laingen had gotten reassurances from Prime Minister Bazargan that the government would, as Laingen reported in his summary of the conversation, "do its best to provide security for the American embassy."[28] Laingen forwarded these modestly reassuring words to the State Department in Washington. Laingen, of course, had no way of speaking directly to some of the more radical elements in the revolutionary movement. If he had found a way, he would have been even more worried than he already was.

The Iranian provisional government did not control the revolution; it had limited authority and no genuine popular support. After the Shah had been deposed, the Ayatollah Khomeini had authorized a secular government to run daily affairs while he and other religious leaders supplied overall guidance in the transition to an Islamic state. Sovereignty, in such a situation, was uncertain. As a result, dozens of political factions ranging from the pro-Soviet Tudeh Party to the liberal, moderate Freedom Party to the religious Islamic Republican Party vied for leadership and control of the state. Khomeini's role was uncodified, even as his popular support was extraordinary.

So, in the days after the Shah was admitted to the United States anti-Americanism was rampant and only weakly controlled by the fragile government. Right after word that the Shah had arrived in the United States spread in Iran a million or more people gathered to protest in Tehran. Few believed that the Shah was really admitted to the United States for medical reasons; a photo of a healthy-appearing Shah appeared in a Tehran newspaper next to an article explaining that the Shah could not have lymphomatic cancer, as the Americans claimed, because everyone knew that Iranians did not even get that kind of illness. Clearly, the Americans were plotting with the Shah to overturn the revolution. Embassy officials had no way to argue with that kind of logic.

Repeated marches and protests were aimed at the embassy. Police, at first, kept the demonstrators away from the immediate proximity of the embassy but by October 26 protesters simply pushed through the police, who let them go. After that, demonstrators massed at the embassy's iron front gates screaming, "Marg bar Amrika!" Still, as Corporal William Gallegos, one of the Marines charged with protecting the embassy, recalls: "There wasn't any violence, and they didn't try to jump the over the walls or anything. . . . [W]e just went on with our regular duties."[29]

Some Iranians were not at all pleased that the U.S. embassy was able to go on with its "regular duties." Nor were they pleased by signs that the provisional government seemed, in the words of an Islamic militant, "helpless, paralyzed, unable to act, as though reluctant to stand up to the United States." A small group of Islamicist students had decided that something had to be done to challenge the Americans and to show both the Iranian government and the Iranian masses that the United States could not be allowed to plot with the Shah to destroy their revolution.[30]

Iranian university students had been at the forefront of the anti-Shah upheavals. The political left-wing, pro-democracy activists, and Islamic groups all were strongly represented on Iranian campuses. University dormitories were described by one student as "incubator[s] for revolution." Carter's decision to admit the Shah had galvanized the revolutionary student body. Some of the most militant were appalled that the government did nothing to retaliate against the American slap in the face. They worried that the government's placidity indicated one of two things: the provisional government had been bought off by the Americans or the government was simply afraid of the American bully. At least two separate groups of students—one left-wing and the other Islamic—began to plan a retaliatory action aimed at the U.S. embassy.

The Islamic group had members from all four major Tehran universities. On November 2, about a dozen of the Islamic students held their first major planning meeting. The group's leader, a civil engineering student known as Mohsen, opened the meeting. He began with the Islamic revolutionaries' customary salutation, "In the name of God." Then he got down to the business at hand: "By allowing the shah to enter the U.S. the Americans have started a new conspiracy against the revolution. If we don't act rapidly, if we show weakness, then a superpower like the U.S. will be able to meddle in the internal affairs of any nation in the world. . . . We've been under the thumb of the U.S. for more than fifty years. Now, it's our chance to do something about it." Mohsen's colleagues grimly agreed. As one later recounted: "In the back of everybody's mind hung the suspicion that with the admission of the shah to the United States, the countdown for another coup d'état had begun. . . . We now had to reverse the irreversible."

Mohsen explained the plan devised by the inner working group: "What we are proposing is a peaceful occupation of the American embassy—without arms. This will mean taking the embassy personnel hostage not as diplomatic personnel, but as agents of the American government. They are deeply involved in their government's conspiracies in any case."[31] The students decided they would break into the embassy, take the Americans hostage, and use the symbolic power of the event to show everyone—in Iran, in the United States, and around the world—that "God is the ultimate power," not the American government.

The plan was simple. First, they reconnoitered the embassy to figure out the layout and the best ways in. A few, pretending to be visa seekers, studied the embassy from the inside. Others gained rooftop views of the embassy compound to draw maps of the grounds. They prepared enough supplies for a three-day occupation—none of the students expected the takeover to last longer. They gathered sufficient pictures of Imam Khomeini and red armbands with the phrase "Allah-o Akbar" printed on them for two hundred and fifty students. Three students met with one of the imam's key advisors, Mousavi Khoeiniha, to ask him to inform Khomeini of their plan and get his approval.

According to the account of these events given by Massoumeh Ebtekar, the young woman who served the student group as the primary translator and English-language spokesperson, the ayatollah never received the message. However, on November 3, just hours after the students' meeting with Khoeiniha, Khomeini issued a public message commemorating the anniversary of a 1978 student protest against the Shah in which the police had murdered several young people. Khomeini stated: "It is incumbent upon students . . . to expand their attacks against America and Israel. Thus America will be forced to return the criminal deposed shah."[32] The students believed they had been given the Imam's approval for the takeover of the U.S. embassy. All the students involved were members of the Muslim Students Association and that was the only common organizational identity that any of them claimed. None of the left-wing political groups was allowed to participate, nor were members of any of the other political factions that vied for power on campus. The leaders of the takeover called their group "Muslim Students Following the Line of the Imam." They wanted to make sure that everyone inside and outside of Iran knew where their allegiances lay.

On November 4, at 10 a.m. the Muslim Students Following the Line of the Imam converged on the U.S. embassy. Many had pinned images of Khomeini to their chests so if they were martyred— shot—by the Americans, Khomeini's bloodied image on their dead bodies could be shown to the world via the mass media. They could easily identify one another by their distinctive red armbands. Some had been marching with a much larger group of students who were part of a mass student demonstration—about thirty thousand— that had been planned for that day in central Tehran. The protest march passed right by the embassy. The Muslim Students Following the Line of the Imam split off from the official protest—and so did thousands of other protesters who knew nothing of the student group's plan but who wanted to make their presence felt outside the American embassy. Two women raised a banner reading "Allah-o Akbar." It was the signal. The fifteen or so Iranian police guarding the embassy gates were advised to step aside. They did. Women took out heavy bolt-cutters hidden beneath their chadors and the chains securing the embassy gates were snapped. The students were in. It was easy.

There was no pandemonium though emotions ran high. As quickly as the gates had been opened they were secured with a new chain and lock. Only students who were part of the takeover plans were allowed in through the gate—there were printed lists with names to be checked off. While the Muslim Students Following the Line of the Imam diligently admitted their crew, other students watched in amazement, thrilled by the audacity of the core group. At first, only the organized group of about 150 students filed into the embassy through the secured gate. Over the next hour, others, mainly high school and university students from the mass protest march, laboriously climbed the unguarded fence surrounding the embassy grounds. It has been estimated that by the early afternoon some 3,000 young Iranians were inside the embassy walls. They were there, however, without any purpose or plan.

With adrenalin flowing, the Muslim Students Following the Line of the Imam began to implement their plan. Each member had an assignment. They knew exactly what they were doing and where they were going.

It was a Sunday morning and little was going on inside the stripped-down U.S. embassy. Since the February 14 invasion of the compound physical security of the embassy had been greatly beefed up and the number of personnel greatly reduced. Windows had been covered with steel bars, sand-filled bullet traps had been installed all over, and strict security protocols of all kinds had been created. Secret documents of all kinds were supposed to be destroyed or shipped out of Iran according to rigid schedules. Despite such precautions, embassy personnel were not prepared for a serious assault nor had all security measures been carefully followed. Despite the rules pertaining to sensitive materials, a great many intelligence or politically sensitive documents were still in the embassy on November 4. And only thirteen Marines guarded the entire embassy and not all of them were on duty that Sunday morning. None of them was stationed at the main gate. Neither the number nor the location of the guards was an indicator of poor planning—it was normal for that pre-September 11 era; basic external perimeter embassy security was the responsibility of the host nation, even a host nation with a new revolutionary government.

When the Iranians came in through the gates, the Marines almost immediately saw what was happening via closed circuit televison monitors. As trained, they fell back to a central position, the embassy's most important and best-secured building, the chancery. They put on combat gear and weaponed up. But what were they supposed to do?

While the Marines waited for the Iranians to challenge their position, the students efficiently moved through the compound. Some secured the various gates and guarded the fences to prevent any Americans from escaping. A larger number began searching for Americans—as well as important-looking documents—in the various other embassy buildings.

John Graves, the public affairs officer, watched the students from the press office. He wasn't afraid. The students were not armed, most of the ones he saw were women, and he noted an English-language sign they were carrying: "Don't be afraid. We just want to set in." "Set in"; it was almost cute. It was as though they thought they were the Iranian twin to the African American sit-in movement of the early 1960s—only they missed the part about not taking hostages. Graves thought he could have ducked out the back gate before they spotted him but, he later recounted, "I was curious. I thought I'd hang around for another five or ten minutes and see what was going on. Which was a big mistake."[33] Graves was grabbed and like the other Americans found outside the chancery he was blindfolded with his hands tied behind his back and led to a pair of small buildings at the southwestern corner of the compound. None of the Americans fought back physically. Some shouted at the students, telling them, "You don't know what you're doing," and, "The police will come." Most were resigned to the nerve-wracking situation, assuming that it would, like the February 14 incident, get sorted out fairly quickly.

The students knew that most of the embassy personnel, as well as the more important American documents, were in the chancery. It took a small group almost an hour to smash the lock on one of the building's basement windows and pry apart the steel bars. About forty students squeezed through the bars. They were shouting, "Marg bar Amrika!"

The Marines were waiting at the top of the stairs. Corporal William Gallegos heard the Iranians pouring into the basement and went down the stairs right at them. He racked his shotgun and aimed it squarely at the Iranians. He had no intention of firing—the Marines had standing orders from chargé Bruce Laingen not to fire unless their lives were in imminent danger—but he hoped they didn't know that. It worked for a very short while. The Iranians kept moving forward and it was all women in the front ranks. As Massoumeh Ebtekar—whom the hostages would soon know too well as "Mary"—later wrote: "[S]ince martyrdom was not a threat, but rather the ultimate salvation, they all marched right on up the stairway."[34] The Marines did their best to slow down the advancing Iranians with tear gas and threatening gestures with their weapons. But the order to retreat came fast and the Marines joined the remaining Americans in the building on the second floor behind heavy steel doors.

On the second floor, in the ambassador's suite, Political Officer Ann Swift was on the phone with Washington. She had called the Ops Center at the State Department within minutes of the embassy attack. The emergency Ops Center patched her through to the home phones of Assistant Secretary of State for Near Eastern and South Asian Affairs Harold Saunders and two other high-ranking State Department officials. It was just after three o'clock in the morning in Washington. They could do little to help but they stayed on the line with Swift for the next two hours. Quickly they spread word of the break-in; Secretary of State Vance hurried in to his office and the president was alerted to the situation.[35]

Most of the Americans in the chancery were doing their best to destroy communications equipment and documents that they did not want to fall into the Iranians' hands. They were fairly sure no immediate help was on the way. Political Officer John Lambert had been on the phone with the Iranian prime minister's office and been told only that they were absolutely going to have a meeting that very same afternoon to sort out the problem. So, while no one in the embassy expected a long-term situation, they did expect a serious short-term mess. They had to anticipate the takeover of the embassy. The most highly classified intelligence material was being fed as fast as possible into the burn furnace. Unfortunately, it broke down and documents had to be simply shredded instead. The Iranians would later do a mind-boggling job reassembling most of those documents. Worse yet, some of the most important material—a great deal of material—was in a very large safe in the charge's office. He was off embassy grounds at the time of the attack—at the Iranian Foreign Ministry, ironically—and no one else had the combination to the lock. These documents would all end up in Iranian hands and, among other things, they revealed the names of many Iranians who had worked with the United States or, more often, simply had contact with embassy personnel; in revolutionary Iran such disclosures were dangerous, often terminally dangerous.[36]

Some fifty or so of the students massed outside the steel doors on the second floor of the chancery. After they tired of pounding on the doors, they decided to use one of the captured Americans to compel his colleagues to surrender. One of the hostage-takers marched the blindfolded Security Officer Al Golacinski, captured earlier when he attempted to negotiate with the students, to the door and placed a handgun against his head and made it clear that he would kill him unless his colleagues opened up the steel door. So much for the unarmed and nonviolent aspect of the "set-in." Golacinski, not in the best spirits, yelled through the door, letting the other Americans know what was happening to him.

John Lambert, who spoke Farsi, volunteered to go out and try to negotiate with the hostages. He slipped out the door and was greeted with chaos. Nobody was in charge. Within minutes, Lambert was also blindfolded and informed he, too, would be killed if the doors were not opened. An English-speaking hostage-taker screamed through the door that now both men were to be killed if the others did not surrender.

Inside, the Americans were on the phone with Bruce Laingen at the Iranian foreign ministry. He told them that they had no choice; they had to surrender. They surrendered.

Immediately they were blindfolded and their hands were tied behind their backs. It was a strange and terrifying few moments. The
hostage-takers were, generally, quite polite and gentle. All around
them, and then ever more so as they were led outside of the chancery, mobs of people were chanting "Allah Akbar! Allah Akbar!"
A couple of the Marines, who had hidden their weapons before
surrendering, were being threatened with death unless they turned
over their weapons. They refused. Several of the Americans were
fairly sure that they were being marched outside to be executed.
Bruce German, a budget officer, was told he must make a statement
condemning President Carter. He said he would not. "I was es-
corted down the steps and out onto the grounds," he later stated,
"toward the screaming mobs. I thought we were going to go in
front of a firing squad."

Even as most of the chancery group were taken hostage, a small
group continued to destroy documents in the CIA's vault area. For
two hours they continued to work, destroying, they hoped, everything of any potential value to the Iranians. Then, with no other
choice, they too, gave themselves up to the students.

A few Americans, in the consulate building several hundred
yards from the main gate, had stayed put for a couple of hours
while all hell broke loose on the capacious embassy grounds. On
orders from Ann Swift, they destroyed the U.S. visa plates to prevent the Iranians from getting hold of them. Then, still undetected,
they decided to make a break for it. They successfully slipped out
of the embassy gates but were not sure where to go. They split into
two groups. Out on the streets, the first group was spotted before
they got more than a couple of blocks away, probably by students
on the consulate roof. Some of the students gave chase, accompanied by an armed Iranian revolutionary guard. The guard fired a
warning shot and the Americans froze. They were grabbed and
forced to march back to the embassy where they were taken hostage. But the other five Americans successfully made their way to
a nearby apartment. They were safe, at least for the moment. All
together, nine American embassy personnel had not been captured.
In addition, chargé Bruce Laingen and two others were, seemingly,

safe at the Iranian Foreign Ministry office. Laingen kept the State Department apprised of the situation. Two miles from the embassy, at the embassy-run Iran-American Society, two other American officials also kept a line open to Washington.[37]

The Students Following the Line of the Imam had captured sixty-three Americans. They were ecstatic. They had never believed the takeover would be so easy, but they were ready for their success. They had their first of many messages ready for the world's mass media. From the beginning the idea had been to make the capture of the American embassy a symbol for the world. They wanted an Islamic theocratic government but they were also young people completely savvy about the workings of modern television and journalism. Joyously, they released—in Farsi—"Communiqué No. 1." They quoted Khomeini's speech of November 3—the one about the need for students to "expand their attacks against American and Israel." Then they got down to business:

> The Islamic Revolution of Iran represents a new achievement in the ongoing struggle between the people and the oppressive superpowers. . . . Iran's revolution has undermined the political, economic, and strategic hegemony of America in the region. . . . We Muslim students, followers of Ayatollah Khomeini, have occupied the espionage embassy of America in protest against the ploys of the imperialists and the Zionists. We announce our protest to the world; a protest against America for granting asylum and employing the criminal shah. . . . for creating a malignant atmosphere of biased and monopolized propaganda, and for supporting and recruiting counterrevolutionary agents against the Islamic Revolution of Iran. . . . And finally, for its undermining and destructive role in the face of the struggle of the peoples for freedom from the chains of imperialism.[38]

The students had won the day. Now the Iranian government, the ayatollah, the Carter White House, and the American people would have to decide what to make of the facts on the ground.

444 DAYS

In November 1979, Roone Arledge was the president of both ABC Sports and ABC News. He'd made his mark in the television business by inventing ABC's Wide World of Sports *and* Monday Night Football. *One show featured oddities like Irish hurling and pulled in viewers by hyping, "The thrill of victory and the agony of defeat." The other turned football into a circus with the part of the ringmaster played by the pompous blowhard Howard Cosell, the announcer Americans loved to hate. Arledge had, as he said, added "show business to sports!"[1] While allowing for certain unstated differences, he believed the news division needed that same pizzazz.*

When Arledge first met the ABC News team in 1977 he was not warmly welcomed. He had no background in journalism. He had never demonstrated any commitment to the serious issues of the day. At his first meeting with the news professionals he wore a polka-dot shirt unbuttoned to reveal a gaudy gold chain around his neck. The man gave every appearance of not being a serious, sophisticated student of American society.

Of course, he was. He understood better than almost anyone what Americans liked to watch on television. Whether it was rodeo barrel racing or war in Zaire, he told his new subordinates, they had to make viewers care viscerally about the story. The evening news was not supposed to be warmed-over newspaper headlines. It was television—and good television grabbed you by the heartstrings. It was supposed to be entertaining. ABC News had always run a distant third to the other national television network news shows; Roone Arledge was going to turn that performance around.

By November 4, 1979, Arledge's news division had deployed a jazzier, more opinionated broadcast style. He'd grabbed more viewers for ABC but he had not had a major breakthrough moment. He wanted to try something different. For a couple of years he'd been telling his bosses that a late-night news show would draw more viewers to ABC. The higher-ups balked; ABC local affiliates were happy filling the 11:30 p.m. slot with reruns of Police Woman, Baretta, *and* The Love Boat. *They all got slaughtered by Johnny Carson's* The Tonight Show *but they cost almost nothing to broadcast.*[2]

Nobody at ABC (or the other networks) took great interest in the November 4 Tehran embassy takeover, at first. It looked to be a flash-in-the-pan crisis. But ABC had a piece of luck. CBS and NBC hadn't been able to get camera crews into Tehran (in the turmoil, Iranian officials had decided to close their borders to Americans) so their immediate coverage was light. Only ABC had gotten a news team in on the first day. The day after the takeover, ABC's World News Tonight *showed the American people exclusive footage of an Iranian mob setting fire to an American flag outside the U.S. embassy. A couple of days later, Americans watching the ABC evening news saw one of their own, blindfolded, hands tied together, led around like a beaten dog by the bearded Iranian hostage-takers.*

Roone Arledge looked at that footage and he saw drama. He ordered the news division to air an Iranian special after the local late-night news show. Working fast, the World News Tonight *producer pulled together a team. He summarized the potential news hook: "Look what's happening to the psyche of the American people. We really are being held hostage by this thing." Lightbulb moment: the special got a name, "America Held Hostage." For one segment of the show they did man-in-the-street interviews. The last man interviewed put an exclamation mark to the unfolding events: "When I watch TV, the news, and I see what they do to that flag, it gets me in the heart."[3] Roone Arledge heard Americans make that same angry, emotional declaration everywhere he went. He went back to the brass at ABC, made his pitch, and he got the late-night news show for which he had been lobbying. Eleven days after the American hostages had been taken, ABC began regular, unrelenting late-night coverage of "America Held Hostage." Attached to the title, that night and every night for the next many months, was the number of days the hostages had been held. Each show opened with a heartbreaking still shot of a blindfolded American hostage. Roone Arledge and his people knew how to tell a story (enough so that the show sometimes beat Johnny Carson in the ratings). The bad guys did their part by burning American flags, hanging effigies of the president, and screaming, on cue for the cameras, "Marg bar Amrika!" (sometimes they even yelled out their anti-American chants in English). The only question was when were the good guys going to ride to the rescue? The drama was set; the problem was that President Carter didn't know how to play his part.[4]*

Everybody, including the Students Following the Line of the Imam, expected the U.S. embassy takeover to be a short-lived affair. The students had only brought enough food for themselves to last three days. They wanted to make a symbolic stand. First, they intended to show the world that they would not be cowed by American power. Second, they wanted to electrify the Iranian people and mobilize support for an uncompromising Islamic revolutionary government that neither feared nor accommodated itself to Western interests and intrigues. Self-consciously, the students perceived the embassy takeover as "propaganda of the deed." They had no clear demands. They really were just students and they did not expect to find themselves in the middle of an immensely complicated, chaotic, and seemingly endless factional power struggle within Iran in which their little escapade would take on immense weight. In Iran, the hostage-taking became a singularly vital episode in a tale of national self-determination and revolutionary grit.

President Carter, who was at Camp David when he received word of the embassy takeover from Secretary Vance, assumed that the proper Iranian authorities would exert control as they had in February and put a stop to the student militants' actions. Carter's chief of staff, Hamilton Jordan, apprised of the situation at 4:30 a.m., groggily told the president's secretary, over the phone, to make sure that Carter paid attention to the incident: "[T]he press will be looking at this in the context of the campaign. It'll be over in a few hours, but it could provide a nice contrast between Carter and our friend from Massachusetts [Senator Ted Kennedy] in how to handle a crisis."[5] Jordan believed that the White House had a simple political story to tell: Carter stands tall during the crisis and shows voters he can lead the nation.

The State Department officials who were on point from the beginning of the ruckus went immediately into gear. Anticipating a quick resolution, they formed a crisis task force—the Iran Working Group (IWG)—set up shop in the State Department, and went to work. Their mission was straightforward: communicate with Iranian officials and negotiate an end to the gross breach of international law. They would struggle to untie the political knots that kept the Iranian government from releasing the hostages. Somehow the right combination of pressure, promises, persuasion, and personalities would be found. It seemed, at first, like the kind of high-stakes, all-night poker game that took cool nerves and a steady hand. They were professionals and they were confident that they had what it took to get their people home.

Unfortunately, the major actors in the hostage crisis did not perceive the rapidly unfolding events the same way. They often were not acting in the same drama but did not realize it. President Carter's political needs matched up poorly with those of the Ayatollah Khomeini. The State Department's quest for efficient, rational negotiations based on the rule of law were stymied by the hostage-takers' seemingly irrational willingness to die as martyrs and by the fragile Iranian government's inability to act as a negotiating partner. For all practical purposes, the Iranian government did not exist as a stable force—Iran was in a state of revolutionary chaos in which power was a prize not yet secured by anyone. Television network news producers had little interest in either Iranian political in-fighting or in the rational disputations and legal argumentation of American bureaucrats. They put up pictures of Americans in harm's way. They showed Iranians spewing hate. Their news correspondents incessantly asked President Carter and his men what they were going to do to bring the hostages home. They wanted people glued to their televisions and they wanted daily news that would give viewers a reason to tune in.

For most Americans the hostages were a simple way of thinking about the state of their nation and the men who were supposed to lead it. It mattered that this was an election year—that the hostages were taken exactly one year before the 1980 presidential election. That story, a narrative of Americans suffering and no one willing or able to put a stop to it, was the one that ultimately captured the nation in the last year of the Carter presidency.

In Iran, the takeover of the American embassy, "the den of spies," was explosive news. Prime Minister Bazargan and Foreign Minister Ibrahim Yazdi, both of whom had stated that they would protect the American embassy and who had just met in productive if uneasy talks with Zbig Brzezinski in Algiers, opposed the takeover. Within a few hours' time, the Students Following the Line of the Imam issued a flurry of anti-American communiqués justifying their actions. In one of their very first actions, they invited Khomeini inner-circle member Hojjatoleslam Mousavi Khoeiniha, whom they had trusted with their plan prior to the action, to join them. He did. So, too, did the ayatollah's son, who pointedly congratulated the students on their action. The signal was clear—the imam approved. Khomeini subsequently made his position clear with the special invective and odd cadence that would become all too familiar to the American people: "The great Satan is the United States of America. It is making much commotion and fuss . . . today underground plots are being hatched in these embassies, mostly by the great Satan America. . . . They must sit in their places and return the traitor [the Shah] soon."[6]

Within forty-eight hours of the takeover, Bazargan and Yazdi resigned. Their attempts to end the takeover had been rebuffed by Khomeini's inner circle and reports had been circulated in Tehran that Bazargan had been conspiring with the American Brzezinski. The provisional government, which had included a range of anti-Shah factions, was finished. Khomeini interjected himself more forcefully into the political maelstrom and stated that all power must be placed in the hands of the Revolutionary Council—the staunch advocate of an Islamic theocracy that had up until that time taken a back seat to the more secularly oriented provisional government. The Carter administration had only the weakest of contacts among the leading figures of the Revolutionary Council, whose members took to heart the fate of Prime Minister Bazargan and Foreign Minister Yazdi: negotiating with the Americans was, at the very best, not good for your political health.

The students were elated. Their takeover had been the lever that had dislodged the reformist government of Bazargan and led to a true Islamic revolutionary regime. Now, taking their cue from the imam, they declared that they would hold the Americans until the Carter government returned the despised Shah to Iran where revolutionary justice would be visited upon him. No one doubted what that would mean. All of Iran watched with excitement and fascination. The Americans had been humiliated and humbled by a small group of university students. The Islamic revolution was producing a never-before-seen fearless national fighting spirit. The students were riding the back of the American tiger and, for many in Iran, it was a wonder to behold.

Inside the White House, Carter's men did what they had to do. On November 5, Brzezinski ran a cabinet-level meeting of the Special Coordination Committee on the Iranian hostage-taking. Nobody anticipated, then, that this meeting was the first of hundreds. Gary Sick had briefed Brzezinski, reporting that the situation in Iran was a mess. His analysis was astute: Khomeini would use the hostage-taking coupled with the Shah's presence in the United States to crack down on moderate forces within the revolution. Khomeini was nothing but trouble and he would not be a good-faith negotiating partner. It would take a great deal of pressure to get the ayatollah's attention. The hostages, Sick emphasized, were political tools that Khomeini would use to further his own ends. Further complicating the situation, the United States had no clear line for communicating with Khomeini or his key advisors. In Sick's published account of the hostage crisis, he observes: "Although it was painfully evident that the United States had very limited means of exerting any direct influence over events inside Iran, there was a deep reluctance at every level in Washington to admit that a great power, with all the diplomatic and financial resources at its disposal, was unable to protect the interests of its citizens in such a flagrant violation of international law. The impulse to act was overpowering."[7]

Jimmy Carter entered the arena to battle the Iranian revolutionaries holding Americans hostage at a very precarious point in his presidency. In early November, he was not even certain of winning his own party's nomination for a reelection bid. Congress, including many key Democrats, had turned on him. Senator Ted Kennedy, gilded with his family name, was openly challenging Carter for party leadership and the 1980 Democratic presidential nomination. Only a few weeks earlier, Carter had been warned by Brzezinski, his chief international advisor, that the world saw him as weak and ineffectual. The American economy was a wreck and his efforts to fix it had largely failed. His attempt to reinvigorate his role as national leader during the summer—with the Camp David domestic summit and the subsequent "crisis of spirit" speech—had almost completely backfired. The press was merciless: "Carter has often seemed an inadequate and dispiriting figure" (*Time*); "assaulted and pushed . . . by his most feared competitor at home and the country's most feared political competitor abroad. . . . Whatever else these developments may mean, they surely reflect an assumption about the condition of the Carter presidency—that it is malleable and weak" (*Washington Post*); and "Carter has no more than 60 days to somehow revive his faltering presidency. . . . [Carter] faces the real possibility of turning into a lame duck even before the first primary vote is cast" (*Newsweek*).[8] A year before the presidential election, Carter had banked little public, political, or international support to carry him through a difficult time.

Despite the political pressures he was under, Carter first responded to the embassy takeover by hoping that the crisis would essentially de-fuse itself. The national security team decided to send a two-man negotiating team to Iran. It was composed of former attorney general Ramsey Clark, who had dealt previously with Khomeini and who had been an outspoken critic of the Shah's human rights record, and William Miller, staff director for the Senate Select Committee on Intelligence, who had some marginal contacts with the Khomeini-ites and, unlike Clark, a savvy understanding of Iran. Carter handwrote a letter directly to Khomeini, asking him to meet with the two Americans and arrange for the release of the "Americans detained in Iran . . . based on humanitarian reasons firmly based on international law." Carter then assured Khomeini that he wished to pursue good relations with the Iranian government "based upon equality, mutual respect and friendship."[9] This gracious letter to Khomeini (which Ramsey Clark was to deliver personally), couched in proper, if not exactly heartfelt diplomatic prose, was the last of its kind.

Khomeini refused to see the American emissaries. Even before Khomeini's brusque dismissal of the American diplomatic effort, Carter and his men had correctly concluded that the hostage takeover was going south in a hurry. In a November 6 Oval Office 8 a.m. meeting, Carter asked his key men—Secretary of State Vance, NSC Advisor Brzezinski, Secretary of Defense Brown and a few others—to begin exploring all possible options, including military, for getting the hostages out safely. Bottom line, the president said to "get our people out of Iran and break relations. Fuck 'em."[10] Before the day was over, the Iranians announced the resignation of the moderate provisional government and the takeover of the Revolutionary Council. Though no one on either side yet knew it, the die had been cast.

Around the world, the embassy takeover was big news. International newspaper and magazine writers wondered what the United States would and should do. Responses were by no means uniform, though many anxiously pondered the effect of American actions on the already precarious global oil market. In Paris, a *Le Figaro* editorial spoke for many: "[W]hat is important in this affair is the uncertainty over oil supplies, with the risk of a new price increase . . . a military raid must be excluded." The Japanese Foreign Ministry, according to the Tokyo newspaper *Asahi*, concurred, stating that oil exports must be maintained and that Japan would, as a result, maintain a "stable" relationship with Iran despite the unfortunate difficulties. German editorialists focused on the geopolitical fallout of the hostage-taking. The Berlin paper, *Der Abend*, observed: "[A] Lilliputian is binding a giant. Such an example invites followers." On a different note, a German television news anchor, following a report from Tehran that featured footage of protesters at the U.S. embassy in Tehran—both angry, shouting demonstrators and peacefully praying men and women—stated that President Carter "desperately needs a success to improve his image [and] that could be . . . rescue of the hostages from the fanatic Moslems." In Korea, the government-controlled press heaped praise on President Carter's approach, congratulating him on his "firm position" not to turn over the Shah to the Iranian revolutionaries and commending "America's humanitarian spirit." In America's one-time colony, the Philippines, editorial comment was less accommodating. The *Times-Journal* of Manila declared: "[W]e can all learn a few lessons from what is happening in Iran. Not the least of these is that fact that the Iranians are taking up the cudgels for their own native land." A collection of such international editorial observations circulated among the pertinent staffers at the NSC. Not surprisingly, international opinion offered no clear guide to American policy—some would damn America for acting too aggressively while others would snidely point out American inaction as a sign of impotence. Probably the only clear international signal from American allies was that the world oil market had to be assiduously protected, regardless of what developed between the United States and Iran.[11]

The Soviet government, surprising no one in the Carter White House, used its state-directed mass media during the initial weeks of the crisis to create as much difficulty for the United States as it could. Subtlety and truthfulness were not high priorities. Using their puppet radio network, the National Voice of Iran (NVOI), the Soviets broadcast vicious anti-American propaganda throughout Iran. The United States was "mad and bloodthirsty." The student takeover of the American embassy was a just and necessary measure because "there is a difference between an embassy and a nest of espionage and conspiracy." Indeed, the broadcasts urged, "occupation of the U.S. Embassy and taking hostage of its employees is not and cannot be the final goal. . . . [A]ll potentialities and means . . . must be used." The Soviets, another broadcast sweetly announced, would stand by the Iranian revolution in its struggle against the United States.[12] The NVOI broadcasters even found time to single out one of the Soviet government's least favorite Americans, Zbigniew Brzezinski, for special treatment, warning Iranian listeners that Carter's right-hand man was "the mad dog of Imperialism and Zionism." Paul Herze, the NSC staffer attending to the Soviets' broadcast operations, told his boss, "Nice friendly and helpful people, these Russians."[13] In the early days of the embassy takeover, the Soviet government still saw the fall of the Shah and the rise of the Khomeini government as a cold war victory. Soon enough they, too, would realize that the fury of Islamic fundamentalism in their part of the world was not such a good thing after all.

An interesting side note: the NVOI summaries circulated in mid-November among members of the Special Coordinating Committee. Vice President Mondale, in particular, was struck by the Soviets' propaganda reach into the Muslim world. He asked Brzezinski about American broadcasting capacity in the region. In late November, Brzezinski reported back to the vice president that the United States had "not much" and that "the Soviets are far ahead of us in this field." Iran had been the target of Voice of America broadcasting in the immediate post-coup years but service was dropped in 1958. In April 1979, a daily half hour, Farsi-language program resumed on the Voice of America; it was expanded to one hour in late November. Other than some quite lame, weak-signal broadcasts aimed at Muslims in the Soviet Union, the United States had nothing going on. Brzezinski told Mondale that for two years he had been urging the State Department to make a major push in getting its message out via radio broadcasting to the Muslim world but that higher budget priorities had stopped the effort cold. Brzezinski, backed explicitly by Carter, did succeed in the coming months in increasing American international radio broadcasting in Arabic and Farsi. In the big picture, it was too little, too late and probably not the most viable tool for turning around public opinion.[14]

At home, the American people almost immediately responded to the hostage-taking with widespread outrage. ABC News had been first to broadcast the images that fixed the embassy takeover in the American imagination. The day after the hostages were taken, ABC showed their viewers a howling mob in front of the U.S. embassy burning an American flag. Men with black beards and women shrouded in chadors screamed and raged while the American flag went up in flames. The story of the hostage-taking headlined almost every newspaper in the country: Americans, protected by international law, had been taken hostage by Islamic students and the Iranian government, led by a religious fanatic who held the United States in contempt, refused to intervene. Americans, already bleeding from an economy hemorrhaging jobs, were in no mood for any more wounds to the body politic. Carter administration officials were caught short by the American public's immediate emotional reaction to the hostage-taking.

Hamilton Jordan, who had run Carter's first presidential campaign, wised up quickly. On November 6 he left the White House after a mercilessly long day and was being driven home when his limousine was caught in a traffic jam on Massachusetts Avenue. Outside of the Iranian embassy, spontaneously, hundreds of Americans had come together to demand that the Iranian government free the hostages. Jordan, surprised by the outpouring of anger he was witnessing, watched spellbound. "I was glad that the people cared," he later wrote, "but bothered that they cared so much."

Carter's chief of staff had good reason to worry. An amazingly large number of Americans took the hostages, right from the beginning, to their hearts. The fate of the hostages became, vox populi, a vital part of how Americans looked at the fate of the nation. And, as Jordan understood from the beginning, many Americans charged Carter with making the story come out right.

Jimmy Carter wanted to play the part of hero. By November 6 he understood that the Iranian government was complicitous with the hostage-takers. He had also decided that he would not be an accessory to murder; the United States was not going to send the Shah back to Iran so that the ayatollah and his people could execute him. That option was off the table. Everything he had learned about Khomeini over the past few months increased his concerns about the hostages' situation. In his diary, he expressed his fears about negotiating with Iran's beloved spiritual leader: "It's almost impossible to deal with a crazy man."[15] Carter knew no easy answer existed. And he also knew that the American domestic politics of the hostage-taking was potentially explosive.

Within hours of the embassy takeover, Carter and his closest advisors were pondering those politics. By day 4, Hamilton Jordan knew that the hostage-taking had become a crisis. He strongly urged his boss to cancel a long-planned diplomatic trip to Canada. Concern over the hostages had become the focal point of American public opinion and the White House had to show the electorate that the president was doing his utmost to bring them safely home: "We must also be in the correct public position to minimize the public and political damage to your presidency . . . if we have a bad result and/or to maximize the benefit of a good result," wrote Jordan.[16] A bad result would be the death of any or all of the hostages—a possibility the White House had to take seriously. A good result, of course, was the release of the Americans. Carter concurred with Jordan's analysis and cancelled the Canada trip and all other upcoming diplomatic and political visits. He would stay close by the White House and take personal responsibility for resolving the hostage crisis. It was good politics and it was, bottom line, what he felt in his gut he must do.

As was his way, Carter threw himself into the process. Both publicly and privately he personally identified himself with the plight of the Americans held hostage and with bringing them home. Soon after the hostage-taking he attended a prayer service for the hostages in Washington's National Cathedral. Four days later, he made his way over to the State Department and met with about twenty family members of those held hostage in the embassy in Tehran. Both events were widely covered by the press. Carter's press secretary, Jody Powell, made sure that the press understood that the president was personally in charge of getting the hostages home safely. Emotionally and politically, the president was wedding himself to the hostages.

Americans overwhelmingly approved of their president's commitment. In the immediate aftermath of the hostage-taking the American people rallied around Carter and his efforts to bring their fellow citizens home. Carter's efforts and the Iranians' anti-American deeds were paired stories in the news accounts that the American people followed.[17]

While Carter and his advisors well understood the immediate political advantage the crisis was creating for the commander in chief, there was nothing cynical about the process. Carter's public and private feelings about the situation were identical. At a private Thanksgiving meal for his key staffers at Camp David, Carter gave a heartfelt prayer that ended with a plea for the hostages' safe release. The president also expressed his feelings about the crisis more profanely. Long before, while running for the presidency in 1976, Carter had admitted to "lusting in his heart" after beautiful women; a lot of American people probably would have appreciated the fact that the president, when angry about Iranian intransigence, also tended to use language (including the "f"-word) that his God-fearing mother would not have liked.

Behind the scenes, the Carter administration was a whirlwind of activity. Right from the start, two approaches were initiated, a diplomatic one and a military one. Carter wanted to have as many options open as were possible to cover as many contingencies as were foreseeable. Potentially influential or helpful people around the world were contacted. And all sorts of individuals who thought they could help approached the White House or people they perceived to have White House connections. Most of these efforts and contacts were kept secret in order to maximize the possibility that negotiations could proceed without either the Iranians or the White House risking adverse domestic political pressures.

Secrecy in such things was difficult to maintain. In the post-Watergate era, journalists were extremely wary of following government officials' lead on what was and was not appropriate for the American people to know. So, for example, when Press Secretary Jody Powell tried to convince NBC News that they should not reveal that the White House had sent ex-attorney general Ramsey Clark and congressional staffer William Miller to negotiate with Khomeini, NBC rejected his request. The story ran and White House officials believed that the coverage contributed to Khomeini's refusal to see the American negotiators. As a result, certain aspects of the Carter administration's handling of the Iran hostage crisis, most critically military planning, ensued under extreme security precautions.[18]

Far more publicly, a number of Iranian students living in the United States decided to hold rallies in the immediate aftermath of the hostage-taking. The demonstrators sided with their student comrades in Iran, demanding that Carter turn over the Shah to Iran's Revolutionary Council. Rallies were held in several university towns, as well as in Los Angeles, Houston, New York, and right in front of the White House.

President Carter was appalled by the protests. He ordered his staff to disallow any future Iranian student protests near the White House. But the day after his order the protesters were back. Carter exploded. Unable to do anything about the hostage-taking Iranian students in Tehran, the president called in his staff and blew off enough steam to run a riverboat. According to notes taken at the meeting, Carter stated that "in his own view no American citizen could consider their President doing his job adequately if he allowed a demonstration by Iranian students in front of the White House while their colleagues in Iran were holding our diplomatic representatives hostage."[19] Carter was under tremendous pressure. He was fighting for his political life; he felt personally responsible for getting the hostages home alive. Despite the whirlwind of activity in the week after the embassy takeover he had no results and no sense that he was making any real progress.

The staff got the message and did everything it could to ensure that no more demonstration permits were issued. Attorney General Benjamin Civiletti did his part by ordering all Iranian students in the United States, some 50,000 (many of whom were no fans of the Ayatollah Khomeini's Islamic revolution), to report to immigration officials to have their visas checked. Students with visa irregularities were to be immediately deported. Several congressmen got into the act by introducing resolutions calling for all Iranian students to be thrown out of the United States. Some American citizens decided to take matters into their own hands. In Los Angeles, a mob used baseball bats on Iranian student demonstrators, sending several to the hospital. On city streets any young man who looked vaguely Iranian—and that was not a clear image for most Americans—stood an excellent chance of receiving angry epithets from passing motorists and pedestrians urging him to commit a physically impossible act. Televised images, newspaper reports, and firsthand experiences of protesting Iranian students in American towns and cities in the days right after the hostage-taking helped heat up the anger and frustration felt by a great many Americans. Rational thought and cool-headed analysis were in short supply.[20]

In the first weeks of the hostage-taking it seemed like everyone in the United States tried to find a way to help the hostages. People wanted to be, somehow, involved and to show that they cared about their captive countrymen and women. In the 1970s, a slew of social critics accused Americans of being narcissists, self-absorbed, and indifferent to the plight of others. The hostage crisis belied those accusations. Post-Watergate, a lot of Americans may well have been skeptical, even cynical, about the morality and competency of their national political leaders and distrustful of most other forms of established authority. But that did not mean that patriotism was dead. Far from it.

During the hostage crisis, within days of the takeover, Americans demonstrated both a sometimes fierce, even xenophobic nationalism and an emotional bond to their fellow Americans held captive in Iran. Just a few days after the embassy takeover longshoremen spontaneously decided not to load any cargo bound for Iran. At the widely publicized request of the hostages' families, millions of people kept their car headlights on during the day to show their solidarity. Church bells rang at midday to honor the captives. At the urging of church leaders, labor union officials, civic groups, and political leaders, many of whom were coordinating the effort with the White House, hundreds of thousands of Americans wrote letters to the Iranian embassy and the Iranian U.N. delegation. Dozens of popular songs about the crisis played on the airwaves, many of them country and western tunes, including the fiery "Go to Hell Ayatollah!" Among the most popular was "The Hostage Prayer," by Christian pop star Pat Boone. On release of the song, he wrote to the hostage families, via the State Department, voicing a common sentiment: "I believe this crisis has really made us one family, in concern and love, in anguish and in prayer."[21]

Six weeks into the hostage crisis, the *Washington Post* ran a short article about Penne Laingen, the wife of embassy chargé Bruce Laingen, who was still holed up in the Iran Foreign Ministry. She told the *Post* reporter that she had, in tune with a 1973 hit song, "Tie a Yellow Ribbon Round the Ole Oak Tree," tied a yellow ribbon around the oak tree in her yard: "So I'm standing and waiting and praying . . . and one of these days Bruce is going to untie that yellow ribbon. It's going to be out there until he does."[22] As word of her action spread through the mass media, Americans began to follow her example and tie yellow ribbons around trees, telephone poles, street lamps, car radio antennas, and numerous other inanimate objects. Americans pinned little yellow ribbons to their clothes and pasted yellow-ribbon bumper stickers to their cars. On Super Bowl Sunday in January 1980, a stupendously long yellow ribbon was wrapped around the entire stadium. Soon after, at the request of the hostages' families, the official White House Christmas tree (the decorative lights of which had been left unlit by President Carter to commemorate the hostage-taking) was bedecked with fifty yellow ribbons. (At that point the American public believed fifty hostages were held by the Iranians—three other Americans were residing in a limbo state at the Iranian Foreign Ministry and six others were hiding in the Canadian embassy. The Carter administration kept the number of hostages unclear to protect the status of the Americans in Iran who were not held in the embassy.) The yellow ribbon had become a ubiquitous symbol of Americans' concern for their captive compatriots.

The mass media tended to personalize the hostages as individual Americans in harm's way. While plenty of articles and evening broadcast segments, especially ABC's late-night "America Held Hostage" specials hosted by Ted Koppel, explored the larger context of the Iranian revolution, America's longstanding support of the Shah, and even the reasons behind many Iranians' disdain for the United States, reports on the hostages almost always treated them as innocents abroad, caught up in the violence of a chaotic revolution, simple victims of unscrupulous Islamic fanatics. Stories about the hostages ignored or glossed over their professional responsibilities or governmental roles at the embassy. Instead, media coverage usually portrayed each hostage as a fellow citizen, a regular American with fearful parents, an anxious spouse, and scared children.

Daytime talk shows on both television and radio competed with one another to interview hostage family members. Even Ted Koppel's more intellectually oriented ABC nightly update on the crisis resorted to such tactics and scored a ratings coup when it squared off a hostage family member with an Iranian government representative. Often, the object of such interviews was to elicit an emotional response—a tearful wife or mother seemed to be the "money shot."[23] In mid-December, more than a month into the captivity, the *New York Daily News* and *Newsweek* both ran long articles about the hostages as individuals. The articles featured a picture of each hostage and a brief, humanizing story about each person.

The same week, the *New York Times* covered a prayer vigil for the hostages in Madison, Wisconsin, attended by a host of local politicians, including the state governor, and quoted from the remarks made by Mrs. Maureen Timm, the mother of one of the captive Marine guards: "I don't understand government workings. . . . I don't understand political things. . . . [We] are here because we are all human beings."[24]

Melanie McAlister, in her critical account of American mass media coverage of the Middle East, argues that the hostages' families were treated by the mass media "as moral agents in the realm of politics." Rather than focus on the relevant government-to-government issues involved in the standoff, she continues, the media used the families as stand-ins for the actual hostages: "These families represented their husbands or children in the Tehran embassy, but they also become more broadly representative; they were not the nation-state as political institution but the national community constituted through its families, and now under siege. The hostages were identified with the private sphere, allied with family, emotions, and domesticity, rather than diplomacy, officialdom, or politics." For McAlister this kind of news coverage created a "moral geography" that supported "U.S. expansionist nationalism."[25] She means that the American mass media portrayal of everyday Americans suffering at the hands of foreigners—Islamic foreigners, in particular—resulted in a widespread public misunderstanding of American foreign policy. Thus, the American mass media coverage of the Iran crisis helped persuade Americans to see themselves as victims of "terrorists" who irrationally hate "us," rather than to recognize that Iranians had attacked the U.S. embassy in response to American policy in Iran.

McAlister's insights are analytically astute (the mass media focus on the hardships faced by families of American troops serving in Iraq during the "war on terrorism" further supports her claim). It is worth underlining that she is not arguing that the people behind the mass media coverage of the hostage-taking were purposefully working to convince their audiences to see the crisis as a simple tale of American "innocents abroad" caught up in a nightmare not of their own making. Most Americans in 1979 and 1980, including news producers, simply considered hostage-taking—whether of diplomats and embassy guards or just plain folks—as beyond the pale of moral, fair-minded behavior. And most Americans were inclined to see the hostages as individuals, not as representatives of U.S. government policy and not as culpable for U.S. actions in the region—especially those that occurred decades before. After all, the Iranians had not charged any individual with a specific misdeed. Roone Arledge, president of ABC News, not a particularly political person, explained his decision to pursue the hostage story in an oft-quoted remark: "[M]y elevator man, the taxi driver, the pilot on the plane . . . all these people care about now are the hostages in Iran."[26] As he saw it, the hostage story had "legs" because a great many Americans were furious that their fellow citizens—individual Americans—had been snatched from their regular lives by a group of politically motivated, American-hating, Islamic fanatics. That was the news he wanted his network to cover because he knew a lot of Americans would watch it and increase his news shows' ratings. However, just because Roone Arledge and the audience he sought to reach believed that the Iranian hostage crisis story was, above all, the plight of individual Americans and their families does not make it the only story.

Iranian supporters of the Islamic revolution that brought down the Shah's regime saw the story quite differently. They saw the U.S. embassy officials they had captured as representatives of the American government, which had subverted their political system, supported a dictator who had tortured and killed dissidents, and sought to destroy their revolution. Where the American people saw individuals and their families, the Iranian revolutionaries saw a superpower that had always treated their nation, their culture, and their religion as expendable pawns in a bigger game. The Khomeini regime had its own "moral geography."

The Ayatollah Khomeini and the Muslim Students Following the Line of the Imam were well aware of the effect the mass media had on how the world perceived their actions. The students almost obsessively issued press communiqués, sometimes half a dozen a day. Having grown up on the American television shows broadcast in Iran and schooled in the power of the Western media to influence world perception, they believed that one of their most important duties was to counter their enemies' control of the news. "Mary," the student with primary responsibility for communicating in English with both the hostages and the world press, later wrote in her memoir: "We knew that the major radio and TV networks and publishing houses were owned by American media multinationals, often with strong Zionist sympathies."[27]

Not surprisingly, the students' attempts to gain positive coverage of their takeover and their demand that the Shah be returned to Iran for trial often backfired. From the start, the students had been interrogating and attempting to indoctrinate many of the hostages. On November 10, with some fanfare, they presented the assembled press corps with a letter printed in block capitals, they said, by one of the Marines held hostage. The letter, addressed to the Marine's parents, read, in part: "I think that the newspapers are not speaking truthfully back home nor elsewhere. Just now I was interviewed by the leaders who are holding us and they had a paper which we could sign (if we wanted to) to ask the U.S. government to send [the] shah back here in return for our release. I did sign it and am glad I did." The letter then went on, rather ominously, to state: "We will not be set free until shah is released and the longer we stay here like this the better is a chance for something terrible to happen." The letter was quoted in American newspapers, along with a statement by the Marine's stepfather that his son had not written the letter. Even if he had, it would be an odd American who would read the letter's passages and, knowing the conditions under which it was produced, feel more sympathetic to the Iranians' cause.[28] This tin-ear for how their messages would be heard in the United States did not help the hostage-takers win over the American people whom, they constantly intoned, were not their enemy. The flag-burning and the chants of "Marg bar Amrika," as the Iranians involved must have at least dimly understood, greatly intensified Americans' disgust with the Iranian "terrorists" and their sympathy for the hostages and their families.

   The Ayatollah Khomeini had his own ideas about how to demonstrate the morality of the hostage-taking to the American people
and others around the world. Just short of two weeks after the
hostages were seized, Khomeini had a message delivered to the
young students. They were to release the women and the black
Americans held hostage, unless they were proven spies. Blacks, he
observed, were themselves victims of American injustice and, thus,
were not to blame for their government's policies. Islam, he further
noted, always treated women with respect and decency.

   The hostage-takers hurriedly began stepped-up interrogations of
the targeted groups to make sure no CIA spies slipped through their
fingers. They understood embassy procedures well enough to know
that the five black Marine guards were not likely to be spies. So
rather than question them, they set up two long sessions, which
included films, about the crimes of the Shah and the nature of the
Islamic revolution. One of the Iranians involved was quite familiar
with the autobiography of Malcolm X and had high hopes that the
black Marines would understand the need for Islamic revolution.
Thirteen hostages, five white women and eight black men, were
scheduled to be released.

   In Tehran on November 19, three of the hostages, prior to their
release, were selected by their captors to hold a press conference.
Indicative of the magnitude of the story, some two hundred reporters from around the world attended. The woman hostage, Kathy
Gross, a twenty-two-year-old Farsi-speaking embassy secretary who
had struck up a friendship with one of her female guards, gave a
statement sympathetic to the Iranian revolution: "If the American
people were put in touch with the developments in the third world
and America's interference in the internal affairs of the countries,
they would certainly protest to the American government." Twenty-
four-year-old black Marine Seargent William Quarles was even
more outspoken. He praised the Iranian revolutionaries, noting,
"[F]reedom isn't just handed to you on a silver platter." And then,
in explicit terms, he condemned American policy: "I think the American people have a lot to turn around and look at. . . . Having been
kept hostage here for two weeks, I got a look at American imperial-

ism. . . . I'd like to, if I could, tell the American government to re-evaluate their foreign policies. A lot of them are terribly wrong and a lot of people are suffering for a few people at the top." While Quarles may have been that day highly influenced by his captors, his critique of American policy in the third world was well within the mainstream views of many intellectually aware young black men and women. The political language of black militancy was still very much alive and well in late-1970s America. Quarles was quoted at length in the *New York Times* story on the hostage release. Also quoted in newspaper accounts of Quarles's comments was a coun-terstatement made by Vernon Jordan, head of the venerable civil rights organization, the National Urban League. Jordan denounced the release of the black hostages as "a cynical attempt to divide the American people. Black citizens refuse to be pawns in the Ayatollah Khomeini's insane game."[29]

Khomeini's order to the hostage-takers to release the African American and women captives was not just an off-hand decision. While Carter and a number of other opinion leaders in the United States genuinely seemed to view the imam as "crazy," "nutty," or "insane," he was not. He was a savvy strategist who was pragmatic in his single-minded effort to create an Islamic state based on the laws of *shari'a*. To solidify his hold on power, he believed, it was necessary to first neutralize the powerful leftist forces active in the revolutionary anti-Shah coalition. He was well aware that even most of the devout Muslim students who had seized the American embassy were fervent leftists who believed that the new revolution-ary Iranian state must be economically progressive and stand in unity with the third-world anti-imperialist struggle. Thus, Kho-meini worked carefully, in word and deed, to use the embassy take-over to demonstrate the Iranian revolution's anti-imperialist mis-sion and its solidarity with third-world people. Releasing the black hostages was such a symbol and Seargent Quarles's press confer-ence statement condemning American imperialism, which reached a worldwide audience, was icing on the cake.

As Khomeini biographer Baqer Moin writes, "By supporting the takeover openly, Khomeini was . . . easily able to distract the atten-

tion of the leftist guerrilla organisations who were still enthusiastic
in their belief that the priority was to support Khomeini's anti-imperialist stand. In short, Khomeini viewed the occupation of the American embassy in terms of domestic policy."[30] He stated the matter
bluntly to one of his closest advisors, Bani-Sadr, who would become
Iran's first elected president: "This action has many benefits. The
Americans do not want to see the Islamic Republic taking root. We
keep the hostages, finish our internal work, then release them. This
has united our people. Our opponents dare not act against us. We
can put the [Islamic] constitution to the people's vote without difficulty, and carry out the presidential and parliamentary elections.
When we have finished all these jobs we can let the hostages go."[31]
More than twenty-five years earlier, Iran's feisty nationalist prime
minister Mossadegh, caught up in intrigues over ownership of Iran's
oil fields, had tried to instruct American negotiator Averell Harriman about the subtleties of revolutionary politics. Harriman had
understood Mossadegh's main point: "Any settlement of the dispute
would end his [Mossadegh's] political career." Much had changed
in Iran since the CIA-sponsored coup against Mossadegh in 1953,
but not everything. Khomeini benefitted politically from the embassy takeover. He had no interest in negotiating a quick end to it.

Khomeini and the hostage-takers kept up a steady drumbeat of
fierce anti-American and pro-nationalist rhetoric. Two weeks after
the takeover, Khomeini agreed to be interviewed by all three American television networks. He used the opportunity to defend the
student hostage-takers and to lambast the Carter administration:
"[W]hat our nation has done is to arrest a bunch of spies, who
according to the norms, should be investigated, tried, and treated
in accordance with our own laws. As for what Carter has done, it
is contrary to international laws; for the criminal [the Shah]—a
criminal who has acted against a country—should come to the
country concerned and be tried. . . . It is Carter who has acted
against international norms, not us."[32] A few days later, basking in
the imam's attention, the students issued a warning to the American government: "If it is felt that the U.S. threats are becoming a
reality, all the hostages will be killed at once." Specifically, they

warned that if a military rescue attempt was made, "the embassy, which has been a place of espionage, will blow up."[33] In less than three weeks the students had totally repudiated their original stance of nonviolent protest. They were not only ready to die for their Islamic revolution; they told the world that they were willing to kill unarmed hostages as well.

For Jimmy Carter and all the members of his administration working to free the hostages, the weeks flew by in a blur of increasingly infuriating and frustrating actions. Carter seemed to do everything right. He tried to use the weight of international opinion to pressure the Iranians. At Carter's request, the French, the Germans, the English, and other European allies stepped up and unequivocally condemned the hostage-taking. Carter got the U.N. Security-Council involved and it, too, condemned the Iranian action. Surprising no one in the White House, the Soviets abstained from the vote. At President Carter's request, U.N. Secretary-General Kurt Waldheim visited Iran. Secretary Vance, who had pushed for the secretary-general's visit, had not expected much from it but he did hope that Waldheim would demonstrate to the Iranian Revolutionary Council how isolated it stood in world opinion. Waldheim, however, did not even meet Vance's low expectations. Vance privately blasted the secretary-general as a weak, "obsequious" man who "tried to identify with the Iranians at [the] expense of representing the world community."

Carter also tried to make moot the Iranian demand that the United States return the Shah to Tehran. As soon as the Shah's physical condition stabilized he was whisked out of the country. Mexico, in a show of third-world solidarity with the Iranians, would not take him back. So Hamilton Jordan, personally, had to convince the Panamanian government, grateful to Carter for his handling of the Panama Canal turnover, to take in the pariah Shah. They did, though the despondent Shah was fleeced once again, this time primarily by the estimable Panamanian military leader, Colonel Manuel Noriega, to the tune of $135,000 a month. But even with the Shah gone, as of December 15, the Khomeini government did not budge, insisting that the United States still had the power to return the Shah to Iran. Substantively, they were right: when it came to the question of whether or not to extradite the Shah the Panamanian government was following the recommendations of the Carter administration.

Carter, working closely with Vance, Brzezinski, and other key members of the administration, set into motion a series of escalating measures against Iran. In mid-November the United States stopped buying oil from Iran. Unfortunately, the Carter administration could not convince other nations to follow the American lead. Then, Carter ordered that all Iranian assets in the United States, including deposits in American banks and even Iranian deposits in the foreign branches of American banks, be frozen until the hostage crisis was resolved. Billions of dollars in Iranian assets were affected. This measure was taken expeditiously, despite some concern about the legality of the measure, on November 14 after Brzezinski received word at 5 a.m. that the Iranian foreign minister had announced at a press conference that the government planned to withdraw all Iranian assets from American banks and deposit them in Iranian banks. A legal brief demanding an end to the Iranian state-sponsored hostage-taking was filed with the International Court of Justice. None of these measures made any noticeable difference—except that the Iranian government was irate about the frozen assets. With billions at stake, a great deal of energy over the next year would go into unsnarling the Iranian-American financial relationship.

The student hostage-takers, in their running stream of communications, constantly threatened to put their American captives on trial to prove to the world that the U.S. embassy was nothing more than a "den of espionage." In even harsher terms Khomeini made the same threat: "[I]f Carter does not send the Shah, it is possible that the hostages may be tried, and if they are tried, Carter knows what will happen."[34] Khomeini's menacing pronouncements, so unlike the usual diplomatic phrases crafted by heads of state, infuriated American government officials who feared the impact they might have on the Students Following the Line of the Imam. American television viewers became unpleasantly accustomed to Khomeini's glowering countenance and his attacks (in translation) on their president and their nation. Khomeini's term for the United States, the "Great Satan," was used so relentlessly by the imam and his followers that it became an ironic bit of dark humor for Americans in the dreary winter of late 1979 and early 1980.

While the U.S. government sought political and economic leverage on Iran the student hostage-takers were painstakingly working their way through the tens of thousands of documents they had seized. They were positive that they had proof of dastardly deeds committed by embassy personnel. One of the worst crimes they discovered was that one of the hostages, who actually did work for the CIA, had a fake passport. They never did find any documentary proof that the captive Americans were plotting to overthrow the revolutionary Islamic government.

The Carter administration was worried that the students and Khomeini would make good on their threat and conduct a kangaroo court. At the request of White House advisor Lloyd Cutler, the prestigious law firm Cravath, Swaine, and Moore prepared a 106-page memo, "On the Rights of American Hostages in Iran," and gathered an impressive amount of documentary material the firm's lawyers thought might be useful in the event of a trial, though what made the firm think that the Iranians would let them participate in a "revolutionary tribunal" is not clear.[35] Experts in Islamic law were consulted. More pointedly, Carter made sure the Iranian government knew that the United States would retaliate with all necessary means if any of the hostages were executed. As publicly as possible, some twenty warships were moved into the Arabian Sea, a show of strength that prompted huge rallies in front of the American embassy in Tehran; thousands of protesters wore white burial shrouds to make clear their willingness to die as martyrs if the Americans attacked. The Carter administration believed that it had to cover every contingency and the number of man-hours spent tracking down experts, consulting with people, holding meetings, drafting position papers, coordinating military capacities, and simply trying to follow every lead and every development was herculean. And none of it was paying off.

With every passing day, Carter's critics multiplied. At first, the only hard questions came from reporters asking the White House to explain why the American embassy personnel were not safely evacuated before the takeover and why the embassy was not better guarded and fortified. Increasingly, however, the president was second-guessed by members of the press and Congress about his decision to admit the Shah to the United States for medical treatment. By late November harsher criticisms aired. On November 27, NBC News reported that Henry Kissinger had given a speech stating "that the people of the United States are tired of being pushed around, and that the fall of the Shah was a debacle."[36] While not getting down to details, Kissinger seemed to be condemning Carter for not unleashing U.S. military might on the Iranian revolution. In early December, Andrew Young, who several months earlier had been forced to resign as American ambassador to the United Nations because he had held an unauthorized meeting with a leader of the Palestine Liberation Organization, attacked U.S. policy in Iran from the political left. He told reporters: "We were wrong in our long support of the Shah. We were wrong to overthrow the government of the Mossadegh and install the Shah. . . . We were wrong . . . to allow SAVAK to torture and persecute Iranian students."[37] Senator Kennedy, gearing up for his presidential primary campaign, blasted Carter's decision to allow the Shah entry into the United States and hyperbolically attacked the Shah's rule as "one of the most violent regimes in the history of mankind."[38] While Kennedy's remarks were widely condemned as not helpful to the problem at hand—and the more Kennedy spoke publicly in late 1979 and early 1980, the less support he generated—they did get under Carter's skin.

In the face of growing criticism, including grumbling from within his own political party, Carter met privately with select congressional leaders and laid it on the line: "If you will excuse my expression, I don't give a damn whether you like or do not like the shah. I don't care whether you think he is a thief or not. . . . I don't care whether you think I . . . was wise or not wise in accepting the shah as one of our allies." "The issue," Carter lectured, "is that

American hostages, 50 of them, are being held by kidnappers, radical and irresponsible kidnappers, with the encouragement and support of the Iranian government. . . . I cannot abide Americans confusing the issue by starting to decide whether the history of Iran before the shah left was decent or indecent, was proper or improper. . . . I don't care about that." Carter then made an extraordinary admission. The safety and return of the hostages, he told the congressional leaders, "is constantly a burden on my mind, no matter what I am thinking about. If I am worrying about an announcement that I am going to be a candidate for president or if I am worrying about the windfall profits tax or if I am worrying about anything else, I am always concerned about the hostages."[39] It was a powerful and compelling unscripted talk, an emotional side of Jimmy Carter that the American people rarely, if ever, saw.

Through the first two months of the hostage crisis, the American people rallied around the president. Carter's standing in public opinion polls skyrocketed. But as Carter told the congressional leadership, "[T]he patience of the American people is not a characteristic of America. People are inclined to be impatient here." And by January, their impatience was growing.

An ABC-Harris Survey released January 7, 1980, indicated Carter's political predicament. When asked if Carter's policy in Iran should be judged a failure if the hostages were still captive in three weeks' time, 53 percent agreed and only 27 percent disagreed. When asked the same question, but if the hostages were still captive in three months time, 74 percent agreed. Only 12 percent disagreed. Worse, from a political standpoint, the survey indicated that Americans had come around to Senator Kennedy's viewpoint that the Shah was a thief and a despot, by better than a two-to-one margin. Carter's stance as commander in chief at a time of crisis had given him a two-month honeymoon with the American people. Carter had ridden that wave of support by announcing in early December that in order to focus his attention on resolving the hostage crisis, he was postponing his campaign for reelection for the foreseeable future. However, just a few days into the new year, with day 62 come and gone, as CBS News anchor Walter

Cronkite reminded his viewers, the bloom was off the rose, and people were only willing to give the president a few more weeks to resolve the crisis.[40]

President Carter, though ever-mindful of the hostages, had another crisis on his hands. Christmas week, the Soviet military, with some 85,000 troops, had invaded Afghanistan. The Soviet government blandly stated that it had sent military assistance, at the request of the Afghan government, to safeguard the regime against a growing internal Islamic revolutionary threat. To put it most pointedly, the Soviets had done for their closely allied communist friends (less charitably, puppet regime) what the Carter administration had chosen not to do in Iran.

Zbigniew Brzezinski was not surprised by the Soviet action. He had been warning the president for months that the Soviets were pushing hard to maintain control in Afghanistan. Somewhat ironically given U.S. policy nearly a quarter century later, Brzezinski had given a major speech in August 1979 in which he had publicly warned the Soviets not to intervene in Afghan internal affairs, insisting that the Soviets stop all efforts "to impose alien doctrines on deeply religious and nationally conscious peoples."[41] Brzezinski had kept an eagle eye on the Soviets' Afghan policy and had urged his boss to "publicize Soviet activities so that the Islamic world would be mobilized, and also to continue to demonstrate our sympathy for the Afghan freedom fighters."[42] Brzezinski saw the blatant Soviet military intervention as proof positive of his concerns that the Soviet government had become emboldened by the Carter administration's relative timidity. He feared that the Afghan move was only the first step in a Soviet campaign to insert itself into the Persian Gulf region. From this position, the Soviets could threaten the rest of the industrial world's oil supply. This threat, Brzezinski and the president agreed, could not stand. Brzezinski had been warning Jimmy Carter for years that the Soviets were never to be trusted and that the worst could always be expected of them. The invasion of Afghanistan seemed to have proved him right. President Carter's trust in his longtime advisor rose accordingly.

President Carter harshly condemned the invasion and took a series of steps against the Soviets. The Carter administration instituted economic sanctions, including a grain embargo (infuriating wheat-growing farmers) and a boycott of the 1980 Summer Olympics in Moscow. The American people responded positively to their president's leadership, which is almost always the case at a time of perceived crisis. The proof came on January 21 at the Iowa Democratic presidential nominating caucuses. Carter buried Senator Kennedy. Two nights later, confident that he was on the right track, President Carter gave his 1980 State of the Union Address and announced what came to be called the Carter doctrine.

Carter warned the American people that the Soviet invasion of Afghanistan was not only an outrage against the Afghan people. It was also a deliberate, threatening move by the Soviets into the Persian Gulf region. "Let our position be absolutely clear," he told the American people. "An attempt by any outside force to gain control of the Persian Gulf region will be regarded as an assault on the vital interests of the United States of America, and such an assault will be repelled by any means necessary, including military force." To back up his sharp words, Carter called for a sustained increase in the American defense budget to meet the new Soviet threat. Here was a new, tough Carter. Talk of human rights abuses was fast being replaced by old-line anti-Soviet rhetoric and policy. Rather than focus on the American policies in the Persian Gulf region that were fostering anti-American sentiments among its Islamic populations—clearly demonstrated in the Iranian hostage-taking—the Carter administration focused on the external Soviet threat to the Gulf's oil.

Carter did not ignore the Iran hostage crisis in his State of the Union speech. But he did try to put a new face on the increasingly old problem. While warning the Iranian government that it would be held responsible for any harm done to the hostages, Carter also tried to shift the focus, stating that the American government must somehow demonstrate to "the Iranian leaders that the real danger to their nation lies in the north, in the Soviet Union and from the Soviet troops now in Afghanistan, and that the unwarranted Iranian quarrel with the United States hampers their response to this far greater danger to them."[43]

Carter presidential historian Burton Kaufman argues that the president overreacted to the Soviet invasion of Afghanistan: "[H]e may have acted out of frustration over other differences between Moscow and Washington and a more generalized despair over the Iranian hostage crisis as out of foreign policy considerations."[44] Kaufman is right that nobody in the Carter administration was happy with Soviet behavior over the prior year and that the Afghan invasion was perceived as part of a pattern of duplicity and aggressive actions in the "crescent of crisis" extending from the Horn of Africa through Southwest Asia. For a long time, Carter had done relatively little about Soviet actions; suddenly, he saw the need to do a great deal. As for the Iran crisis, however, the Carter administration was actually in quite a hopeful mood by late January. When he alluded in the State of the Union speech to better days ahead between the United States and Iran based on a common concern about the "far greater danger" represented by the Soviets, he meant it.

Through a private French back channel as well as via American professor Richard Cottam, an expert on Iran sympathetic to the revolution, the Carter administration had been communicating with Iranian Foreign Minister Sadegh Ghotbzadeh. The foreign minister, like so many elite Iranians, had studied in the United States and had actually been Professor Cottam's student. While Ghotbzadeh spent a good deal of his time expressing his fears about his precarious position within the revolutionary government, he also made it clear that he wanted to return the hostages to the United States so that Iran could move forward politically, both domestically and internationally. Four days after Carter's address to the nation, the State Department IWG received word that Ghotbzadeh believed that "progress could be quite fast now and there should be movement on many fronts."[45] To ensure a settlement, Ghotbzadeh wanted the United States to allow the United Nations to investigate Iranian claims against American policy, to go slow on sanctions, and to unfreeze certain Iranian assets held in the United States. The United States was also hearing through intermediaries that Khomeini insider and the man most likely to be the new president of Iran, Abol-hassan Bani-Sadr, wanted to resolve the hostage situation as well. Problems still existed. First, Ghotbzadeh's own political power was, like most everyone else's in Iran, precarious. Second, Khomeini personally hated Carter for his public support of the Shah and for not reaching out to Khomeini prior to the revolution; no one knew what he might say or do next.[46]

By mid-February, the IWG in the State Department and a number of White House staffers felt a deal was close to being struck. Chief of Staff Hamilton Jordan, in a hush-hush, secret meeting in London, had met the two French lawyers who were dealing directly with Ghotbzadeh. Jordan had high hopes that the crisis was soon to be resolved. Only the NSC remained dubious. Brzezinski told Jordan, "I don't think the Iranian government will challenge the militants, and there is such chaos in Iran that ultimately only Khomeini has the power to order the release."[47] Regardless of such well-founded skepticism, on February 15, 1980, a statement for use "after the Hostages are Released" was drafted. In part, it read: "The United States hopes it will now be possible to move toward a constructive relationship with the government and people of Iran. Such a relationship must be based upon a mutual respect for the lawful rights and total independence of each state. . . . We are devoutly thankful that the hostages are now free."[48]

But they were not. As Brzezinski had predicted, Khomeini would not allow it. The Revolutionary Council had tried to gain control of the hostages but the students in the embassy, supported by Khomeini, refused to hand them over. A U.N. Commission inquiry into Iranian grievances against the United States that the Revolutionary Council had demanded as a step aimed at releasing the hostages arrived in Tehran in late February. But at Khomeini's order the commission members were not allowed to visit the hostages (a demand the American government had made before giving its okay to the U.N. effort and to which the Iranian government had agreed—or at least certain members of the Iranian government had agreed). Stymied, after eighteen days in Tehran, the U.N. investigators left on March 11. The more moderate or, at least, pragmatic

Iranians suggested that the matter was still in hand. They asked the United States to be patient while internal issues—most importantly an upcoming parliamentary election—were resolved. Soon, they insisted, the hostages would be released. For the Carter White House, it was mind-bogglingly frustrating.

The president had already paid a public opinion price for dickering with the Iranians over the hostages. Conservatives had roundly condemned his willingness to use a U.N. inquiry to resolve the crisis and had attacked the suggestion that the U.S. government might be willing to provide Iran with aid once the hostages were released. Syndicated columnist George Will, never a fan of President Carter, wrote, "[T]he administration has hinted that aid might be part of Iran's reward for releasing the hostages. Arguably, the United States is so weak, militarily, and so isolated, diplomatically, that it never had any choice but to devise an agenda of appeasement. But such agendas never stop lengthening." In an extravagant rhetorical flourish, he concluded by comparing the American people's acceptance of Carter's policy of appeasing the Iranians with that of the French in 1938 when faced with the Nazi threat. William Safire, a one-time speechwriter for Richard Nixon and a strong supporter of Israel, writing in the *New York Times*, was even harder on Carter. He accused him of "rewarding terrorists" and letting all "terrorist groups" know that they risked nothing by kidnapping Americans.[49] Carter was willing to take such blistering rhetoric if his gamble paid off with the release of the hostages. But it had not and now Carter simply looked weak and ineffective.

While Carter had weathered the Kennedy challenge by late March 1980—luckily for Carter, the Massachusetts senator had proved to be a terrible campaigner who constantly stuck his foot in his mouth—he was fast losing public support. Public opinion polls showed him in deep trouble just seven months before the presidential election. The rally-around-the-president phenomenon produced by the crisis was brief, lasting just into the new year. By March the Iran hostage crisis to which the president had *deliberately* tied himself had become a millstone around his neck.

Zbigniew Brzezinski insisted that the time had come to act decisively. The United States had to exercise its military option. The March 14 Iranian elections had only strengthened the hand of the Islamic hard-liners; they would not now give up the hostages without some kind of abject measures taken by the United States. Several weeks earlier, a touch of black humor had still seemed possible and a Farsi-English list of useful phrases had circulated among White House staffers. Included in the list was the Farsi for, "If you will do me the kindness of not harming my genital appendages, I will reciprocate by betraying my country in public."[50] But Jimmy Carter was not willing to abase himself or the nation in order to get the hostages home. By the beginning of April, he had come to accept that Brzezinski was right and that it was time to up the ante.

For the March 25 Special Coordinating Committee meeting, Brzezinski circulated a report on the general direction of American foreign policy. It warned that "*our policy is neither coherent nor constant*; on a number of specific issues, notably Iran and the Middle East, we are in fact *losing momentum*, with potentially very destructive consequences for our interests." The policy paper called for a "unfiying theme" to give clarity and purpose to American policy: "The theme we propose is that the Soviet invasion of Afghanistan must focus our attention on a major new order of politico-economic-military threat to the non-communist world security—Soviet domination of Middle East oil." To counter Soviet aggression, according to Brzezinski's report, the United States had to dramatically reassert in its global leadership through an "integrated approach" and demonstrate its "deterrent capabilities so that we can sustain a credible overall response." Iran policy had to be at the symbolic heart of that reassertion of credible deterrence. Critically, the report concluded, "[W]e have essentially run out of peaceful steps we can take to put pressure on the Iranians, are we prepared for more significant military actions?"[51]

Between March 25 and April 11, Jimmy Carter, in essence, gave the Iranians a last chance to resolve the hostage crisis peaceably. At a Camp David meeting held on March 22, he was briefed by

Chairman of the Joint Chiefs of Staff General David Jones about the military option, a hostage-rescue plan that had been in the works, as a contingency, since November. He knew that the military was ready. He also understood that Secretary of State Cyrus Vance remained fully committed to a peaceful, patient solution to the imbroglio.

On April 11, Carter met with his National Security Council to work through the military option. Two days earlier, Brzezinski had given Carter his views in the bluntest possible language: "In my view, a carefully planned and boldly executed rescue operation represents the only realistic prospect that the hostages—any of them—will be freed in the foreseeable future. Our policy of restraint has won us well-deserved understanding throughout the world, but it has run out. It is time for us to act. Now."[52] For months, Carter had been under pressure to act more boldly. Early in the crisis, his right-hand man and key political advisor, Hamilton Jordan, had told him that a "punitive" response to the crisis was "absolutely essential to your own re-election and to America's image in the world." Jordan warned, "[I]f after such an outrageous act directed against us by another country, we are compelled to sit silent and not retaliate, then perhaps we really have become a helpless giant."[53] By mid-April, Carter felt he had to act. A surgical insertion of a commando rescue team that would free the hostages, kill only as many hostage-takers as was absolutely necessary, and produce as little collateral damage in Iran as was possible seemed the best solution to a crisis that had dragged on for over 150 days. As of April 11, the operation was on.

Carter knew that Vance and his people in State were opposed to this action but he no longer cared. Indeed, humiliating Vance, the final meeting on the military option was taken while the secretary of state was vacationing in Florida. He was not called back for the meeting or even told for several days about its outcome. Upon his return to Washington Vance was stunned by the decision and by his exclusion from the critical meeting that had changed policy. Ten days later, after failing to convince the president that the military option was the wrong option to take, he submitted his letter of resignation, effective after the hostage-rescue attempt—whether it succeeded or failed.

Since signing up to work for Jimmy Carter, Vance had been dueling with Zbigniew Brzezinski for the mind of the president. The sometimes unpleasant competition and occasionally public sniping between Vance and Brzezinski had been an inside-Washington story for better than two years. Carter even kidded about it, at one point joking at a correspondents' dinner that he was being urged by foreign policy experts to discuss "linkage" (in fact, with the Soviet Union) but that after discussing the matter with Vance and Brzezinski, "They say it is much too early to have that much relationship between the State Department and the NSC."[54] By April 1979, the joke had worn thin. For the first years of the Carter administration, Vance had won more battles than he had lost—pushing an agenda of human rights, engagement with the Soviets, and a generally patient and prudent approach to international problems. With the Soviet invasion of Afghanistan and the continuing intractability of Iran in State Department–led negotiations, the president had lost faith in his secretary of state's judgment. Carter turned to Brzezinski, embracing his certainties about Soviet malevolence and the need to show the world America's steely strength. Judging by the election of 1980, a majority of the American people believed that this turn came too late.

On April 24, President Carter began a normal day at the White House. In a low-key manner, he moved through routine meetings and appearances. While Carter was no professional actor, all day he gave no hint of the tremendous anxiety he was feeling.

Some five months earlier an elite team of American fighting men, Delta Force, led by Colonel Charlie Beckwith, had begun training to rescue the hostages. Delta Force had begun operations only two years earlier. It was specifically created as the U.S. military's first counterterrorist unit. Chosen personally by Beckwith after enduring an extraordinarily rigorous and competitive process, the men of Delta Force learned an array of skills that ranged from driving an SSB-1200 diesel locomotive to picking locks to scaling mountains. Every man in the unit went through weapons training at least three to four hours a day, five days a week. Above all, they trained relentlessly to neutralize hostage-takers, airplane hijackers, and other nonconventional threats to American security.[55] The meaning of "neutralize" was made clear by a sign Colonel Beckwith kept on his desk: "Kill 'em all. Let God sort 'em out." To prevent leaks to the mass media, the operation maintained extraordinary levels of OPSEC—operational security—throughout the training period. Later, the military concluded that the stringent security concerns had gotten in the way of proper preparation for the mission. Too few people had been consulted about mission planning and the various groups of men involved in the rescue understood too little about how each piece of the operation fit together.

The rescue plan—code-named Eagle Claw—was not simple. Using eight helicopters, an assault force of 118 men would make their way from the carrier *Nimitz* in the Gulf of Oman to a desert location in Iran—Desert One. There, they would refuel their huge RH-53D Sea Stallion helicopters from C-130 fuel-carrying planes. Then, through a several-step process, aided by operatives already in place in Tehran, the team would stealthily make their way to the U.S. embassy. Through human intelligence capacities the exact location of the hostages in the embassy was known. The Delta Force commandos would enter the embassy compound, kill every armed guard they encountered—two head shots each—extract the hostages, and return the hostages home safely. Everybody understood that each phase of the operation entailed risks and nobody thought it would be easy.[56]

Task Force Commander General James Vaught personally briefed President Carter on the overall operation just a few days before it was to be launched. Carter listened with his usual intensity. Delta Force commander Colonel Beckwith then specifically explained to the president how his people would rescue the hostages. The president asked the colonel how many casualties he anticipated. General Vaught replied for Beckwith. No one could answer that question, he said, but suggested that maybe six or seven Delta Force men might be wounded and perhaps two or three of the hostages. Warren Christopher, with his usual careful deliberation, asked what would happen to the guards. Beckwith replied that his men would "take the guards out." Christopher wanted to make sure that the president understood: "What do you mean? Will you shoot them in the shoulder or what?" Beckwith clarified his statement: "No, sir. We're going to shoot each of them twice, right between the eyes."[57]

As the meeting came to a close, President Carter asked to speak privately with Colonel Beckwith. The president said, "I want you, before you leave for Iran, to assemble all your force and when you think it's appropriate give them a message from me. Tell them that in the event this operation fails, for whatever reason, the fault will not be theirs, it will be mine."[58]

The mission failed. Three helicopters, on their way to the Desert One refueling location, suffered mechanical problems or perceived problems. An unexpected, severe dust storm likely caused those mechanical difficulties. Better meteorological information might have prevented the mission from flying into the dust storm. Two of the helicopters turned around and a third, while making it to Desert One, had hydraulic problems. Mission planners had built in two extra helicopters to cover mechanical failures but a minimum of six helicopters was necessary to move the team forward. Only five were fully functional at the Desert One refueling site. With only five helicopters, twenty men would have to be left behind. In the middle of the desert, Colonel Beckwith had to make a brutal decision. He knew the president was counting on him. But the rescue, he believed, could not be accomplished with twenty of his men left behind. In all probability, hostages would die, his men would be killed, and nobody would get home. The colonel radioed in his recommendation to abort mission. At the top of the chain of command, President Carter, back in the Oval Office, mournfully agreed.[59]

It got worse. After the abort order was issued, a helicopter lifted off in the dust storm and collided with a refueling plane at Desert One. An explosion tore apart the helicopter and the C-130; flames shot three to four hundred feet into the night sky. Eight Americans were killed. There was nothing to do but get the survivors out on the remaining C-130 aircraft and leave the five helicopters, partially destroyed plane, and dead bodies behind as macabre trophies for the Iranian revolutionaries. The mission had gone from unlucky failure to tragic disaster.[60]

In the United States, as Carter historian Mark Rozell notes, press coverage of the rescue mission was more mournful than anything else. Meg Greenfield, in her *Newsweek* column, set the tone, "Let's Avoid Scapegoats." But *Time* magazine's cover story on the failed mission pointed out the obvious: "While most of Carter's political foes tactfully withheld criticism, his image as inept had been renewed." Other media outlets hammered home the same message. The *Washington Post*'s Joseph Kraft put it most bluntly: Carter, he wrote, is "unfit to be President at a time of crisis."[61]

In Iran, masses of people thrilled to the Americans' botched rescue attempt. The Ayatollah Khomeini told his followers: "Those sand particles were divinely commissioned. They had a mission: to destroy the aggressor's planes." "Carter," he said, "still has not comprehended what kind of people he is facing and what school of thought he is playing with. Our people is the people of blood and our school is the school of *Jihad*."[62] The joyous students at the embassy made sure everybody understood the imam's Koranic reference. In their media statement after the failed rescue attempt they told of the failed attack on "God's House" in Mecca by the evil Abraheh, ruler of Yemen, whose assault was to be led by elephants and horsemen. But God destroyed that mighty force by sending "birds with stones of clay aimed at the aggressors." As "Mary" later wrote, "divine intervention had saved Iran" as it had saved "God's House" fourteen centuries earlier in Mecca.[63] Americans had long grown accustomed to football coaches, clergymen, and political leaders telling them that God was on their side. Now the other side was making the same claim. To make sure that God was not called on again soon for another miracle, the students and the Iranian government, in full cooperation, removed the hostages from the embassy and imprisoned them individually all over Iran. After the failed rescue attempt nobody in power in Iran was in the mood for a deal.

In the 1970s, helicopters were associated with some of the American people's darkest visions and most hopeless hours. On August

9, 1974, Americans had watched President Richard Nixon board a helicopter, one step ahead of impeachment. Just before he ducked his head to leave the White House in ignominy, he plastered a wretched smile on his face and incongruously flashed a V for Victory sign. Less than a year later, with the unelected president Gerald Ford standing uneasily at the nation's helm, Americans watched footage of another helicopter: this one lifted off in a cloud of tear gas from the roof of the American embassy in Saigon in the final stage of Operation Frequent Wind; the last Americans in Vietnam beat their terrified Vietnamese allies off the helicopter skids as they fled, one step in front of the triumphant communist army. Five years and six days after the United States had been driven out of Vietnam in defeat, the American people had to imagine a third image: a helicopter on fire, its rotors churning uselessly, American soldiers screaming, dead bodies piled up in a godforsaken Iranian desert.[64]

Most Americans had seen enough. They were hungry for new leadership. That summer the Republican Party nominated Ronald Reagan to be their torchbearer in the 1980 presidential election. Reagan had first tried for the nomination in 1968. He had tried again in 1976, and after that failure the pundits and political professionals had counted Reagan out. By 1980, Reagan was sixty-nine years old and had not held an elected office for five years. But in the minds of many Americans his absence from the national political stage during the late 1970s counted in his favor.

"I will not stand by and watch this great country destroy itself under mediocre leadership that drifts from one crisis to the next, eroding our national will and purpose. . . . We need a rebirth of the American tradition of leadership at every level of government and in private life as well," said the former Hollywood actor and ex–California governor at the convention that nominated him.[65] Four years earlier, an unknown Georgia governor had captured the Democratic nomination and then the White House by offering a humble pledge, "I will never lie to you." Reagan, a national celebrity in one form or another for some forty years, promised a very different kind of leadership. Promoting love of country at every opportunity, he unrelentingly derided the competency of the federal government, in general, and the presidential leadership of James Earl Carter, in particular. Though he had been rejected by his own party twice before, suddenly the time seemed right for the sunny platitudes, moral certainties, and anti-government rhetoric of Ronald Reagan.

Throughout the election campaign the hostage crisis dragged on. The Carter administration, in the weeks and then months after the failed rescue operation, tried—at last—to draw attention away from the hostages' plight and the government's inability to get them home. Though Carter continued working hard to resolve the crisis, publicly, he drew away from the seemingly endless debacle. But CBS News anchor Walter Cronkite kept counting out the days of the hostages' captivity and ABC continued to remind the American people of the hostages' plight on its nightly news program, rechristened *Nightline*. While host Ted Koppel occasionally featured other breaking news stories, the focus remained on Iran. With dirty yellow ribbons hanging everywhere in the United States, the American people had grown numb to the ordeal—if no more satisfied with Carter's failure to bring the hostages home.

There had been some good news. Besides the thirteen hostages released in mid-November 1979, the six Americans who had made a successful run for it the day the hostages were taken and spent over two months hiding at the Canadian embassy had escaped in late January 1980 through the good offices of stalwart Canadian diplomats in Tehran. That July the Iranian hostage-takers had shown a bit of humanity by releasing another hostage who was suffering from multiple sclerosis. But for the other fifty-two Americans still in Iran, scattered around the country, the months went by in dull misery.

Iran remained mired in instability. In June fierce armed clashes broke out between leftists and Islamic fundamentalists. Political divisions within the Iranian military upped the anxiety level throughout Iranian society. Control of the revolution was by no means finalized. President Bani-Sadr attributed the factional troubles to U.S. meddling.

Then on September 22, 1980, catastrophically for the people of Iran, a major war broke out between Iraq and Iran. After a series of border skirmishes and troop escalations, Iraq opportunistically invaded Iran's Khuzistan province, hoping to take advantage of the Iranians' political disarray. Many in Iran blamed the United States for the bloody confrontation.

The Shah's whereabouts, meanwhile, had become a moot point in the seemingly endless and pointless negotiations that continued between Iranian officials and American diplomats. The Shah's health had continued to worsen and his situation in the hostile and larcenous environs of Panama became increasingly unpleasant. By late March 1980 he feared that the Panamanians would cut a deal with the Iranians to extradite him and he no longer trusted Carter to keep him safe. After Panamanian officials refused to allow his doctors to perform a necessary operation and the Carter administration refused to help, the Shah fled Panama. His old friend, President Anwar Sadat, had taken pity on him and, despite the domestic risks from militant Islamicists, had invited the Shah to end his days in Egypt. On July 27, Reza Pahlavi died in Egyptian exile.

Iranian leaders, though cheered by the Shah's death, were far too embroiled in the internal political factional fighting that had overtaken the revolution to focus on the hostage negotiations. In addition, those Iranians who were looking to resolve the hostage situation had concerns beyond the Shah's return: they wanted their nation's frozen assets back, as well as the American-based assets of the Shah's family. They wanted the military supplies for which Iran had already paid the United States under the Shah's regime, now a pressing concern as Iran was at war with Iraq. And they wanted ironclad guarantees that the United States would not subvert, in any way, the Iranian revolutionary government.

In the weeks right before the presidential election, Carter's men worked desperately to free the hostages and give the president a last-minute electoral boost. The NSC's Gary Sick has since argued that Reagan's election team, with future CIA director William Casey in the lead, tried to engineer its own "October Surprise" by meeting secretly with Iranian officials and promising them military equipment if they held back any hostage release until Reagan won the election.[66] While no hard evidence has emerged to back up Sick's thesis and nothing in recently declassified documents available at the Carter Library supports the allegation, unanswered questions about Casey's activities before the election have kept the "October Surprise" scenario alive. What is certain is that despite the Carter administration's faith that they had cut a deal with the Iranians for a hostage release right before the November election, nothing happened.

Carter tells the story of the election himself in his diary entries. November 3, 1980: "Pat [Caddell, the pollster] was getting some very disturbing public opinion poll results, showing a massive slippage as people realized that the hostages were not coming home. The anniversary date of their having been captured absolutely filled the news media. . . . This apparently opened up a flood of related concerns among the people that we were impotent."[67] Carter was right to be worried. The next day he lost the presidency to Ronald Reagan. Carter won only six states and Reagan received a large plurality of the popular vote.

The hostage crisis was by no means the only reason that Carter lost. The continuing economic problems, the energy crisis, and even the infamous spiritual "malaise" all played a part. But in the end it was the hostage crisis, the single event that took up more of the president's time and public energies than any other, that crushed his hopes for reelection. The American people had been bullied, successfully, by the Ayatollah Khomeini, whom most perceived as a crazy, religious fanatic, and his Islamic fundamentalist followers. The seemingly endless crisis driven by people who, from an American perspective, were operating in a thousand-year time warp, spoke to Americans' sense that the nation had come unglued and the people in charge did not know what to do about it. Carter, as he put it, appeared "impotent." Having an impotent man as leader did not tend to make Americans feel good about their country or themselves.

Ironically, the hostage crisis did not directly affect almost anyone in the United States. It was a foreign policy mess the likes of which most Americans could safely have ignored. And, in fact, over the next decade, as Middle East terrorists held a number of other U.S. citizens hostage, few Americans maintained the same kind of continuous concern over their fates as they had exhibited during the Iran hostage crisis in the last year of the Carter presidency. I would argue, however, that it was precisely *because* the hostage crisis did not directly affect the American people that it became a metaphor for the massive changes in American life that made the 1970s so unsettling to so many people. While Americans worried a great deal about the energy and economic crises that affected their daily lives, the hostage crisis allowed them to worry about something larger than themselves: as singer Pat Boone put it, the national "family." The man who followed the peanut farmer from Georgia as president would proudly tell the American people that he did his best thinking "with a horse between his legs." A majority of the American electorate decided it was time to try out a man who, at least, knew how to play the part of a cowboy.

Epilogue

THE HOSTAGES finally were freed on January 20, 1981. Fifty-two of them had been in Iranian hands for 444 days. Just before the hostages were to fly out of Tehran, Bruce German, who had been the embassy budget officer, insisted that they take a count to make sure that all were present and accounted for. They counted again, and again. German remembers: "We wanted to make sure that everybody was on that plane. We weren't about to leave anyone behind."[1]

The route home was circuitous. At their first stop, in Algeria, the Americans were amazed and unsettled by the media attention focused on them. Camera crews and reporters were there in full strength, desperately trying to do interviews and get footage of the newly freed hostages. Charles Jones, who had been a communications officer, asked what was going on. He was told that he and the others were heroes. "Heroes?" he said, "We're not heroes. We're survivors. That's all. Just survivors."[2] It was a very end-of-the-1970s comment.

Deputy Secretary of State Warren Christopher led the American team that finally worked out a deal with the Iranians. In November 1980, Algerian diplomats took on the role of mediators and, according to Christopher, they were outstanding. Two decades earlier, Algerians had been the region's great revolutionaries; now, with aplomb, they served as cultural brokers for the United States and Iran. Christopher was later uncharacteristically effusive about the Algerians' competence and commitment to a successful outcome: "The Algerians served an indispensable function in interpreting two widely disparate cultures and reasoning processes to each other. . . . All in all, no one performed with more energy, skill, commitment, or honor than did members of the Algerian team." Christopher, who was one of the few primary actors in the crisis who emerged from it with his reputation enhanced, drew a useful conclusion about the Algerian diplomats' role: "So the crisis demonstrated that we have much to gain from responsible international citizenship and also that ours is far from the only society that aspires to lofty ideals."[3] For Christopher, Algeria's fruitful role in resolving the crisis gave yet more evidence that U.S. foreign policy must embrace a multilateral perspective.

The details of the deal were, for most Americans, anti-climactic. Most of the final negotiations involved complex financial concerns. The Iranians wanted their frozen assets back and American banks wanted the new Iranian government to pay off loans made to the Shah's regime. Since the American banks had a good deal of Iranian financial assets in their possession, they had significant negotiating power. The U.S. side explained that they could not simply give the Shah's estate to anyone—even the new Iranian government. Disposition of the Shah's assets was, instead, a legal matter to be decided by the courts. The Iranians, after much dickering and rhetoric, conceded that the dead Shah's assets did not have to be returned to the Iranian people. The U.S. government did, however, meet one of Iran's fundamental demands. The final agreement stated that the United States would not in any way attempt to overthrow the revolutionary Iranian government or intercede in Iranian internal affairs.

While these issues were very real, in the end the hostages were released because the Khomeini-led government no longer had any use for them. Khomeini, to his mind, had successfully humiliated Jimmy Carter, the president who had supported the Shah and then given him political asylum (short-lived as it was) in the United States. In Tehran, the newspaper headlines read: "America Bows to the Nation's Conditions: Hostages Released."[4] While the headline was not literally true in all regards, from the Iranian militants' perspective it was true enough. They had defeated the "Great Satan."

Poor Jimmy Carter had worked tirelessly, as was his wont, in the last days of his presidency trying to finalize the deal that would free the hostages. He had intended to spend his last weekend in office at the Camp David retreat that had been the site of his greatest triumph, the Begin-Sadat negotiations. Instead, he literally camped out in the Oval Office, waiting to hear that the hostages would be freed while he was still president. At 4:44 a.m. on January 19, the day before he was to leave office, he thought a final deal had been struck. He even made an announcement to a very groggy press corps. But he was wrong. Not until the next day, five minutes after Carter turned over the presidency to Ronald Reagan, were the hostages freed by their Iranian captors.

Reagan sent Carter and the core group of men who had worked for so long on the hostage crisis to Germany, where the ex-hostages flew after their brief stop in Algeria. It was an emotional meeting. Some of the hostages had hard questions for the former president, asking why he had allowed the Shah into the United States despite warnings from the embassy and why he had attempted a military rescue that could have endangered their lives. Cyrus Vance, who had resigned over that mission, was also there with the freed Americans, spending some time, as he said, "with my people." On the way home, Carter turned to Hamilton Jordan, the man who had been with him since he had started his presidential odyssey, and said: "You know, Ham, if we had had a little luck back in March or April and gotten 'em out then, we might be flying back to Washington instead of Plains."[5] Probably not, given all the other troubles too many Americans blamed on Carter's presidency, but who can say for sure?

It would be President Reagan, not President Carter, who ceremoniously welcomed the hostages back to the United States. And it would be Reagan's State Department, under the direction of Secretary of State Alexander Haig, that would snub its metaphoric Foggy Bottom nose at Carter's people by stating unequivocally: "The present Administration would not have negotiated with Iran for the release of the hostages."[6] As the Iran-Contra scandal (in which Reagan White House officials provided weapons to Iran in exchange for their help in returning American hostages held by Iranian-supported terrorists in Lebanon) would later prove: words are cheap. Nobody in the Reagan White House, or in those presidential administrations that followed, had any certainties about how to prevent terrorist acts from being committed against the United States.

Despite the incredible attention the Iran hostage crisis had attracted during its 444-day run, in its immediate aftermath few Americans thought much about what lessons it might hold for the American people. In part, the brutal war between Iran and Iraq refocused the American public's attention away from the revolutionary nature of Khomeini's regime and that regime's desire to spread its theocratic revolution throughout the Islamic world. Instead, newspaper stories recounted nightmarish scenes of Iranian human-wave attacks, involving tens of thousands of casualties, against heavily armed Iraqi troops. The focus was on nation-to-nation war, involving two neighboring Islamic countries. Coverage of this war allowed events in Iran to be seen, once again, as a story of third-world chaos, not as a revolution. Little heed was paid to Khomeini's promise: "We shall export our revolution to the whole world. Until the cry 'There is no God but God' resounds over the whole world, there will be struggle."[7]

Militant Iranian Islamicists did their best in the 1980s to maintain their revolutionary ardor and spread their creed—including a fierce anti-Americanism. In 1982 a kind of Islamic International, not unlike the Communist Internationals held in Moscow after the Bolshevik Revolution, convened in Tehran. Some 280 Islamic clerics from 70 nations met to discuss "the ideal Islamic government" and how "to rid the region of foreign infidels."

As Robin Wright reports in *In the Name of God*, her telling account of "The Khomeini Decade," after the Iranian revolutionary regime failed to incite Shi'ites in Iraq and Bahrain to overthrow their respective governments, Iranian hard-liners set their sights on Lebanon. Israel had invaded Lebanon in early 1982 in order to destroy the Palestine Liberation Organization's bases in the southern part of the country. In the violent chaos and anti-Israeli fervor, the Iranians hoped to assist Lebanon's Shi'ites in taking over the nation and establishing another militant Islamic government.

The Reagan administration, trying to broker an Israeli withdrawal from Lebanon and help the Lebanese restore political order, became caught up in this Middle East inferno. Radical Islamicists in Lebanon believed that the United States was siding with the Israeli-allied Lebanese Christian factions. After four Iranians were seized by a Lebanese Christian militia group, Iranian-linked militants retaliated by kidnapping a U.S. citizen, the president of the American University of Beirut (he was held for more than a year before being freed). Over the next few years some 130 foreigners were taken hostage by Lebanon-based militant groups, most of which were supported by Iran. On April 18, 1983, a new, shadowy terrorist group known as Islamic Jihad (seemingly composed of Shi'ite radicals linked to Iran) sent a suicide car-bomber to attack the American embassy in Beruit. The ensuing explosion blew off the entire façade of the embassy and killed 63 Americans and Lebanese. A phone call to Western news agencies warned that more attacks would follow unless all Americans withdrew from Lebanon.

Six months later, with the U.S. diplomatic community and a small Marine command still operating in Lebanon, Islamic Jihad executed an even more horrifying attack. At the request of a besieged Christian-led Lebanese Army unit, the U.S. military command authorized the USS *Virginia* to offer the unit protection by opening fire on an attacking Islamic militia. Robin Wright concludes: "By pushing the peace pact with Israel, the United States had been perceived by militant Muslims to be using diplomatic muscle to entrench Christian domination; now it was seen to be deploying military might to the same end. And that had to be stopped."[8] On the morning of October 23, 1983, an Islamic Jihad suicide bomber drove a large truck filled with explosives into the building at the Beirut airport where most of the U.S. military contingent slept. In the massive explosion 241 Americans died.

In Iran, the men who sought to spread Islamic revolution throughout the region were pleased. Later, a high Iranian official stated: "In Lebanon, we trained the people who drove a bomb into the American Marine barracks, but we didn't tell them to do such an act. . . . We only trained the Lebanese to defend their country. When we heard about the bomb, we were happy. But we didn't plan it. It was their right. Ask yourself. Why were the Americans in Lebanon?"[9]

Almost exactly four years earlier, Jimmy Carter had admitted the Shah to the United States for medical help. At the time, the U.S. embassy press attaché Barry Rosen categorically opposed the decision. "Having failed so often," he later wrote, "to recognize the power of symbols to Iranians—and the significance in particular of the Shah as the symbol of evil—to do so again would announce that we understood nothing about the revolution. Those who bruited the possibility probably didn't understand that admission would be a seemingly calculated insult to an entire nation."[10] In 1983, the revolutionary regime in Iran and the militant extremists it supported in Lebanon were still ever ready to see American actions as diabolical plots aimed at destroying them.

The Reagan administration, which had taken power in part because of Carter's inability to manage the Iranian debacle in all its dimensions, had failed spectacularly in Lebanon. Of course, preventing the attack would have required extraordinary political precautions and highly perceptive diplomatic actions—just as preventing the hostage crisis would have required. Instead, the United States blundered into the bloody abattoir of fanatics. But, ironically, by 1983 few Americans blamed U.S. government policy for the Lebanese bloodbath or, more generally, the firestorm that was engulfing swaths of the "crescent of crisis." Americans considered the Iran-Iraq War, the Soviet-Afghan clash, the Israeli-PLO battles, and the Lebanese maelstrom from multiple perspectives but few saw any simple solutions. Some American evangelical and fundamentalist Christians, not an insignificant percentage of the electorate, even took solace in the regional violence, seeing the conflicts as the sign of a coming apocalypse (as prophesied in the Bible and popularized in best-selling books) that would usher in the messianic age. Most Americans felt that the United States should simply do its best to stay out of harm's way in the Middle East.

President Reagan, having been burned badly in his forays into the Middle East, simply turned his attention to the struggle to which he had been dedicated for so long: the cold war. Secretary of Defense Caspar Weinberger supplied a policy analysis to undergird that turn. The Reagan doctrine, as it was called, echoed President Jerry Ford's post-Vietnam approach. The United States would not send troops around the world to fight in regional conflicts unless the United States faced direct threat. Instead, the United States would send guns and money to anti-communist "freedom fighters." So, among other actions, the Reagan administration—with the general support of both parties in Congress—armed Islamic fundamentalists in Afghanistan to fight a guerrilla war against the Soviet Union. Once again, top American policymakers decided it was easier to see Red than try to gain a clear view of Islamic Green.

History books will note the role President Reagan played in ending the cold war with an American victory. It is still too early to tell if his administration's policies in the Islamic world, including actions in Lebanon, support of Iraq, and funding of the Afghan "holy warriors," will be seen as major contributors to what is now called in the United States the "war on terrorism" or to what political theorist Samuel Huntington sees as the "clash of civilizations" between the Islamic world and the West.[11]

The Iran hostage crisis, in retrospect, was a wake-up call for the American people and the nation's leaders. Some lessons were obvious. For example, do not trust dictators to tell you the truth about their problems. Nor should you allow the intelligence service of other nations—a euphemism in many countries for repressive internal security forces—to serve as your main source of information about their country. Here, the Reagan administration and the presidential administrations that followed learned from President Carter's mistakes. Thus, in 1986, when Philippines' dictator and longtime American ally, Ferdinand Marcos, faced a "people power" revolt, cool heads in Washington, led by Iowa Senator Dick Lugar, rejected the Marcos regime's claims about communist subversion, as well as its pleas for help. Though the U.S. government, including President Reagan himself, had long supported

Marcos, during the critical stage of the revolt the Reagan administration cut ties to the dictator. They embraced—even if stiffly—the new reform government. The next year, the Reagan administration showed similar flexibility when it urged the South Korean government not to use force on pro-democracy demonstrators (whom the Korean government insisted were communists) and, instead, to move toward more representative and open government. Both decisions led, on balance, to good results.

Other lessons proved harder to learn or apply. The political scientist Chalmers Johnson, in his provocative book, *Blowback: The Costs and Consequences of American Empire*, argues that "[i]t is typical of an imperial power to have a short memory for its less pleasant imperial acts, but for those on the receiving end, memory can be long indeed."[12] In the United States, the relatively "short memory" of the American public is complicated by the democratic electoral cycle. Mistakes may have been made by their predecessors, American elected officials might admit, but now everything is different. President Carter certainly intended the world to understand that, unlike the hard-hearted international policies of his predecessors, he embraced a more humanitarian ethos. Revolutionary forces in Iran, conditioned by decades of American involvement in their country and Carter's generally supportive policy toward Shah Pahlavi, saw little difference between Carter and the presidents that came before him. Even when the United States did not intervene in the overthrow of the Shah, the new regime anxiously awaited signs that the superpower would soon subvert their revolution. Giving shelter to the Shah was, to them, that sign. In the late 1970s, Americans were so caught up in their immediate present—a drama of perceived national decline—that the long-term trauma of the Iranian people in which the United States qua superpower played at least some role was largely invisible. The Iranian public's memories of American actions and the American public's general ignorance of U.S. policy in Iran were so asymmetrical as to preclude mutual understanding.

American policymakers, at the least, have to reckon with the shadow the past casts on their present policies. Thus, Iranian-linked elements in the Middle East in the 1980s were not going to give the new American president, Ronald Reagan, the benefit of the doubt; instead they had been conditioned to see almost any American move in their region as sign of dark and deadly intrigue. In that historically conditioned context, American policymakers needed but failed to practice extraordinary care.

An even harder lesson to learn for the generally (even in the 1970s) optimistic and universalistic American public is that other people often see the world differently. Carter administration officials were well aware that the Ayatollah Khomeini did not share their worldview but, as a result, they tended to dismiss him as a historical anachronism who was, for all practical purposes, crazy. Samuel Huntington, in his controversial and influential essay, "The Clash of Civilizations?" argues that "differences among civilizations are not only real; they are basic. The people of different civilizations have different views on the relations between God and man, the individual and the group, the citizen and the state, parents and children, husband and wife, as well as differing views of the relative importance of rights and responsibilities, liberty and authority, equality and hierarchy."[13] Relations between the Islamic regime in Iran and the Carter administration gave evidence of such differences. Whether those differences are as timeless, essentialized, and civilization-based as Huntington claims is, I would think, dubious. (For example, one thinks of the popular and divisive movements in the United States to make Christian biblical law fundamental or to pass a constitutional amendment to ban gay marriage—religious fundamentalism versus secularism seems to cut across so-called civilizations, much complicating Huntington's claims.) Still, Huntington's attempt to treat seriously differences in worldview—even if such views can overlap, change, and be contested not just across "civilizations" but within nations, cultures, and "civilizations" themselves—is critically important, especially for those Americans who take as a matter of fact that their culture and their nation (as well as their military) represent the future of all of humanity. Such typical American attitudes do not play well around the world. Nor does an unreflective belief in American-based universalism aid policymakers or the American public in understanding certain significant actors in the world. Finally, I want to add, recognizing that other people may have different worldviews is not the same as accepting all views as equally valid, moral, or just. Some differences will and should result in conflict, even violent conflict. But understanding the significance and power of such differences offers at least the possibility of useful, informed negotiation.

Specifically, the most immediate lessons of the Iran hostage crisis went largely unheeded. Who knows what good might have come if American policymakers, supported by the American people, had paid greater attention to the lessons of the Iranian debacle. A simple first step would have been to take political Islam seriously by paying respect to its advocates and seeking to understand it as a force in the world. A massive foreign aid investment in the educational and vocational infrastructure of the Islamic world would have been, in retrospect, a cost-effective and change-directed policy. And lastly, a genuine American commitment to creating a just settlement in the Palestinian-Israeli struggle could have changed regional perception of the U.S. global role.

Historians usually are accused of exercising 20–20 hindsight. But in this case, at this time, the historian's vision can also be used to look forward into the perilous future.

Notes

Chapter 1: Crisis, Chaos, and Jimmy Carter

1. This account is taken from William Daugherty's compelling memoir, *In the Shadow of the Ayatollah: A CIA Hostage in Iran* (Annapolis: Naval Institute Press, 2001), 103–8.

2. One can hear Walter Cronkite intone those words at the CBS Web site: http://www.cbsnews.com/stories/2001/01/19/iran/main265565.shtml

3. Massoumeh Ebtekar, as told to Fred A. Reed, *Takeover in Tehran: The Inside Story of the 1979 U.S. Embassy Capture* (Vancouver: Talonbooks, 2000), 51–52. This memoir by one of the key student militants is written for maximum political utility—all quotes and accounts have to be taken with a mound of salt.

4. For the women's movement in the 1970s, see Ruth Rosen, *The World Split Open* (New York: Viking, 2000), pts. 3, 4. For statistics on African American progress and controversies in the 1970s, see Stephan Thernstrom and Abigal Thernstrom, *America in Black and White: One Nation Indivisible* (New York: Simon and Schuster, 1997), especially 288–89.

5. Kathleen Hall Jamieson, *Packaging the Presidency* (New York: Oxford, 1996), 326.

6. I have pulled the facts and statistics from the U.S. Census Bureau Web page, census.gov. The dollar figure is, as reported in Household Income Tables, in constant 2001 dollars.

7. Examples taken from Haynes Johnson, *Sleepwalking through History* (New York: Anchor Books, 1992), 116–17.

8. For an overview of the nation's economic plight in the 1970s and the regional dislocations produced, see Bruce Schulman, *The Seventies* (Cambridge: De Capo, 2001), chaps. 4, 5. For the poll data, see http://www.gallup.com/poll/state Nation/default.asp?Version=p

9. Judith Jones Putnam and Jane E. Allshouse, "Food Consumption, Prices and Expenditures, 1970–97," April 1999, Economic Research Service, U.S. Department of Agriculture, http://www.ers.usda.gov/publications/sb965, table 96.

10. The statistics are drawn from Norman Rosenberg and Emily Rosenberg, *In Our Time* (Englewood Cliffs, NJ: Prentice Hall, 1995), 206–07; and John C. Barrow, "The Quest for a National Energy Policy," in *The Carter Presidency*, ed.

Gary Fink and Hugh Davis's Graham (Lawrence: University Press of Kansas, 1998, 161.

11. Quoted in David Frum, *How We Got Here* (New York: Basic Books, 2000), 313.

12. Barrow, "The Quest for a National Energy Policy," 160–67.

13. Ibid., 169.

14. Nicholas Lemann, "How the Seventies Changed America," in *A History of Our Time*, ed. William Chafe, Harvard Sitkoff, and Beth Bailey (New York: Oxford University Press, 2002), 110, and, for an overview of conditions, 109–11. See also, Barrow, "The Quest for a National Energy Policy," 169–71.

15. Quoted in Michael Barone, *Our Country* (New York: Free Press, 1990), 545.

16. Quoted in William Leuchtenberg, "Jimmy Carter and the Post–New Deal Presidency," in *The Carter Presidency*, ed. Gary Fink and Hugh Davis Graham (Lawrence: University Press of Kansas, 1998), 11.

17. Chris Matthews, *Hardball* (New York: Vintage, 1989), 33–34.

18. Sidney M. Milkis, "Remaking Government Institutions in the 1970s: Participatory Democracy and the Triumph of Administrative Politics," in *Loss of Confidence: Politics and Policy in the 1970s*, ed. David Brian Robinson (University Park: Pennsylvania State University Press, 1998), 59. Watergate-era Congresses had passed numerous bills, most importantly the Budget Control Act of 1974, which was aimed at reducing the power of the so-called imperial presidency.

19. James Fallows, "The Passionless Presidency," May 1979, *Atlantic Monthly*, http://www.theatlantic.com/unbound/flashbks/pres/fallpass.htm. The piece remains the most illuminating sketch of Carter written.

20. All quoted in the useful compendium, Mark Rozell, *The Press and the Carter Presidency* (Boulder: Westview Press, 1989), 125.

21. Quoted in Burton Kaufman, *The Presidency of James Earl Carter, Jr.* (Lawrence: University Press of Kansas, 1993), 137. I rely, in this section, on Kaufman's analysis of the 1979 crisis. In general, I have been guided by Kaufman's compelling Carter biography.

22. Rosalyn Carter, *First Lady from Plains* (Boston: Houghton Mifflin, 1984), 302.

23. The quoted words are Jimmy Carter's paraphrase in his aptly titled memoir, *Keeping Faith* (New York: Bantam, 1982), 115.

24. Carter, *Keeping Faith*, 115–20; Kaufman, *Presidency of James Earl Carter*, 144–45. Clinton is quoted in Leuchtenburg, "Jimmy Carter and the Post–New Deal Presidency," 21.

25. Jimmy Carter, "Energy and National Goals," July 15, 1979, http://www.presidency.ucsb.edu/site/media/play.php?id=135.

26. Hamilton Jordan, "A New Approach and Attitude about Government and Governing," July 16, 1979, box 34, Office of the Chief of Staff Files (hereafter OCS), Jimmy Carter Presidential Library (hereafter JC); and on drug use, Jimmy Carter to Senior Staff, July 24, 1978, box 34, OCS, JC.

27. Fallows, "The Passionless Presidency."

28. Hamilton Jordan to Jimmy Carter, "Change Analysis," July 16, 1979, box 34, OCS, JC.

Chapter 2: The Shah, Khomeini, and the "Great Satan"

1. My account closely follows the version narrated in James A. Bill, *The Eagle and the Lion: The Tragedy of American-Iranian Relations* (New Haven: Yale University Press, 1988), 180–82. This chapter draws on Bill's outstanding analysis. Material on David Rockefeller comes from David Rockefeller, *Memoirs* (New York: Random House, 2002), 356–58. Rockefeller devotes a chapter to his relations with the Shah but chooses not to mention the Tehran Investment Seminar.

2. Gary Sick, *All Fall Down: America's Tragic Encounter with Iran* (New York: Penguin, 1986), 5. Sick's book is the best of the insider accounts of the Iran hostage crisis; not only did Sick have the advantage of personal experience and contacts, he did a great deal of research.

3. Marvin Zonis, *Majestic Failure* (Chicago: University of Chicago Press, 1991), 222. Zonis is referring more generally to Iranians' views of the West, but I think the focus, here, on the United States is accurate for the late 1970s era.

4. Kermit Roosevelt, *Countercoup: The Struggle for the Control of Iran* (New York: McGraw Hill, 1979), 199.

5. The Religious Community of the City of Isfahan to President James Carter, May 16, 1977, file CO-71, Box CO-31, White House Central Files (hereafter WHCF), JC.

6. Department of State memo for Zbigniew Brzezinski, June 23, 1977, file CO-71, box CO-31, WHCF, JC.

7. Quoted in Peter N. Carroll, *It Seemed Like Nothing Happened* (New York: Holt, Rinehart, and Winston, 1982), 168–69.

8. Ibid., 198.

9. Ibid.

10. All quotes are found in Gaddis Smith, *Morality, Reason, and Power* (New York: Hill and Wang, 1986), 29–30.

11. The quote and background on the Trilateral Commission come from its Web site: http://www.Trilateral.org; see especially the section titled "FAQ." For Carter's invite to the commission, see Zbigniew Brzezinski, *Power and Principle* (New York: Farrar, Straus Giroux, 1983), 5.

12. Quoted in Hamilton Jordan, *Crisis* (New York: G. P. Putnam's Sons, 1982), 45.

13. Zbigniew Brzezinski, exit interview, JC; see also Gerry Argyris Andrianopoulos, *Kissinger and Brzezinski* (New York: St. Martin's Press, 1991), and Walter Issacson, *Kissinger* (New York: Simon and Schuster, 1992).

14. Brzezinski, *Power and Principle*, 7.

15. Marilyn Berger, "Cyrus Vance, a Confidant of Presidents, Is Dead at 84," January 13, 2002, *New York Times*, http://www.nyt.com/2002/01/12/obituaries/13.vanc.html. See also Cyrus Vance, *Hard Choices* (New York: Simon and Schuster, 1983), and George Ball, *The Past Has Another Pattern* (New York: Norton, 1982).

16. "Overview of Foreign Policy Issues and Positions," appendix 1, in Vance, *Hard Choices*, 441.

17. Vance, *Hard Choices*, 30.

18. Ibid.; Brzezinski, *Power and Principle*, 4.

19. Peter Goldman, "Mr. Carter Goes to Washington," *Newsweek*, December 6, 1976, p. 21.

20. The Shah of Iran (Reza Shah Pahlavi) to President Roosevelt, Tehran [August 25, 1941, 10 p.m.?], translation, in *The United States and Iran; A Documentary History* (Frederick, MD: University Publications of America, 1980), 77–78.

21. Much of this section is derived from the compelling account offered by Barry Rubin in *Paved with Good Intentions: The American Experience in Iran* (New York: Penguin, 1981), chap. 1.

22. Both quotes are taken from Rubin, *Paved with Good Intentions*, 39, 41–42.

23. I rely on the epic history by Daniel Yergin, *The Prize* (New York: Simon and Schuster, 1991), 134–64, 450–53.

24. Again, I am relying on Yergin, *The Prize*, and should point out that my sentence on the British perspective is similar in nature to a sentence composed by Mr. Yergin; it appears on page 433 when he discusses oil companies' perspectives on profit distributions. I've also relied on Bill, *The Lion and the Eagle*, chap. 2; the Fraser quote appears on page 72.

25. For the Mossadegh remark to Harriman, see Bill, *The Lion and the Eagle*, 65. For the public Mossadegh statement, see Yergin, *The Prize*, 455. Both books supply the underlying narrative here.

26. Bill, *The Lion and the Eagle*, 78.

27. For the Harriman remark, see Yergin, *The Prize*, 462; page 463 for the "day of hatred." The Boston Tea Party remarks are from Bill, *The Lion and the Eagle*, 76.

28. Quoted in Bill, *The Lion and the Eagle*, 80.

29. Quoted in Rubin, *Paved with Good Intentions*, 59.

30. Quoted in Chester Pach and Elmo Richardson, *The Presidency of Dwight D. Eisenhower* (Lawrence: University Press of Kansas, 1991), 76.

31. Rubin, *Paved with Good Intentions*, 84; my account is primarily based on chapter 3 of Rubin's work. For a rich overview of the coup, see Stephen Kinzer, *All the Shah's Men* (New York: John Wiley and Sons, 2003).

32. Zonis, *Majestic Failure*, 103.

33. Rubin, *Paved with Good Intentions*, 89.

34. My summary of the coup is based on Rubin, *Paved with Good Intentions*, chap. 3, and Bill, *The Lion and the Eagle*, chap. 2.

35. Rubin, *Paved with Good Intentions*, 87.

36. Bill, *The Lion and the Eagle*, 98–99.

37. Zonis, *Majestic Failure*, 107.

38. I am following the argument made by Bill, *The Lion and the Eagle*, chap. 4.

39. Baqer Moin, *Khomeini: Life of the Ayatollah* (New York: St. Martin's Press, 2000), 88.

40. Ibid., 55; and Robin Wright, *In the Name of God* (New York: Simon and Schuster, 1989), 43–44.

41. I am following the analysis of Daniel Brumberg, *Reinventing Khomeini: The Struggle for Reform in Iran* (Chicago: University of Chicago Press, 2001), chaps. 1–3. For a more personal account of why Iranians found Khomeini's Islamic message powerful, see Ebtekar, *Takeover in Tehran*, 42–45.

42. Moin, *Khomeini*, 60–62.

43. Ibid., 104.

44. Ibid., 121–22. Moin hammers home this point while Barry Rubin, in *Paved with Good Intentions*, lets this episode pass with little comment.

45. Moin, *Khomeini*, 122–27. The lengthy speech is quoted at great length.

46. "National Security Council Report on United States Strategy for Iran," undated [circa 1963], in *The United States and Iran*, 353–61.

47. Ball, *The Past Has Another Pattern*, 435–36. Barry Rubin states that per capita income in Iran in 1971 was $350. Rubin, *Paved with Good Intentions*, 133.

48. The party is described by William Shawcross, *The Shah's Last Ride* (New York: Simon and Schuster, 1988), 38–48, and by Bill, *The Lion and the Eagle*, 185, which is the source for the Khomeini and the Shah quotes.

49. I am following Rubin's narrative in *Paved with Good Intentions*, 15.

50. Sick, *All Fall Down*, 16. I am also relying on Bill, *The Eagle and the Lion*, 200–214; and Rubin, *Paved with Good Intentions*, 129–57.

51. Rubin, *Paved with Good Intentions*, 128–37, and Bill, *The Eagle and the Lion*, 200–204, 208–209. A little authorial perspective as well; I draw on my 1996 Fulbright experience living in Jakarta.

52. Yergin, *The Prize*; the quotes appear on pp. 582, 585.

53. Quoted in Yergin, *The Prize*, 626.

Chapter 3: Takeover in Tehran

1. Mozaffar Firouz, interview by Habib L. Adjevardi, December 6, 1981, Iranian Oral History Project, Harvard University Center for Middle Eastern Studies, http://www.fas.harvard.edu/~iohp/firouz.html. The quote appears on pp. 12–13 of transcript 2. The Khomeini middleman piece comes from Abol Hassan Bani-Sadr, *My Turn to Speak* (New York: Brassey's, 1991), 62.

2. Mozaffar Firouz to Jimmy Carter, December 6, 1979, File 60–71, CD-31, WHCF, JC. In this letter he quotes generously from his 1977 letter.

3. The *60 Minutes* piece aired March 6, 1977.

4. Carter, *Keeping Faith*, 65.

5. Frank Moore, Dan Tate, and Bill Cable, Memo for the President, July 27, 1977 (the date is scrawled and might be July 29), box 34, OCS, JC. The administration's congressional problems are ably analyzed, if not solved.

6. Jimmy Carter, inaugural address, January 20, 1977.

7. See the nuanced treatment of Carter's Soviet human rights views in Robert A. Strong, *Working in the World: Jimmy Carter and the Making of American Foreign Policy* (Baton Rouge: Louisiana State University Press), chap. 3.

Strong makes a useful case for Carter's reliance on earlier foreign policy initiatives, in general.

8. Strong, *Working in the World*, chap. 6; the Reagan quote is on page 154. Carter comments on the political price in *Keeping Faith*, 184.

9. Carter, *Keeping Faith*, 273.

10. Vance, *Hard Choices*, 318–19.

11. Jimmy Carter to Muhammad Reza Shah Pahlavi, November 28, 1977; regarding oil prices, Arthur Burns to Jimmy Carter, November 28, 1977; for Mondale, Suggested Toast for Vice President and Mrs. Mondale's Luncheon for the Shah and Shahbanou of Iran, November 16, 1977, all located in folder CO–71, box CO-31, WHCF, JC. The Religious Community of the City of Isfahan to President James Carter, May 16, 1977. See also R. Carter, *First Lady from Plains*, 305–6.

12. Quoted in Smith, *Morality, Reason and Power*, 186. According to Sick, *All Fall Down*, 405n. 7, the overripe language was the result of a rewrite penned by a Carter speechwriter on Airforce One just before arrival in Tehran.

13. Gary Sick to Zbigniew Brzezinski, November 30, 1977, folder CO-71, box CO-31, WHCF, JC.

14. Sick's concerns had appeared in Carter's briefing book—and Carter read his briefing books; Sick, *All Fall Down*, 35.

15. The preceding paragraphs draw on Kaufman, *Presidency of James Earl Carter*, chap. 8.

16. Brzezinski, *Power and Principle*, 354–55. For an overview in the archival record, see the fascinating, recently declassified State Department Evening Reports (hereafter SDER) for summer and fall 1978 in box 39, Plains File (hereafter PF), JC.

17. Jordan is quoted in the memo from Frank Moore to President Carter, August 8, 1978, box 99, Staff Offices, Office of Staff Secretary, JC.

18. Cyrus Vance to Jimmy Carter, August 15, 1978, SDER, box 39, PF, JC.

19. Paul Hoffman, "Behind Iranian Riots, a Web of Discontent," *New York Times*, March 5, 1978, p. 7; Nicholas Gage, "Shah of Iran Facing Growing Opposition," *New York Times*, May 18, 1978, p. 1; Nicholas Gage, "Shah of Iran Faces Challenge Headed by Moslem Clergy," *New York Times*, June 4, 1978, p. 1.

20. Senators in 1977 and 1978 kept pressuring the White House, on behalf of defense contractors in their states, to sell weapons to the Shah; see "Trade" TA-9, folder TA 3, CO-71, box CO-31, WHCF, JC. File CO-71 also contains letters mixed in from senators on behalf of Iranians living in the United States.

21. Bill, *The Eagle and the Lion*, 234.

22. Ibid., 216–88.

23. Brumberg, *Reinventing Khomeini*, 62–63.

24. Ibid., 64.

25. Ibid., 63.

26. I follow Ebtekar's own story as told in her memoir, *Takeover in Tehran*, 40–45. The Shari'ati material is drawn from Moin, *Khomeini*, 172–74. Ebtekar does not mention the anticlerical aspects of Shari'ati's teachings, nor his emphasis on democracy. According to Moin, Shari'ati did not urge people to follow the line

of Khomeini, as Ebtekar writes, but to pursue instead a radical Islam that did not give clerics overriding authority. Again, Ebtekar's memoir is a politically loaded document.

27. Material is drawn from the SDER written at this time by Warren Christopher to Jimmy Carter, August 7, 1978, September 8, 1978, and September 13, 1978, box 39, PF, JC. Alas, these documents are declassified only through February 1, 1979.

28. Sick, *All Fall Down*, 44–45.

29. For the Shah's health, see Mohammad Reza Pahlavi, *Answer to History* (New York: Stein and Day, 1980), 19; for Vance's view, see Christopher to Carter, September 9, 1978, SDER, JC.

30. Rubin, *Paved with Good Intentions*, 207.

31. Warren Christopher to Jimmy Carter, October 24, 1978, SDER, JC.

32. This dialogue comes straight from Zonis, *Majestic Failure*, 90. Zonis had amazing access to key figures in the Shah's regime both during the late 1970s and after, while he was researching his psychobiography. The quoted passage is based on an interview he did in 1982.

33. Carter, *Keeping Faith*, 438.

34. Ahmad Mohamadi to Walter Mondale, September 12, 1978, and Peter Tarnoff, memo for Christine Dodson, September 30, 1978, file CO-71, box CO-31, WHCF, JC.

35. Taken from November and December, SDER, JC.

36. The November 6, 1978, edition of the *New York Times* is loaded with Iranian news. The NSC followed the domestic response to the Iran debacle; see Gary Sick to Zbigniew Brzezinski, November 11, 1978; for the "heartland" quote, see Samuel Hopkins to Zbigniew Brzezinski, December 4, 1978, CO-71, box CO-31, WHCF, JC.

37. Brzezinski, *Power and Principle*, 367–68; Sick, *All Fall Down*, 80–84.

38. "Shah Addresses Nation," November 6, 1978, Tehran Domestic Service, box 38, Zbigniew Brzezinski (hereafter ZB), JC.

39. Cyrus Vance to Jimmy Carter, December 26, 1978, SDER, JC.

40. On January 11, 1979, the Shah basically conveyed these feelings to General Robert Huyser; Robert E. Huyser, *Mission to Tehran* (New York: Harper and Row, 1986), 78.

41. Brzezinski, *Power and Principle*, 370–71; Ball, *The Past Has Another Pattern*, 457–59.

42. Blumenthal's account appears in Shawcross, *The Shah's Last Ride*, 22. The list of people appears in Rubin, *Paved with Good Intentions*, 229. The Byrd quote and story come from William H. Sullivan, *Mission to Iran* (New York: W.W. Norton, 1981), 196–98.

43. Haig wrote a blistering attack on the Carter policy in the introduction to Huyser's memoir; General Alexander M. Haig, introduction to *Mission to Tehran*, vii. The more genteel quoted language is from "The Huyser Mission in Iran, January 4 to February 4, 1979," a briefing paper presented at a spring 1980 meeting—no date given—of Vance, Brzezinski, and Brown, file 3/80–9/80, box 34, ZB, JC.

44. Huyser, *Mission to Tehran*, 32–35.
45. Ibid., 35.
46. Ibid., 45.
47. Huyser's information about the military leaders' coup plans was not as timely as the reports the president was receiving through other channels. The president was well aware of coup plans by January 5, before Huyser had even had a chance to meet with the Iranian generals. For Carter's awareness, see "(in Guadeloupe, January, 1979)," January 5, 1979, Iran 6/75–12/79, box 23, PF, JC; for Huyser's discoveries, see Huyser, *Mission to Tehran*, 21–76.
48. *Pravda* quoted in Huyser, *Mission to Tehran*, 2. For the coup talk, see, for example, the bottom of page 57 and the top of page 66.
49. As late as October 28, 1978, Sullivan had strongly opposed any overture to Khomeini; Carter, *Keeping Faith*, 439.
50. The last-minute dickering over policy options is smoothly summarized in A. Moens, "President Carter's Advisors and the Fall of the Shah," *Political Science Quarterly* 106, no. 2 (summer 1991): 211–38. Like much of the academic literature on the Carter administration and the fall of the Shah, Moens blames feuding officials for the policy mess. He singles out Brzezinski for not giving Carter a clearer sense of the policy options available. While I am not particularly concerned with the presidential policy advice debate, I would argue that Vance could have presented the State Department position more forcefully to the president. Also, Carter was well aware that his administration was divided over policy and it was finally his decision to make. He chose, essentially, to muddle through rather than make a clear and decisive policy choice. In Carter's defense, often enough muddling through works.
51. "(in Guadeloupe, January, 1979)" In the document, Carter used a shorthand symbol for the bracketed word *with*.
52. Incoming Telegram, Sullivan, William H., to Secretary of State, January 10, 1979, Iran 6/75–12/79, box 23, PF, JC. Sullivan explains his views in *Mission to Iran*, 221–25.
53. Carter, *Keeping Faith*, 446.
54. "Khomeini Hopes to Be Iran's 'Guide'," January 10, 1979, 1/79–12/79, box 11, ZB, JC.

Chapter 4: *Shaslik Nerg Bessawari Azerbaiyan* or
"The Red Blindfold Would Be Lovely"

1. Background on Robert Ode is supplied in box 11, Robert Ode Collection (hereafter RO), JC.
2. The Jonestown events are summarized on Court TV's excellent Web site, Crimelibrary.com. See also the Jonestown Memorial Project, http://www.Jones-town.org.
3. Carter received quotes from these editorials while he was in Guadeloupe monitoring the Shah's travails; newspaper editorial summaries, Iran 6/75–12/79, box 23, PF, JC.
4. Moin, *Khomeini*, 190–91.

5. Ibid., 15, 33–34.

6. Zbigniew Brzezinski to the President, NSC Weekly Report #87, Weekly Report 12/78–3/79, box 42, ZB, JC.

7. The general American image of Arab terrorism was not invented during the hostage crisis. During the 1972 Summer Olympic Games in Munich, Palestinian guerrillas took a group of Israeli athletes hostage and killed them. But mass media coverage placed that event squarely in the geopolitical realm and did not suggest that Islam was somehow connected to the events.

8. Both of the preceding quotes appear in Rubin, *Paved with Good Intentions*, 249.

9. Shawcross, *The Shah's Last Ride*, 106–7.

10. Television news coverage can be followed by searching the Vanderbilt University on-line archive of television:http://tvnews.vanderbilt.edu. Word searches provide the exact dates, segment time, and summary of every news story.

11. Besides reading the *New York Times*, for mass media treatment of Iran and the Iranian revolution I rely on information distilled from Hamid Naficy, "Mediating the Other: American Pop Culture Representation of Postrevolutionary Iran," and David Detmer, "Covering Up Iran: Why Vital Information Is Routinely Excluded from U.S. Mass Media News Accounts," both in the very useful collection, Yahya R. Kamalipour, ed., *The U.S. Media and the Middle East: Image and Perception* (Westport: Greenwood Press, 1995). I am also indebted to the far-ranging analysis provided by Melanie McAlister, *Epic Encounters: Culture, Media, and U.S. Interests in the Middle East, 1945–2000* (Berkeley: University of California Press, 2001). I encountered more coverage by the television networks of Iran, beginning in November 1978 right through November 1979, than some scholars' treatments suggest. Stories included U.S. government involvement with the Shah's regime, especially as it related to arms sales and SAVAK.

12. "AM-Iran-Kissinger," Iran Meetings, 11/2/75–1/31/79, box 12, ZB, JC.

13. Carter, *Keeping Faith*, 202.

14. Tim Wells, *444 Days* (New York: Harcourt Brace Jovanovich, 1985), 10.

15. Ibid., 12.

16. Ibid., 15.

17. Kaufman, *Presidency of James Earl Carter*, 131. I am drawing, generally, on Kaufman's history of events in 1979.

18. Ibid., 132.

19. See David Farber, "The Torch Has Fallen," in *America in the Seventies*, ed. David Farber and Beth Bailey (Lawrence: University Press of Kansas, 2004).

20. Zbigniew Brzezinski to the President, NSC Weekly Report #109, September 13, 1979, box 42, ZB, JC.

21. I write these sentences in early 2004 while awaiting the unfolding of the Bush administration's Kurd policy.

22. Sick, *All Fall Down*, 221–22.

23. Rockefeller provides a rich insider account of these events in Rockefeller, *Memoirs*, chap. 24; the quoted memo appears on p. 368. For McCloy, see Kai Bird, *The Chairman* (New York: Simon and Schuster, 1992), 646–54. John McCloy to Warren Christopher, April 16, 1979 and Warren Christopher to John

McCloy, April 18, 1979, CO-31, CO-71, WHCF-Staff Files (hereafter SF), JC. George Will is quoted in Bird, *The Chairman*, 646. I also rely on Sick, *All Fall Down*, 207–12, and Michael Ledeen and William Lewis, *Debacle* (New York: Alfred Knopf, 1981), 216–19.

24. The quotes are from Bird, *The Chairman*, 648–49.

25. Ashraf Pahlevi to President James Carter, March 21,1980, box 20, ZB, JC—the letter summarizes her letter of August 10, 1979. Also see Bird, *The Chairman*, 651.

26. Zbigniew Brzezinski to the President, October 20, 1979, box 23, WHCF-SF, JC. Brzezinski recommends letting the Shah in for medical reasons; one of the NSC advisor's aides provides a handwritten outline of events in the margins of the memo. The Vance quote is from Bird, *The Chairman*, 651; the Jordan quote is from Jordan, *Crisis*, 31; the Reed quote is from Bird, *The Chairman*, 652.

27. Wells, *444 Days*, 17–18.

28. Ibid., 26.

29. Ibid., 29; the photo story is told by Barry Rosen on page 28.

30. Ebtekar, *Takeover in Tehran*, 51. I rely on this problematic memoir to reconstruct the student radicals' thoughts and acts before and during the takeover.

31. Ibid, 51–53. The quoted sentences are likely modified versions of the actual dialogue that took place but they are the best record available of the students' actions and motives.

32. Ebtekar, *Takeover in Tehran*, 58.

33. Wells, *444 Days*, 39.

34. Ebtekar, *Takeover in Tehran*, 67, and for Gallegos, Wells, *444 Days*, 61.

35. Harold Saunders, "The Crisis Begins," in Warren Christopher, Harold H. Saunders, Gary Sick, Robert Carswell, Richard J. Davis, John E. Hoffman, Jr., and Robert Owens: *The Conduct of a Crisis: American Hostages in Iran* (New Haven: Yale University Press, 1985), 35–37.

36. Gary Sick describes this problem in *All Fall Down*, 223–25.

37. Almost all of this is taken from the priceless oral history compiled by Wells, *444 Days*, 55–83. See also Richard Queen, *Inside and Out* (New York: G. P. Putnam's, 1981), 50–53.

38. Ebtekar, *Takeover in Tehran*, 69–70.

Chapter 5: 444 Days

1. Quoted in Marc Gunther, *The House That Roone Built: The Inside Story of ABC News* (Boston: Little Brown and Company, 1994), 18. Arledge's bio is drawn from Gunther's rich account, 8–30.

2. I continue to rely on Gunther, *The House That Roone Built*, but am more directly drawing here from Ted Koppel and Kyle Gibson, *Nightline* (New York: Times Books, 1996), 4–6.

3. Koppel and Gibson, *Nightline*, 8–9.

4. On March 24, 1980, the show was retitled *Nightline*—the hostage graphic and numbering of the days of captivity continued.

5. Jordan, *Crisis*, 19.

6. Ebtekar, *Takeover in Tehran*, 74.

7. Sick, *All Fall Down*, 242.

8. All quotes are from the indispensable Rozell, *The Press and the Carter Presidency*, 143–44.

9. President Jimmy Carter to the Ayatollah Khomeini, November 6, 1979, Alpha Channel (Misc), 1/80–3/80, box 20, ZBc, JC.

10. I am quoting from Sick, *All Fall Down*, 246.

11. All quotes come from "Foreign Media Reaction," Morning Digest, November 8, 1979, Weekly Reports, 7/79–12/79, box 42, ZB, JC.

12. The broadcast quotations, translated into English, are from [Redacted] to Paul Herze, NVOI Transcripts and Summaries, November 15, 1979, 11/79, box 4, National Security Affairs Staff Material (hereafter NSC), JC.

13. "PBH" to "ZB," November 9, 1979, 11/79, box 4, NSC, JC.

14. Zbigniew Brzezinski to the Vice President, n.d. [circa November 28, 1979], 11/79, box 4 NSC, JC. Other material in this box explores the radio broadcasting issue in detail.

15. Carter, *Keeping Faith*, 458.

16. Hamilton Jordan to President Carter, November 8, 1979, Iran 11/79, box 34, OCS, JC.

17. For these activities and press coverage, see boxes 61 and 62, Jody Powell (hereafter JP), JC.

18. The press coverage problem is discussed by Harold Saunders, "Diplomacy and Pressure," in *American Hostages in Iran*, 76–77.

19. ALM Notes for the Files, 11/8/79, Iran 11/79–12/79, box 13, Al McDonald, JC.

20. The Iranian student protester issue is copiously documented in boxes 86 and 87, especially the file titled "Demonstrators 11/79," box 87, Lloyd Cutler Papers (hereafter LC), JC. For the plight of young men who appeared to be Iranian students, I rely on the firsthand account provided to me by Daniel Frank, a Chicago resident in November 1979.

21. Pat Boone to "Dear Family," January 21, 1980, box 13, RO, JC. In the same box is a list of twenty-five recorded songs about the hostages.

22. Quoted in Gerald Parsons, "How the Yellow Ribbon Became a National Folk Symbol," American Folklife Center, http://www.loc.gov/folklife/ribbons/ribbons.html. The article was originally published in *Folklife Center News* 12, no. 3 (1990); 9–11.

23. Barbara and Barry Rosen, with George Feifer, *The Destined Hour*, (New York: Doubleday, 1982), 161.

24. The *Newsweek* story was in the December 17, 1979, issue, and the *New York Daily News* article appeared on December 12, 1979. The *New York Times* article ran on December 13, 1979.

25. McAlister, *Epic Encounters*, 208, and the second set of quotes appears on p. 201.

26. Gunther, *The House That Roone Built*, 99.

27. Ebtekar, *Takeover in Tehran*, 86.

28. The letter is quoted in the *New York Times*, November 11, 1979; the story is included in the Cravath, Swaine, and Moore Chronology (hereafter CSM), 3/ 3, box 86, LC, JC.

29. Both hostages statements and the general scene are covered in Tehran Domestic Service, November 18, 1979 and November 19, 1979; the Quarles quotes are from the *New York Times*, November 19, 1979; all are included in CSM, box 85, LC, JC. The entire "Vernon Jordan statement," November 19, 1979, is in box 62, JP, JC.

30. Moin, *Khomeini*, 227.

31. Ibid., 227–28. The quoted passage is according to Bani-Sadr's account and he is, alas, not always a perfect source of information.

32. Khomeini interview text, November 18, 1979, CSM, box 85, LC, JC.

33. "Excerpt from Statement No. 45 of the Muslim Student Followers of the Imam's Policy," November 21, 1979, CSM, box 85, LC, JC.

34. "Excerpts from Khomeini speech," November 20, 1979, CSM, box 85, LC, JC.

35. "On the Rights of American Hostages in Iran," December 16, 1979, CSM, box 85, LC, JC.

36. "Today Program," November 29, 1979, transcript, box 61, JP, JC.

37. *Financial Times*, December 9, 1979, clipping, CSM, box 86, LC, JC.

38. Quoted in Kaufman, *Presidency of James Earl Carter*, 162.

39. President with Select Members of Congress, December 5, 1979, transcript, pp. 4–5, 10, box 61, JP, JC.

40. ABC News—Harris Survey, January 7, 1980, box 63, JP, JC.

41. Brzezinski quotes himself in Brzezinski, *Power and Principle*, 427.

42. Brzezinski, *Power and Principle*, 428.

43. President James Earl Carter, "State of the Union," January 23, 1980, http:// jimmycarterlibrary.org/documents/speeches/su80jec.phtml.

44. Kaufman, *Presidency of James Earl Carter*, 165.

45. Harold Saunders, To the Secretary [Cyrus Vance], January 28, 1980, box 34, OCS, JC.

46. A fascinating series of documents declassified and redacted mostly in 1997 provide a detailed narrative of the secret communications between Bani-Sadr and Ghotbzadeh and the various intermediaries and the subsequent discussions within the Carter White House and the State Department. They are located in the folders titled Iran 1/80 and 2/80, box 34, OCS, JC.

47. Brzezinski is quoted in Jordan, *Crisis*, 122.

48. Hedley Donovan, To Mr. Jordan, February 15, 1980, box 34, OCS, JC.

49. George F. Will, "What Next on the Agenda of Appeasement?" February 21, 1980, *Washington Post*, and William Safire, "Terrorism Triumphs," February 21, 1980, *New York Times*.

50. "For persons of the American Persuasion traveling to or in Iran," 11–12/ 79, box 95, LC, JC.

51. "Foreign Policy: Coherence and Sense of Direction," March 25, 1980, SCC 293, box 32, ZB, JC.

52. Quoted in Sick, *All Fall Down*, 341. I am relying on Sick's account of the final decision-making that led to the rescue operation attempt, on pp. 338–48.

53. Hamilton Jordan to President Carter, n.d. [late November 1979?], box 34, OCS, JC.

54. "Remarks of the President at the Dinner for Radio and Television Correspondents," March 9, 1978, box 63, JP, JC.

55. Colonel Charlie Beckwith and Donald Knox, *Delta Force* (New York: Harcourt Brace Jovanovich, 1983), 128–29.

56. Beckwith and Knox, *Delta Force*, 226–29.

57. This account of the conversation is provided by Beckwith and Knox, *Delta Force*, 6.

58. Again, I rely on the version of events provided by Beckwith and Knox, *Delta Force*, 8–9.

59. Beckwith and Knox, *Delta Force*, 259.

60. "Rescue Mission Report," Special Operations Review Group, August 1980, box 92, LC, JC; August 24, 1980, box 79, Presidential Diary, JC; Sick, *All Fall Down*, 338–48.

61. Rozell, *The Press and the Carter Presidency*, 164–65.

62. Quoted in "Carter Ready to Commit Any Crime for Election," *Tehran Times*, April 26, 1980, p. 1, box 23, WHCF, JC.

63. Ebtekar, *Takeover in Tehran*, 210–15.

64. I use the helicopter rift in my essay on political leadership in the 1970s, "The Torch Has Fallen," 9–10.

65. Ronald Reagan, "Acceptance of the Republican Nomination for President," July 17, 1980, Detroit, http://www.tamu.edu/comm/pres/speeches/rraccept.html.

66. Gary Sick, *October Surprise* (New York: Random House, 1991).

67. Carter, *Keeping Faith*, 568.

Epilogue

1. Wells, *444 Days*, 431.

2. Ibid., 435.

3. Christopher, Introduction, to *American Hostages in Iran*, 9.

4. Ebtekar, *Takeover in Tehran*, 234.

5. Jordan, *Crisis*, 415, 416.

6. Robert B. Owen, "Final Negotiations and Release in Tehran," in *American Hostages in Iran*, 298.

7. Wright, *In the Name of God*, 108.

8. Ibid., 119.

9. Ibid., 120.

10. Barry Rosen, *The Destined Hour* (Garden City, NJ: Doubleday, 1982), 101–2.

11. Samuel F. Huntington, "The Clash of Civilizations?" *Foreign Affairs* 72, no. 3 (summer 1993): 22–49.

12. Chalmers Johnson, *Blowback: The Costs and Consequences of American Empire* (New York: Henry Holt, 2000), 13.

13. Huntington, "The Clash of Civilizations?" 25.

Index

Cities of Knowledge: Cold War Science and the Search for the Next Silicon Valley by Margaret Pugh O'Mara

Labor Rights Are Civil Rights: Mexican American Workers in Twentieth-Century America by Zaragosa Vargas

Pocketbook Politics: Economic Citizenship in Twentieth-Century America by Meg Jacobs

Taken Hostage: The Iran Hostage Crisis and America's First Encounter with Radical Islam by David Farber